MARCHING WITH SHARPE

MARCHING WITH SHARPE

B. J. Bluth PhD

To those who served, who suffered, who fought, who died
to vanquish the Corsican usurper
Napoleon Bonaparte
and
To Bernard Cornwell
who, in telling their story,
brings them so much to mind.

NOTES ON THE TEXT

This book is based on direct quotations, first-hand accounts, from the diaries, journals, letters and commentaries of the veterans of England's war with France, between 1808 and 1815, and their contemporaries. This technique is called 'stitching passages', where the words are compiled and arranged, combining the ideas of a number of people into a flowing coherent whole — the words, however being mostly original. Where there are no quotations, the words have been mostly paraphrased but are still authentic. The spelling, grammar, syntax, wording and technical and historical errors are thus preserved in the hope that, joined with the photographs and drawings, their spirit and style will rise above the print and years, alive and provoking.

To preserve the progression of ideas being conveyed using the stitching passages technique, footnotes have been omitted as there would be so many they would constantly interrupt the smooth flow of the text.

All of the sources used in writing this book can be found at the end of each chapter, and in the Bibliography. A list of easily obtained books are included in 'Recommendations for Further Reading.'

First published in Great Britain in 2001
by HarperCollins*Publishers* London

This edition published by HarperCollins*Publishers* 2003

© HarperCollins*Publishers*

1 3 5 7 9 8 6 4 2

A CIP catalogue record for this book is available from the British Library

The HarperCollins website address is: www.fireandwater.com

ISBN 0-00-414537-2

Printed and bound in Great Britain

Acknowledgements

The author is deeply grateful to all the many persons who have helped with this book, inspiring its growth and evolution, generously supplying hard to find information, and who read the manuscript at various stages making sound suggestions and observations. Special gratitude goes to Ian Drury, who made it happen, and to Maureen and Irene Shettle, Maureen and Terry Howes, Sherry R. McNeal, Rob and Rich Bluth, and to the staff of the National Army Museum in London, all helping in great and small ways.

The publishers also wish to extend their thanks to the following people and organisations:
The Curator, Major Ken Grey, and his staff of the Royal Green Jackets Museum in Winchester.
Martin Monks and all the members of the Napoleonic Association - particularly the men of the 95th Rifles & the Highlanders for their patience and kind assistance.
Ron Roberts of the 7th Hussars (in North America).
Allan Rooney of Midas Tours for his spectacular views of the peninsular battlefields.
Richard Palmer for his excellent photographic services.

CONTENTS

FOREWORD

BY BERNARD CORNWELL

It was in 1979 that I began to write the adventures of Richard Sharpe. They sprang from the naval adventures of Horatio Hornblower which I had read avidly as a teenager and, when C.S. Forester ended that series, I wanted more and so I began to read the non-fiction histories and discovered that, rich as Britain's naval achievements were in the long wars against Revolutionary and Napoleonic France, the army also had some extraordinary tales to tell. So began a lifelong fascination with Wellington's army. I devoured books about the Peninsular War and Waterloo, but I was a great fan of historical fiction and, for some strange reason, there were very few novels about the soldiers who fought against Napoleon. There were plenty of fictional sailors following in Hornblower's wake, but no soldiers and, after haunting the bookshops for years, I decided I might try and write the books myself. There are now eighteen Sharpe novels and I suspect there will be more.

Most of Sharpe's adventures take place against 'real' backgrounds, from the capture of Seringapatam in 1799 to the horrors of Waterloo sixteen years later. Those real backgrounds are easy to research because there are scores of books that tell us what happened and why it happened, but right from the beginning of Sharpe's career I discovered very few sources that told me what it was really like to be in Portugal or Spain or India during the long wars. There were a few published diaries and volumes of letters and those offered some marvellous clues, but there were still a host of unanswered questions.

What did the soldiers eat and how did they cook it? How did they amuse themselves? How did they mend boots or uniforms? I still remember the joy of discovering one day that the only cloth available in Portugal was brown, and in consequence the army was not really one of redcoats and greenjackets at all, but browncoats. Films often make British armies look resplendent in red coats, but that must have been very unusual because after a few days of marching and sleeping rough they looked more like a horde of tramps. 'I don't know what they do to the enemy,' the Duke of Wellington once remarked about one of his regiments, 'but they frighten me.'

So piece by piece, diary by diary, I assembled a working knowledge of how Wellington's men lived. I started this process long before I began writing Sharpe, back when I was working in television, and I collected the material in a large red BBC notebook that is still my primary source for Sharpe's background. The book is held together with sticky tape and staples, and is totally inadequate because I have never taken the time to organise its material. I did try once. I numbered its 279 pages and started an index, but never finished it, and so the notebook remains a disorganised mess. A page opened at random tells me that a battalion once sailed from the southern coast of England to Lisbon in a mere seven days while another unit, without fair winds, took forty nine days. The same page tells me about 'the pains', the soldier's nickname for the discomfort caused by the standard issue army knapsack that was ill-designed by a Mister Trotter. The next page informs me that a troop of Horse Artillery had 243 men and 206 horses and needed 71 mules to carry bread, 24 for rum, 12 for rice and 69 for forage, spare horse shoes and nails, and those 176 mules needed another 29 to carry their own forage, but I never noted down where I found those figures. I am hopelessly disorganised. Two pages later the book records the common belief that French musket balls were poisoned (they were not), and notes the advice given to British soldiers by their Portuguese allies that they should only drink white wine 'because we know how the red is made'. But how? The very next line tells me that seventeen men from the 71st were all killed by a single French round shot, while in the margin, hastily scrawled in pencil, is an excerpt from a soldier's letter home; Lisbon, he wrote, 'is a dungheap from end to end'.

The notebook is also full of anecdotes. How a British officer stopped a French pursuit by placing barrels of wine on the road and the enemy, sure enough, preferred to stop and get drunk. In the Pyrenees some French troops were about to slaughter a bullock for food when the beast managed to escape. It crossed to the British lines where it was captured and killed by the redcoats whereupon the hungry French soldiers sent some emissaries under a flag of truce to beg for half of the carcass, which was given to them. One of the nastiest tales is how some Riflemen sliced the buttocks from a dead Frenchman and sold them as 'ham' to a Portuguese battalion (the Portuguese had killed the Riflemens' pet dog). The BBC notebook is crammed with such stuff, and I suppose I have used most of it over the years, but I constantly find forgotten things in its pages or, worse,

know that some crucial fact is hidden in the mess and cannot be rediscovered. I have just finished Sharpe's Prey and spent hours searching for the results of tests done on heated shot. You could heat a cannon ball to red heat in a furnace, then let it cool for a long time and douse it in water and it would still retain enough heat to ignite wood, and somewhere in the notebook is the description of that experiment which I remember as astonishing, because a twenty-four pound round shot (or was it an eighteen pound ball?) could be cooled for hours (I think) and repeatedly doused in water and it would still set a battleship alight, but I could not find the details, and still cannot. I did find the results of a Prussian experiment in musketry. They made a target 100 feet long and 6 feet high, which is broadly the size of a battalion in line, and had a regiment fire volleys at the target which is the equivalent of, say, ten barn doors, and at 75 yards (which is 68 and a half metres for those who insist on using French measurements) only 60% of the musket balls hit. At 150 yards (137 metres) it was down to 40% and even that flatters the musketeers because the target was a solid sheet, whereas a battalion has gaps between the men. It is all useful stuff, but so hopelessly arranged. What I have really needed all these years is this book by B.J. Bluth.

For this book, better than any other I have seen, tells you how Wellington's army lived and fought. It was a magnificent army, and it is brought to life in these pages and by the photographs of modern day re-enactors. Life was not easy for Wellington's men, but they helped rid Europe of a tyrant and they did it with forbearance, good humour and a frightening ferocity. This book tells you what their lives were really like and my only regret is that B.J. Bluth did not write it twenty-two years ago.

PREFACE

A LITTLE HISTORY

In 1066, William, Duke of Normandy crossed the Channel from France to claim his throne, defeating Harold, last king of the Old English at Hastings, and thus becoming the King of England. From then on, the English nation became enmeshed in tensions and bloody conflicts with France, as Normandy was only 20 miles from Paris and the French King. After a few generations, the King of England, still the Duke of Normandy, came to rule more than half of the feudal territories of France. War upon war followed, with the English defeating the French, the French defeating the English, in what seemed a never ending cycle of victory, elation, rage and defeat – living out a veritable 'Devil's code of honour'[1], as the Kings of England and France fought over their boundaries, their prerogatives and their crown.

In 1760, George III assumed the throne of England, and in 1774, Louis XVI became King of France. George III lost his English Colonies in America after a revolt which was aided and abetted by Louis XVI. The latter had sent men, weapons and enormous treasure to ensure victory and to achieve his true goal - striking a devastating blow to English power and commerce. However, Louis XVI's actions only aggravated rising tensions in a seemingly prosperous France, resulting in 1789, in the French Revolution.

The affluent and growing middle classes of France held the power of mobile money and expanding capital, financing the government loans. It was also the middle classes, together with the peasantry, whose taxes paid for the adventures of the King and the lifestyle and privileges of his court, his nobility and the princes of the Church. They paid five times more in land taxes than the aristocratic and clerical Estates: they paid tithes to the Church and feudal dues to the lord of the manor; head taxes, income taxes, sales taxes, salt taxes and tolls for the use of the roads.

The middle classes believed that their energy and ingenuity was responsible for France's growing wealth, and consequently, were convinced that they had rightful access to the favours and appointments of the state, equal status before the law and at the royal courts, access to all of the privileges and graces of French society, and an equitable proportion of the burdens of taxation.

The truth was that by 1789, the state was mired in 'an incorrigible system of faulty finance', stemming from the reign of Louis XIV. Its credit was exhausted, with a debt 16 times greater than its total revenue — it was on the edge of complete bankruptcy. The funds spent by Louis XVI to support the American Revolutionaries had been secured by enormous loans, doubling the national debt. In 1789, half of the crown's income was consumed in servicing its debt.

If the King had used a firm hand, reform might have been possible. However, that was not to be. Marie Antoinette sketched her husband:

The King is not a coward; he possesses an abundance of passive courage, but he is overwhelmed by an awkward shyness and mistrust of himself...He is afraid to command.[2]

Every possible reform which might have solved the severe fiscal problems of the crown and the social and financial inequities prevailing throughout the society, interfered with the powerful vested interests of either the Crown, the nobility, the clergy or the various members of the middle class. However, the nobility and clergy were uncompromising, insisting on keeping all of their entitlements, income, exemptions and ancient favours. The middle classes were impatient to expunge the ancient codes. The King was at an impasse and avoided making harsh decisions. France had become an irrational and unworkable system and 'an explosion was inevitable and had long been expected by all inquiring minds.'[3]

Time passed and France became engulfed in crises: bad weather, bad harvests, famine, bread riots, tax revolts, demands from the nobility, the growing deficit, and plots against the throne. The King responded by freeing his own serfs, providing loans for the poor, forbidding the use of torture on witnesses or criminals, reforming the prisons, allowing for considerable religious liberty and refusing to let the government spy on the private correspondence of citizens. It was not enough.

On July 14th 1789, the Bastille fell to a Parisian mob, blood flowed in the streets and heads were raised on pikes. 'In the name of reason irrational forces had been let loose.'[4] Over 200, 000 nobles requested passports to leave the country.

By this time, England had already come through the long process of instituting a constitutional monarchy, and many actually welcomed the rebellion, assuming that the outcome would be a France with diminished military threat and based on many of the same principles as the English Government. Edmund Burke, however, saw the Revolution as a prelude to something more frightening — a creeping threat to the institutions of Christian Europe. He counselled preparation for war.[5]

The massacres began in September 1792 and by the end of that month the first French Republic was declared. Emboldened by victories on the battlefield, on December 15th 1792, the Edict of Fraternity was proclaimed, offering 'fraternity and assistance to all peoples who seek to recover their liberty,'[6] thus actively exporting the revolution and breaking with established international order. While radicals and revolutionaries applauded, the kings and cabinets of Europe 'found their minds wonderfully concentrated.'[7]

One by one, countries broke their diplomatic relations with France. In France, a rebel group marched from Marseilles to depose the King singing the newly composed song, 'The War Song of the Army of the Rhone' or '*The Marseillaise*'.

Though the King and most of the royal family had been held in genteel imprisonment for three months, documents were found in November which implicated the King in treason. His trial opened December 11th 1792. He was convicted by a vote of 683 to 66; the vote for death was 361 to 334. On January 21st 1793, the 'République de France' executed King Louis XVI by guillotine.

They had committed regicide and they broadcast their challenge throughout Europe:

Allied kings threaten us, and we hurl at their feet as a gage of battle the head of a king.[8]

We must establish the despotism of liberty to crush the despotism of kings.[9]

France declared war on Holland and Great Britain on February 1st 1793. News of mass murders of the aristocracy came across the Channel, and what had, at first, been seen as a welcome constitutional reform had turned into a bloody dictatorship. France was threatening the world, and as Prime Minister William Pitt put it: 'We are at war with those who would destroy the whole fabric of our Constitution.'[10]

Control of the Continent ebbed and flowed over the following years, as the nations, striving to subdue the rebellious French were repelled, intimidated or overcome in battle, only to rise up again, continuing the bloody cycle of victory and defeat.

The *République* continued in discord and conflict, but eventually by 1795, managed to create another constitution. It was preparing to inaugurate its new government, when, on October 4th and 5th, a group of plutocrats and royalists assembling a force of 25,000 men rose in revolt, threatening the deputies. Remembered for the clever tactics he used to rid Toulon of the English fleet in 1793, Brigadier-General Bonaparte, who was serving as Director of Military Plans in Paris at the time, was asked to intervene. He promptly sent for Captain Joachim Murat to bring some guns with which to administer a 'whiff of grape-shot'[11]. Napoleon ordered the crowd to disperse and when they refused, he commanded the artillery to fire, killing between 200 to 300 of the insurgents. The rest fled. This action resulted in his promotion to the rank of *Général de Division* with command of the *Armée de l'Interieur*. By March 1796 General Bonaparte was the Commander-in-Chief of the *Armée de l'Italie*, where he soon won spectacular victories and glory by defeating the Austrians. He had risen from obscurity to fame, his portrait filling the Paris shops, showing a haggard young general with classic features, gesticulating to his admiring soldiers against a backdrop of the snowy Alps.[12]

The Italian campaign successfully completed, on October 27th 1797, General Bonaparte was appointed to command the *Armée de l'Angleterre*, assembling in the Channel ports to invade England. He said that:

The English are courageous, meddling and energetic. We must pull down the English monarchy... Let us concentrate our efforts on building up our fleet and on destroying England. Once that is done Europe is at our feet.[13]

The alarm had passed throughout England and by 1798, engravings of the French invasion 'machines' were on view in Fleet Street and St. James Street. Semaphores were erected, serious plans for the defence of the coast, started in 1796, were again updated and empowered in the Defence Act of 1798. Mobilization proceeded. In April of 1798, however, Napoleon decided that a successful invasion was not possible:

Whatever efforts we make, we cannot gain naval supremacy for some years to come. To invade England without such supremacy would be to embark on the most daring and difficult task ever undertaken... If, in view of the present state of our navy, it seems impossible to obtain the promptness of execution which is essential, we can only abandon the expedition, while maintaining a pretence of it, and concentrate our attention and resource on the Rhine... or undertake an eastern expedition to threaten England's trade with the Indies.[14]

In April 1798, Napoleon was given command of the *Armée de l'Orient* and departed for Egypt, where, despite his land victories, his navy was destroyed by Admiral Horatio Nelson at the Battle of Aboukir Bay. This left Napoleon and his army stranded and fostering another European coalition which attacked France, reclaiming many of Napoleon's gains. In August, Napoleon and most of his principal staff officers slipped out of Egypt, reaching the shores of France on October 9th. Another *coup d'état* was imminent in Paris and by November 9th, the streets of the city were filled with troops commanded by Napoleon's officers: Napoleon Bonaparte was nominated First Consul in the new government, first among three. He had been given the power of a king, though without the sceptre.

After years of war, lawlessness, tyranny, executions and massacres, most in France were sick of the Revolution. They wanted peace and stability, and the majority assumed that the chaos of the past could only be brought under control by the hand of a single, powerful leader. General Napoleon Bonaparte, hero of France, seemed to have all the qualities needed to heal the land while standing proud.

One of his first acts as First Consul was to put aside his uniform and adopt modest civilian dress, giving himself to the administration and reordering of the nation. By May, however, he was back in uniform, attempting to reassert the power of France over a hostile Europe, and by 1801 was again planning an invasion of England. England reacted by putting Admiral Horatio Nelson in command of the naval defense of the Thames in July and expanding on land defense work.

The war took its toll, and faced with stalemate, England and France signed a treaty of peace at Amiens on March 25th 1802. In August, Napoleon was made Consul for life with the right to select his successor.

For Bonaparte, peace was the continuation of war by other means. English forbearance lasted until May 1803, when England declared war on France once again. Napoleon believed that the only way to defeat the English was to invade, and a month after war had been declared, he ordered the *Grande Armée* to the Channel ports to begin training for a seaborne invasion. This time, he intended to provide a worthy fleet and ordered 2,000 small craft to be escorted by his ships, carrying 167,590 men and 9,149 horses in one crossing to the shores of England.

French preparations to invade England continued. On May 3rd 1804, Napoleon Bonaparte, First Consul, was proclaimed Emperor of the French.

In 1804, England once again, stood alone, 'unreconciled, unconquered, implacable – sullen fierce and almost unperturbed,'[15] against the threat of French mastery and empire. English ships, her walls of wood, blockaded the French inside the Continental coasts, but the Government believed that the French had to be defeated on land – something they could not accomplish alone. The English Government, once more, began to build a third coalition of allies, united to defeat France.

Devising complex manoeuvres to deceive the English Admirals, Napoleon continued with his plan to cross the Channel under the protection of a joint French and Spanish fleet. However, on news of the strength of the gathering coalition forces, on August 26th, he ordered the *Grande Armée* to leave the Channel ports and march into Germany. On October 21st 1805, Admiral Nelson found and defeated his navy at Trafalgar, ending his naval adventures. Nelson gave his life in this victory.

Napoleon, once again, made his way across Europe, systematically defeating the allies. Unable to attack the English directly, he attacked them by issuing the Berlin Decrees which were intended to strangle their trade and commerce by creating an iron ring of customs guards and decrees stretching from the borders of Russia around the coasts of Northern Europe and Western France, sealing off the whole Mediterranean coastline as far as the Dardanelles. It was a land blockade of English sea power, keeping English goods from entering Europe, and forbidding products and raw materials from getting out. The aim was to stifle the English life blood of trade and commerce. The Continental battles continued, aided and abetted by considerable English treasure.

There were, however, serious cracks in the Continental iron rings. Portugal, which had long been one of England's allies, proved to be a gap of momentous proportions as its sea ports allowed English commerce and information to flow through with relative ease. Threatened by an invasion of French armies, the Portuguese royal party, the Government and the nobles of Portuguese society fled Lisbon to the safety of their colonies in South America. A few days later, Napoleon's troops occupied Lisbon. England expanded her blockade to all French and French-allied ports.

Spain rebelled in a fury of spontaneous insurrection at the duplicity and egregious deceit Napoleon had used to depose and replace the Spanish Bourbon monarchy, placing his brother, Joseph, on the throne. A riot ensued as the remaining Spanish princes and princesses, the King's brother, younger son and daughter, were being taken from Madrid to Bayonne to join the royal party in detention. The angry crowd stoned the French soldiers escorting the royal coach, tearing some to pieces. The French fired upon the mob until they fled, but the insurrection which had begun in Madrid spread throughout Spain.

Peasant bands armed themselves with whatever weapons they could find and killed any French soldier unwise enough to be alone or in a small group. At the time, the Spanish people were governed by local and provincial committees, the Juntas — a covey of alternative, parallel and changing authorities, liberally filled with clergy. Between May 24th and 30th, the committees began to converge at their local centres. They refused to obey any order coming from a branch of the government working with the French. The tiny province of Asturias, acting on its own, drove out the French governor, seized the arsenal, constituted itself an independent government, declared war upon Napoleon and sent their envoys to England to appeal for alliance and aid. On June 6th 1807, they arrived in London, whereupon the English agreed to their request. At that moment the Peninsular War began.[16]

The Spanish armies reformed and defeated some French divisions; on July 18th, in particular, they inflicted upon the French a humiliating defeat at Bailén by taking 22,800 surrendering soldiers prisoner. Andalusia and Galicia also declared war on France. When Joseph arrived in Spain he quickly saw that the situation was extremely dangerous. He told his brother: 'No one has told your majesty the truth. The fact is that there is not a single Spaniard who is for me except the few who came here with me. All are terrorised by the unanimous feelings of their compatriots,' and asked for 'plenty of troops and money.'[17] Napoleon, however, would not hear of it, and he replied: 'Keep fit! Have courage and gaiety and never doubt that we will be completely successful.'[18]

The Spanish invitation gave the English an opportunity to bring their armies into the land war on the Continent. The English could be supplied by sea. French communication lines back across the mountains would be tenuous with the Spanish peasantry in revolt, and Napoleon would have to expend precious men and resources to fight the Allied army and to conquer and contain the rampaging guerillas living in the difficult terrain. Aside from the military opportunity, the alliance with Portugal and Spain would give the British access to Continental sea ports and a new source of gold and silver, especially from Spanish America. This not only helped finance the war in the Peninsula, but also increased funds to support the coalition.

The English Government sent an army led by Sir Arthur Wellesley (the future Duke of Wellington) to offer support to the Spanish insurgents. However, since the Spanish Juntas of Galicia and Andalusia were not yet willing to accept foreign troops, and believing that the French in Portugal could not be reinforced through Spain, the expedition was sent to Portugal, landing August 1st 1808. Wellesley first dealt a severe blow to the French at Roliça and then defeated an army of around 16,622 men with a combined Anglo-Portuguese force of 18,669 at Vimeiro on August 21st. The French were then evacuated from Portugal. The alliance with Portugal now re-established, peace was made with the local Spanish representatives, and the English army was increased to some 40,000 with Sir John Moore in command.

News of the defeats of the French in the Peninsula spread throughout Europe, suggesting that the French were not invincible. Napoleon decided to remedy to this idea by imposing a few crushing defeats himself:

I will conduct this war of peasants and monks myself, and I hope to thrash the English soundly...[19]

I leave in a few days to put myself at the head of my army and, with the help of God, I will crown the King of Spain

Madrid and plant my eagles on the ramparts of Lisbon... It is the special blessing that Providence, which has always watched over our armies, should have so blinded the English that they have left the protection of the sea and, at last, exposed their troops to the continent.[20]

There were 314,612 French soldiers on the roles in Spain, 152,000 of which were under Napoleon's direct command. He was in Madrid by the end of November.

His next goal was to regain control of Portugal and he was planning to move towards Lisbon.

I shall hunt the English out of the Peninsula. Nothing can for long withstand the fulfillment of my wishes.[21]

Spain, which had earlier rejected England's help, asked Sir John Moore to protect Madrid, but unfortunately, it fell the day after the request arrived. Moore decided on a gamble to overwhelm an isolated French force in the north, an action which would also cut the French communication lines back to France. He soon learned, however, that Napoleon knew where he was and was quickly converging with a superior force to destroy him. Rather than be caught between two French armies, Moore elected to retreat over 250 miles of rugged snow-covered mountains, beginning his famous retreat to Coruña. In January 1809, Napoleon was indeed close. However, he was forced to leave immediately when news reached him that serious problems in Austria and Paris were leading to a plot to replace him. He delegated command of his army but the British escaped, although Sir John Moore died in battle as the English troops prepared to embark to their ships.

Once at home, Napoleon declared: 'the Spanish business is finished,'[22] and turned over the war in the Peninsula to his brother and some of his best generals. He never returned. Napoleon belittled the Duke of Wellington as 'Sepoy General', who, having risen in rank in the easy fields of India, would be easy prey. Napoleon sent his veterans to the mountains of the Peninsula, apparently unconcerned about the small allied army, its general or the fierce and angry peasants of Portugal and Spain who hated his soldiers.

Wellington, although numerically outnumbered, proved an artful opponent, who devised tactics which set the battles on his own terms, enabling him to hide and protect his troops. He had an eye for selecting ground that would give him the advantage and he mastered the logistics of supplying his army with food and weapons in an inhospitable land. He did not expend his men uselessly, and for this, they respected him and fought valiantly for him. Napoleon referred to the Peninsular War as his 'Spanish ulcer'. He had not heeded the admonishment of Henry IV that 'Spain is a country where small armies are beaten and large ones starve.'[23]

With bloody and brutal fighting, the allied armies, under the Duke of Wellington, gradually pushed the French out of the Peninsula, pursuing them over the mountains into France in 1814 and Napoleon's fortunes were sinking. His army of a half a million men had been destroyed in Russia in the disastrous retreat from Moscow in 1812. He was routed at Leipzig in 1813. The Allies, knowing him to be hundreds of miles away, seized Paris on March 30th 1814 and the Allied Peninsular Army, under the Duke of Wellington was on French soil. Convinced by his marshals that all was lost, Napoleon Bonaparte, Emperor of the French, abdicated on April 6th and was exiled to Elba.

The story ends with Napoleon's escape from Elba, his resumption of the crown, and finally, his total defeat at the battle of Waterloo on June 18th 1815 and his exile to St Helena. Alone of the European powers, England had 'withstood the whirlwind unleashed by the French Revolution unscathed'[24] and had repelled the grasp of the French crown for its island nation once again — apparently for the last time.

ABOUT THIS BOOK

This book is focused on the campaign fought under the command of the Duke of Wellington against the French and is neither a history nor an analysis of that war.

Using first-hand accounts of the men - and their contemporaries - who fought in the Peninsula and France, illustrated with drawings and photographs, most of which, depictions by re-enactors, this book attempts to convey what the soldiers thought, experienced, and saw — what it was like to march in those fields, to climb across those mountains, to experience new cultures, to

suffer in those climes and to fight in those battles.

The book is intended as a compliment to the fictionalised account that Bernard Cornwell has created of Richard Sharpe, a Rifleman of the 95th Division, the famous Rifle Brigade, which brings home in extraordinary detail the visceral, human and existential dimensions of England's war with France, battle by battle. By providing these authentic reflections of the participants, it is hoped that the supplement will honour the men and bring to those attracted to this human endeavour some further insight into the conditions and the driving motivations which brought these men to action, ready to pay the price required for victory, the men who were — Marching with Sharpe.

1 Thackeray. *Vanity Fair*

2 Durant. *The Age of Napoleon*. P. 9.

3 Churchill. *The Age of Revolution*. P. 268.

4 Churchill. *The Age of Revolution*. P. 278.

5 Lee, Christopher. *This Sceptred Isle*. P. 461.

6 Durant. *The Age of Napoleon*. P. 50.

7 Best, Geoffrey. *War and Society in Revolutionary Europe 1770 – 1870*. Pp. 82-83.

8 Churchill. *The Age of Revolution*. P. 285.

9 Churchill. *The Age of Revolution*. P. 285.

10 Lee. *This Sceptred Isle*. P. 462.

11 Glover, Michael. *The Napoleonic Wars: an illustrated history 1792-1815*. P. 39-40.

12 Oman, Carola. *Britain Against Napoleon*. P. 43.

13 Glover, Michael. *The Napoleonic Wars*. P. 50.

14 Glover, Michael. *The Napoleonic Wars*. P. 53.

15 Churchill. *The Age of Revolution*. P. 314.

16 Churchill. *The Age of Revolution*. P. 317.

17 Churchill. *The Age of Revolution*. P. 318.

18 Glover. *The Napoleonic Wars*. P. 131.

19 Britt, Albert Sidney, III. *The West Point Military History Series. The Wars of Napoleon*. P. 88.

20 Glover. *The Napoleonic Wars*. P. 132.

21 Glover. *The Napoleonic Wars*. P. 134.

22 Glover. *The Napoleonic Wars*. P. 135.

23 Britt. *The Wars of Napoleon*. P. 101.

24 Muir, Rory. *Britain and the Defeat of Napoleon. 1807-1815*. Pp. 374-375.

PREPARING FOR WAR

All you who are kicking your heels
Behind a solitary desk with too little wages
and a pinch-gut Master
– all you with too much wife,
or are perplexed with obstinate and
unfeeling parents…
Join the 14th Light Dragoons

As the 1800s progressed, the English Army was in dire need of recruits. France and England, the two leading nations of the world, were 'both deeply disturbed by angry passions, eager for great events and astonishing dominion.'

The French empire was then so vast that it enabled Napoleon, through conscription, to array an army as numerous as the hosts of the ancient Persians, trained with Roman discipline and led with genius. With seemingly inexhaustible resources and uninterrupted success for so many years, he had created a power with a moral influence doubling its actual force.

By 1808, some 120,000 French soldiers had surged through the Peninsula, occupying all Portuguese and most Spanish fortresses. The entire *Grande Armée*, some 400,000 veterans, stood in reserve, ready to offer support to the troops in the Peninsula, should they require it.

The English Government, still at war with France, decided it imperative that military action be taken to enable Portugal and Spain to throw off this French yoke – to disburse Napoleon's 'hovering eagles' casting their 'gloomy shadow over Spain.' Napoleon immediately rose to the challenge, addressing his troops:

> *Soldiers! I have need of you. The hideous presence of the leopard contaminates the peninsula of Spain and Portugal: in terror he must fly before you. Let us bear our triumphal eagles to the pillars of Hercules!*

Though omnipotent on the ocean, England was, at that time, little regarded as a military power, being inferior in numbers and plagued with past defeat. The Duke of York calculated that Spain would be swept away unless a force of 60,000 thousand men could be sent to defy Napoleon's momentum: in October 1808, however, Parliament sent Sir John Moore to Portugal with an army of only 30,000 men and 5,000 cavalry. By 1809 Moore was dead, and almost all of his devastated army (over 26,000) had embarked back to England. Napoleon's brother, King Joseph, was in now Madrid; the total number of French Soldiers in the Peninsula was over 200,000: 'Portugal, like a drunken man, at once weak and turbulent, was reclining on the edge of a precipice.'

Sir Arthur Wellesley (later the Duke of Wellington) still believed that the French could be expelled with a force of 30,000 men; the Government agreed, staking their faith on the correctness of his conclusions. However, the regiments then quartered in England were meagre in numbers and being battle scarred in the Peninsula were too weak to sail. Large numbers of new men, therefore, had to be recruited into the army and trained.

RECRUITING:

A portrait of Lt Gen Sir John Moore, currently on view at the Museum of the Royal Green Jackets, Winchester.

WANTED

Brisk Lads, light and straight,
and by no means Gummy;
not under 5 feet $5^1/2$ inches, or
over 5 feet 9 inches in height.
Liberal bounty; good uniforms;
generous pay!
Step lively lads and come in
while there is time!

RIFLE CORPS!
COUNTRYMEN!
LOOK, BEFORE YOU LEAP:
Half the Regiments in the Service are trying to persuade you to Enlist;
But there is ONE MORE to COME YET!!!
The 95th; or, Rifle REGIMENT,
COMMANDED BY THE HONOURABLE
Major-General Coote Manningham,
The only Regiment of RIFLEMEN in the Service:
THINK, then, and CHOOSE, Whether you will enter into a Battalion Regiment, or prefer being a RIFLEMAN,
The first of all Services in the British Army.
In this distinguished Service, you will carry a Rifle no heavier than a Fowling-Piece. You will knock down your Enemy at Five Hundred Yards, instead of missing him at Fifty. Your Clothing is GREEN, and needs no cleaning but a Brush. Those Men who have been in a RIFLE COMPANY, can best tell you the comfort of a GREEN JACKET.
NO WHITE BELTS! NO PIPE CLAY!
On Service, your Post is always the POST of HONOUR, and your Quarters the best in the Army; for you have the first of every thing; and at Home you are sure of Respect—because a BRITISH RIFLEMAN always makes himself Respectable. The RIFLE SERJEANTS are to be found any where, and have orders to Treat their Friends gallantly every where.
If you enlist, and afterwards wish you had been a RIFLEMAN, do not say you were not asked; for you can BLAME NOBODY BUT YOURSELF.
GOD SAVE the KING! and his Rifle Regiment!
HULL, January 15th, 1808.
ROBERT PECK, Printer of the HULL PACKET, Scale-Lane, HULL.

The roll of the spirit-stirring drum, the glittering file of bayonets, with the pomp and circumstance of military parade, not unmingled perhaps with undefined thoughts of ultimate promotion, passed in review before my imagination in colours vividly charming; resistance was vain. In fact, on the 6th of April 1806, I enlisted in the 43rd regiment of the line.

Two pounds were given as part of the bounty, which was only eleven guineas instead of sixteen, having been sworn in for seven years and six months.

I was now fairly well off, and with my pocket full of money.

Indeed, one could sign up for life, or choose defined years of service of seven years. Cavalrymen were required to sign on for ten years in the first stretch, with subsequent periods of seven years each. Artillery started at 12 years, followed by periods of five years after that. The Irish tended to sign up for life; the Scots for one period at a time.

The first step made, events for the new recruit moved quickly:

The doctor ordered me to undress, to ascertain if I were sound; and having finished his examination, made his report to the Colonel that I was fit for service. The next day I was before Mr Justice Sheepshanks, to be sworn in the questions being put:

> *Are you already a member of any regiment,*
> *militia, navy or marines?*
> *Have you fits, or a rupture?*
> *Are you in any ways disabled by lameness,*
> *Deafness or otherwise?*
> *Do you have the perfect use of your Limbs and*
> *Hearing?*
> *Are you an Apprentice?*
> *Are you willing to go?*

He then tendered to me the oath:

> *I swear to be true to our sovereign Lord King*
> *George, and serve him honestly and faithfully in*
> *defence of his person, crown and dignity, against*
> *all His enemies or opposers whatsoever; and to*
> *observe and obey His Majesty's orders, and the*
> *orders of the generals and officers set over me by*
> *His Majesty.*

After which he then read to me the Articles of War, relating to mutiny and desertion.

I now mounted my uniform for the first time.

I was that evening parading the town *à la militaire*; **and no one who saw me would have supposed I had only been enlisted that day. How delightful to parade the streets in our splendid uniform, exhibiting**

ourselves as the brave defenders of our country should the Corsican attempt to carry into effect his threatened invasion of England.

Actually, most new regulars in Wellington's army came from the local militias, where there were various plans for inducing men to volunteer into regiments of the line.

The militia would be drawn up in line and the officers, or non-commissioned officers, from the regiments requiring volunteers, would give a glowing description of their several regiments, describing the victories they had gained and the honours they had acquired, and conclude by offering, as a bounty, to volunteers for life, £14; to volunteers for the limited period of seven years, £11. If these inducements were not effectual in getting men, then coercive measures were adopted; heavy and long drills, and field exercises were forced on them; which were so oppressive, that to escape them, the men would embrace the alternative and join the regulars.

Militia were preferable to raw recruits as they were required to have a minimum of drill and discipline, thus being trained soldiers of some little experience, who held 'great indignation at the presumption of the Corsican upstart;' men moved by the wrecks from Nelson's battle at Trafalgar:

Excited by curiosity, I visited Portsea Dock Yard, in which were some of the shattered ships that had been engaged at Trafalgar. One of them called the Timerare, had a breach in her side which extended the distance of three portholes. Her masts and bowsprit all gone.

A sober man might think it better to hazard life and limb abroad in the regular service, than to have poverty and hard-labour accompanying him to a peaceful grave at home. The young thought it:

A very fine thing, no doubt, to be an ensign in the local militia, and a remarkable pretty thing to be the admiration of all the milkmaids of a parish, but while time was jogging, I found myself standing with nothing but the precarious footing of those pleasures to stand on, and it therefore behoved me to think of sinking the ornamental for the sake of the useful.

TAKING A COMMISSION:

General: 'Young gentlemen, would you like to be an officer?'
Orderly: 'Of all things.'
General: 'Well, I will make you a Rifleman, a green jacket, and very smart.'

Before reforms were enacted, most officers came into the Army paying their shilling rather than taking it. Many fathers paid to have their children, nay even infants, commissioned and carried on regimental books, these officers being born to the Army, so to speak. With reforms in place, however, a young man being sixteen years old, literate and able to provide a letter of recommendation from an officer holding the rank of a major or above (or someone of high social standing) could apply for a commission. A resourceful subaltern in the Volunteers or Militia could 'recruit for rank'. If he could persuade other men to enlist with him, he could receive a commission at no cost, providing there were vacancies available. Men from good families with modest means simply went out to the battlefield, fighting in the ranks with a musket and living with the officers until a vacancy occurred – Gentlemen Volunteers. All officers, however, had to be able to afford the cost of uniforms, basic equipment, daily expenses, transport and necessaries for themselves as well as for their horses and servants, for an army salary, even when paid, was generally insufficient. No military experience was required.

REASONS FOR SEEKING A COMMISSION:

From the end of the 18th and beginning of the 19th century, English boys grew up in homes where:

All the talk round the dinner table was military; musters, uniforms, manoeuvres – heady stuff for a small boy. The French landed in Fishguard, there was excitement as the Worcester garrison marched out to the sound of the guns.

The French were ever to mind – French émigrés forming small discomforted colonies throughout England, and newspapers constantly reporting on Napoleon's victories in Europe or the growing French invasion force assembling across the Channel.

William Pitt warned that 'this time the struggle must be for existence', and that Bonaparte intended to break the Spirit of Britain. Semaphores were rigged. Martello Towers, a simple tower, being perfectly round, of brickwork, defended by a handful of resolute men, were built along the coast. Evacuation plans were circulated. Patrols, signal posts, beacons, flags were everywhere, to be used to spread an alarm which could bring, in the course of twenty-four hours more troops than the enemy could possibly land in the same time. There were drills, parades and continuous talk of frigates, fencibles and raft-weather. At Fleet Street in London, one could view startling engravings of Napoleon's machine for the invasion, the 'GIANT raft'. It had four windmills; a battlemented wooden fortress with batteries of 48-pounders at every corner, accompanied by the St. Malo raft which had a dome and carried two tents. It was surrounded by a host of smaller Calais rafts – each 300 feet square and able to carry 60 cannons and 4000 men. The roar from the firing of the French cannons in Boulogne could be heard on the English shores.

Nobles and men of high rank whose ancestors had been knights 'retained by the King for life', often joined the Army through a sense of duty to the King, although by the Napoleonic wars, there were but few of them in the Army. Younger sons of large and noble but not so well-to-do families, not in line to inherit family land or money – Arthur Wellesley being one of them – had commissions arranged for them. They accepted their service as their duty to family and country, as well as a way to earn a living.

Some men simply relished military life, drawn by the excitement, the travel and the wild romantic existence. Others sought in the Army stability and a home:

> Wander where he will, a regiment is ever, to a single man, the best of homes. For him there is no life, save one of travel or military occupation, which can excite feelings of interest or consolation. The hazard of losing life, which a soldier is often called on to encounter, gives to his existence, as often as it is preserved, a value it would otherwise soon cease to possess.

Young men had never known a time without the war. Unsurprisingly, therefore, many sought to wear the red coat so they could help to crush 'the Fiend of the Bottomless Pit, the Serpent of Corsica, the Brigand Chief, the Beast of the Apocalypse'.

THE KING'S HARD BARGAINS:

Finally, swept into the thin red line were the 'King's hard bargains': pickpockets, coiners, footpads and other incorrigible bad characters, 'manumitted goal-birds' forced to choose between the Army, jail or worse. Some bargained they would outwit the Army and took the bounty with every intent to desert and 'jump another bounty': Tom 'The Devil' enlisted, took his shilling and then deserted 49 times before being hanged at the age of 26. Thus, nearly every battalion in the Peninsula had its share of drunkards, plunderers, stragglers and criminals 'whom neither punishment nor any kind of discipline could restrain.'

FROM RECRUIT TO SOLDIER – TRAINING

Drunk or sober, rank and file recruits to the infantry were escorted or found their own way to camp. Advice to the new recruit, given by one who knew from experience, was:

1. *Appearing in your own eyes, with your bounty in hand, to be enormously rich, don't take the trouble to throw your shillings and halfcrowns at people's heads, as if they were of no value;*

2. *You find a comrade particularly civil: begin to suspect he has fallen in love – not with you, but your money; and button up your pockets in exact proportion to the zeal which he manifests for trying their depth;*

3. *Non-commissioned officers are in an especial manner to be shunned, whenever they profess to hold you in favour; … these harpies desire only to make a prey of you. They will first suck you dry, and then grind you to powder;*

4. *Endeavour to begin your career as it is your wisdom not less than your duty to go forward with it. Aim at the character of a sober and steady man, and you will, without doubt, succeed in deserving it.*

5. *Keep your temper, even if you be wronged, especially when the wrong is put upon you by a superior. Truth and justice are sure to prevail in the end; whereas, it often happens that he who is eager to anticipate that end is crushed in the struggle.*

6. *Finally, be alert in striving to acquire all necessary drills, and an acquaintance with your duty in general.*

This advice came hard bought as there were some shameless recruiters who, having quotas to meet, placed the King's shillings into drunken hands, bullied men through their oath and then would 'pounce upon the recruits like a band of harpies'. In a young recruit's words:

> [They] never let us loose from their talons till they had thoroughly pigeoned us, the first step being to extract, in the shape of a loan, whatever happened to remain of our bounty. His next was to defraud us of the better half of our marching-money.

TRAINING RECRUITS:

When the recruits arrived at a depot or camp, they were assigned to a company, issued a knapsack and basic clothing including trousers, cotton drawers, boots, a cap and a red coat with a collar of the facings and the buttons of the regiment. Then they began to drill.

Now I began to drink the cup of bitterness. How different was my situation from what it had been! Forced from bed at five o'clock each morning, to get all things ready for drill; then drilled for three hours with the most unfeeling rigour, and often beat by the sergeant for the faults of others. I who never knew fatigue, was now fainting under it.

THE REGULAR INFANTRY:

For hundreds of years, little had changed in the combination of technical elements that were merged into a lethal force on a battlefield. There were men, horses, edged weapons, muzzle loading cannons and muskets. Advantages could be found in the ground chosen, the tactics used to surprise and deceive, the size of the force, the precision of manoeuvre, the will to fight, the discipline or an unforeseen event. But it was the Infantry that defined the tactics at the heart of the encounter: 'On their steadiness and efforts the decision of events depends.'

THE REDCOAT'S MUSKET:

The firearm of the British infantryman was a smoothbore musket, often called 'Brown Bess', a noble yet horribly inaccurate weapon. It could create a tangle

of bodies in the ranks of an oncoming column – but only at 50 or maybe a 100 yards, and only as a result of a volley of hundreds of muskets firing simultaneously. At a longer range the volley only had the effect of possibly demoralising the troops and scaring them into running away in panic, which was actually the preferred outcome. 'Such explosions may intimidate by their noise; it is mere chance if they destroy by their impression.'

In most versions of the smoothbore musket, the .75 calibre barrel-bore was larger than the spherical lead ball, Ensuring that the gun could be loaded and fired quickly. As a result of this windage and the gap between the ball and the barrel, the shot wobbled and bounced on its way down and out of the barrel. Hitting a chosen target, even at 50 or 75 yards took a lot of skill and luck and was hard to repeat – no one ever knew which direction the ball would take from its last bounce before it exited the barrel. 'You may as well fire at the moon and have the same hope of hitting your object.'

THE MUSKET AND THE LINE:

With such an inaccurate and unreliable weapon there was little point in aimed individual fire. The most effective course of action was to provide a volley of fire from a very large number of muskets firing in unison. This resulted in tactics which required highly disciplined massed columns or lines of densely packed men, using complicated marching manoeuvres to obtain an advantage for this salvo of death followed by a bayonet charge.

Thus, to train a regular infantryman of the line to fight, was to train him to march – the precise, immediate, disciplined execution of deploying, countermarching, retreating, and remaining steady. Firing his musket was secondary; very little time was spent even firing the gun with blanks, let alone teaching a man to aim or giving him enough practice with live ammunition to hit a target. If he could load the gun, point it in the right

direction, stand steady, wait for the order and then fire or charge on command, that was sufficient. Getting the column in place was first and foremost.

DRILL:

When the war with the French broke out, there was no fixed system of drill in the British Army and there was no standard training for officers – if there was any training at all. Officers who purchased their commissions in the 'old days' believed and taught that:

> **Dry books of tactics are beneath of the notice of a man of genius; if therefore, the major or the adjutant advises you to learn the manual, the salute or other parts of the exercise, you may answer, that you do not want to be a Drill-sergeant or corporal – or that you purchased your commission and did not come into the army to be made a machine of.**

The solution was to have the adjunct or sergeant-major write out the words of command in the proper order on a small card so that 'if you cannot retain the manoeuvres in your head, you may at least keep them in your hat'. Any interest shown by an officer in the details of march other than their need to be present at the end of the daily parade, was thus variously exhibited with capricious originality.

Approaches to the control and discipline necessary to drill the complex manoeuvres was open to the personal predilections of the officers, ranging from numbing repetition of drill:

> **Serjeant Major, Do they grumble?**
> **Yes, sir.**
> **Then wheel 'em again!.**

to producing abject fear through frequent flogging (being 'flayed alive' for any 'perceived' mistake) which could often be extremely severe. Military ardour was damped by the cruelty practised on men, many suffering from recent wounds for the slightest breach in the strictest attention to duty and punished with 200 or 300 lashes. 'To see such men tied to the halberts and their backs lacerated, for the most trifling fault, was really horrible.'

This army of the end of the 18th century, so trained and managed, was incapable of concerted action in the field, a situation which Colonel Sir David Dundas, 'Old Pivot', determined to rectify by writing and publishing his *Rules & Regulations for the Formations, Field-Exercise and Movements of His Majesty's Forces*. Long and ponderous, his point, nevertheless, was taken by the Commander of the Army and the Duke of York, and copies were delivered to regiments throughout the Army with the injunction that they be put to use. However, habitual independence of action is not easily repressed, and Dundas' Eighteen Manoeuvres were not seriously practised. In 1795, another general order was issued prescribing not only their use, but also the weekly schedule that was to be followed:

Monday and Friday in every week are to be devoted to the exercise of separate battalions under the personal direction of its own commanding officer; Every Tuesday and Saturday the exercising of troops is to be performed by brigades, under the immediate conduct and command of their respective major generals; On each Wednesday, the commanding general will take out the whole line and make them perform such movements, manoeuvres or other exercises as he may think proper; Thursday is to be set apart as a day of repose for the whole; such Corps only excepted as may have been negligent or irregular in their exercises on the preceding days; or which are otherwise defective or behind hand in their discipline.

THE EIGHTEEN MANOEUVRES:

As their use spread, the Eighteen Manoeuvres gradually became a standard for drilling the Line Infantry, Militia and the volunteers. Troops marched and counter marched towards one another, deployed into lines and commenced fire or charged. This line, two or three deep, could be miles long and it was to be held continuous and straight. Distances had to be exact, commands perfectly timed and troops prompt and correct in executing their movements.

THE EIGHTEEN MANŒUVRES

MANŒUVRE I
CLOSE COLUMN IN REAR OF THE RIGHT COMPANY

MANŒUVRE II
CLOSE COLUMN IN FRONT OF THE LEFT COMPANY

MANŒUVRE III
CLOSE COLUMN ON THE RIGHT CENTRE COMPANY
FACING TO THE REAR.

MANŒUVRE IV
CHANGE OF POSITION IN OPEN COLUMN

MANŒUVRE V
WING THROWN BACK

MANŒUVRE VI
COUNTERMARCH AND CHANGE OF POSITION

MANŒUVRE VII
COUNTERMARCH BY FILES, ON THE CENTRE OF THE BATTALION

MANŒUVRE VIII
MARCH IN OPEN COLUMN

MANŒUVRE IX
ECHELLON CHANGE OF POSITON

MANŒUVRE X
CHANGE OF POSITON

MANŒUVRE XI
CHANGE OF POSITON

MANŒUVRE XII
RETREAT IN LINE

MANŒUVRE XIII
MARCH TO A FLANK IN ECHELLON

MANŒUVRE XIV
HOLLOW SQUARE AND ITS MOVEMENTS

MANŒUVRE XV
RETIRING AND FILING TO THE REAR

MANŒUVRE XVI
FILING, ADVANCING AND CHARGING TO THE FRONT

MANŒUVRE XVII
RETIRING IN LINE

MANŒUVRE XVIII
ADVANCING IN LINE

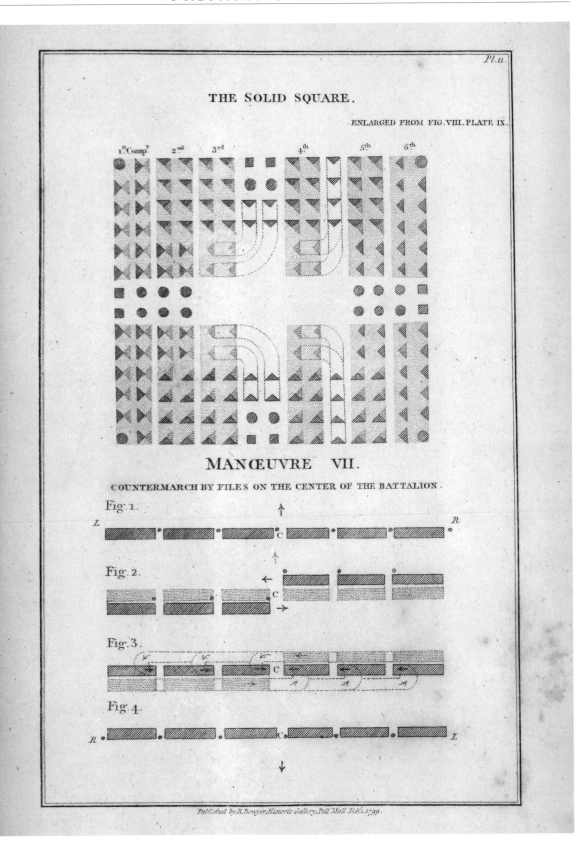

Pl. 11.

THE SOLID SQUARE.

ENLARGED FROM FIG. VIII. PLATE IX.

1.ᵗ Comp.ʸ 2.ⁿᵈ 3.ʳᵈ 4.ᵗʰ 5.ᵗʰ 6.ᵗʰ

MANŒUVRE VII.

COUNTERMARCH BY FILES ON THE CENTER OF THE BATTALION.

Fig. 1.

L .... C .... R

Fig. 2.

C

Fig. 3.

C

Fig. 4.

R .... C L

Published by R.Bowyer, Historic Gallery, Pall Mall Feb.1.1799.

To end pockets of continued wilful deviations or misinterpretations of the drill, in 1804, the Duke of York once again ordered that the regulations be upheld and that 'strictest conformity thereto be observed in every particular of execution'.

According to Dundas, infantry recruits were to be drilled first without arms, secondly with arms (though they did not fire), then with the platoon or company, followed by the battalion and finally, entirely with the line. A file leader or 'fugleman' – an experienced soldier – stood in front of the ranks so his movements could be copied by the troops. Some dedicated officers purchased toy soldiers which could be moved about to help them learn how to conduct the various manoeuvres of a battalion in the field, though the burden of this work usually fell to the non-commissioned officers (NCOs).

Gradually, and with much effort, the Army coalesced into a force capable of coordinated action in the field and their display of a feu de joie had a fine effect upon all. In this case, the line, an extensive line, would commence fire with the right file and each of those on their left taking it up rapidly in succession, so that to an onlooker, it has the appearance of a wild-fire running along the line: 'Every heart present was elated with joy, and beat high to be led on to share in those glorious achievements which we were celebrating.'

Though such attainments were not obtained without struggle: General Sir John Moore, reflecting the widespread sentiments of many of his colleagues, once commented to Dundas about his Eighteen Manoeuvres: 'General, that book of yours has done a great deal of good, and would be of great value if it were not for those damned eighteen manoeuvres.'

ACCLIMATISING OFFICERS OF THE LINE:

To acclimatise the officers and to inculcate steadiness in the men, exercises were held wherein soldiers fired volleys using 20 or 30 blank cartridges: the officers were engulfed in the sounds of the battlefield and the smell of the enveloping smoke and were made to execute manoeuvres – opening and closing columns, forming hollow squares, falling into line again and bayonet charges. Some officers were further conditioned through vigorous riding, swimming, lifting cannon balls and climbing precipices. Overall, however, training for officers was so sporadic, that although many came to the field competent to lead infantry in battle, there were still those who rose to high command incapable of directing even simple manoeuvres; whilst others, who were expert in drill, turned out to be abject failures when faced with the demands of real battle.

Infantry rank and file generally considered the training drill severe, but many embarked for the Peninsula with full confidence in their arms and accoutrements, 'thoroughly understanding the use of [their] weapons, and passing muster without difficulty.'

LIGHT INFANTRY:

The situation was quite different for the Light Infantry, as some of these regiments were part of an experiment addressing the need for effective skirmishing and general reform. At the end of the century, many British officers thought there was a pressing need to:

Revive an appetite for things military in Great Britain, which had become utterly jaded by the military debauch of the last ten years. Most of the war trained soldiers had been either disbanded or had become utterly demoralised. The old rigid discipline had broken down, and the new well-jointed discipline, brought to life by the American War, was entirely dissipated by want of direction want of condensation and want of control.

Reforms were introduced to address the range of problems plaguing the Army in those days. Napoleon's threat to cross the Channel to invade England with his skirmishers attacking like a 'swarm of wasps' amidst the enclosed hedgerows of England, where a battalion could not 'march and attack in front', and where cavalry could 'not charge but on great roads', made these reforms even more urgent. Many British officers remembered Flanders, where 'No mobbed fox was ever more put to it to make his escape than we were, being at times nearly surrounded', or seeing riflemen spitted to trees with bayonets in the American woods. Or Bunker's Hill, where the American riflemen, described as an

undisciplined peasantry, held in check the best dressed regiments in the British service, killing or wounding no less than 1,054 officers and soldiers out of some 2,000.

England needed a disciplined army with skilled skirmishers:

> *A complete renovation must be produced on the public mind with regard to the system of defence, and to the military service in general. So critical a period being therefore arrived, it becomes the more necessary to take an enlarged view of the present state of our land forces. Without a radical change in our present military system, Britain will certainly not long continue to be either formidable abroad, or secure at home.*

The drill of Sir David Dundas was taken as a lever for the restoration of the Line Infantry, while skirmishing and elemental reform was given over to a few units of Light Infantry and the newly established Rifle Corps. These Riflemen, not only trained differently but also looked different.

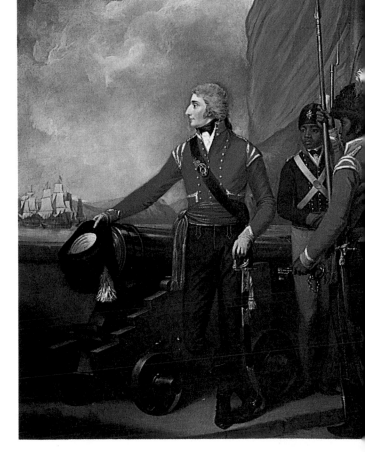

Col Coote Manningham, who established the first written regulations for the Rifle Corps in 1800.

27

THE RIFLE CORPS:

Stationed at Shorncliffe, the men recruited into the Rifle Corps and the 43rd and 52nd Light Infantry units, were to have qualities of a superior order. Sir John Moore wrote that:

A portrait of Lt W. Clarke.

The service of light infantry does not so much require men of stature as it requires them to be intelligent, handy, and active, and they should in the first instance be young, or they will neither take to the service or be easily instructed in it.
'NO WHITE BELTS! NO PIPE CLAY!'

Whilst in Dublin, I one day saw a corps of the 95th Rifles, and fell so in love with their smart, dashing and devil-may-care appearance, that nothing would serve me till I was a Rifleman myself.

Black leather belts, bottle green jackets, a smart cut and growing fame drew so many volunteers to the Rifle Corps in 1809 that a call for 338 volunteers from the militia brought in no less than 1,282 applicants.

There was an abundance of Johny Newcome's tumbling in hourly, for it was then such a favourite corps with the militia men, that they received a thousand men over their complement within the first three days of the volunteering (and before a stop could be put to it), which compelled the horse-guards to give an additional battalion to the corps – the 3rd Battalion.

The differences could be felt the moment of arrival. On first joining the Rifle Corps, a recruit was to be placed in the charge of some good men of his company, who would act not as his comrade but as his instructor in conduct and exercise: 'On my first arrival my whole soul was so absorbed in the interest excited by the service-officers that, for a time, I could attend to nothing else.'
    The recruit was issued an undress uniform which consisted of:

A while flannel jacket;
A green cape and cuff;
A regimental white waistcoat;
Russia duck trousers;
Boots;
A black forage cap edged and lettered in white;
Necessaries;

proportion as armies have been effective, they have uniformly proved themselves to be sources of internal strength. The only means of giving troops this distinctive superiority, is by a judicious course of discipline, which shall, by degrees, mould the intractable passions of men into habits in many respects repugnant to the feelings of ordinary life. It is not so much on mechanical dexterity, as on the acquirement of peculiar moral habitudes that the superiority of regular troops depends.

Nevertheless, it did not follow that discipline was to be lax or defection disregarded. The Regulations for the Rifle Corps stipulated that:

So serious indeed is the trust which it is expected may be put in a Rifleman, that if any man be found, after fair trial and instruction, a dull, stupid, careless character, valuing not his arms and never improving at the target, he will be [...] exchanged out of the corps.

LIGHT INFANTRY TACTICS:

Marching and training with the Riflemen in their green, the Light Infantry wore the same stovetop shako with the bugle and power horn, but also wore a regulation red coat which had wings on the shoulders to distinguish them from the regular redcoats. All the units of the Light Infantry, including Riflemen, mastered the manoeuvres and evolutions of the line battalions, but they also had their unique 'loose and desultory' tactics intended to:

Secure the front, flanks and rear of the army from surprise;
Stop the progress of an army;
Defeat the purposes of the cavalry by quick and irregular firing;
Meet the irregular presentations of the enemy;
Protect and shield the battalion in its advance;
Cover Foraging parties and convoys;
Reconnoitre, scout.

He wore this undress uniform until he was thoroughly instructed by the Regimental Drill Sergeants and Adjutants when, deemed fit for the ranks, he was issued his regimental uniform and his rifle.

Throughout training, a unique approach to the discipline of the recruit was to be followed: 'Lenity and attention will be shewn him every way, in the first instance, nor will severity be adopted until the former is found to fail.'

The Light Infantry and Rifle Corps worked from the proposition that:

Reliance on forces imperfectly disciplined has ever led to disaster, and, on the other hand, in

Thinking of a battalion of heavy infantry in line as a weapon, stretching out over miles, it fell to the Light

Infantry to conceal from the enemy its most important manoeuvres. They were to skirmish out before the line, using concealment, lying in ambush in woods, fields, steep hills and rugged precipices, taking posts, all with rapidity, peculiar to themselves, in order to surprise the enemy, gather intelligence, disrupt their supply and communications or deter their advance. Though appearing irregular, in truth, they pursued their course with order and regularity.

To do this, recruits first learned the basic manoeuvres which included:

LOOSE FILES – Marching six inches apart
from each other;
OPEN ORDER – Marching with two feet
between each file;
EXTENDED ORDER – Marching with two
paces (six feet) between each file;
MOVEMENTS IN QUICK TIME – All
movements of the Light Companies were to be in
quick time (about 120 paces a minute) except
when firing, advancing or retreating.

Pivot men or men best acquainted with the manoeuvres and sounds of the bugle within the line were to be corporals; when possible, this ensured the motions were performed with greater precision and celerity.

Due to the ground covered and the nature of Light Infantry movements in files, the greatest difficulty was in keeping the files 'locked up' and going straight, since a gradual wandering and lengthening out of the files was a 'serious evil' that counteracted the whole design of the tactics. Perfecting the exercise required considerable training and practice:

A perfect cadence and equality of step is to be
preserved, and without the least opening out, or
lengthening of the file. After facing, and at the
word march, the whole step off at the same
instant, each replacing, or rather overstepping the
foot of the man before him, i.e. the right foot of the
second man comes within the left foot of the first,
and thus of every one; more or less overlapping,
according to the closeness or openness of the files,
and the length of step. The front rank will march

straight along the given line, each soldier of that rank, looking along the necks of those before him, never to the right or left, otherwise a waving of the march will take place; and, of course, the loss and extension of line and distance; whenever the body returns to its proper front. The centre and rear ranks must look to, and regulate themselves, by their leaders of the front rank, and always dress in their file. Although filemarching is generally in quick, yet it must also be practised in ordinary time. The above position of feet takes place in all marching in front, where the ranks are close and locked up. With a little attention and practice, this mode of marching, apparently so difficult, will be found, by every soldier, to be easier than the common method of marching by files, when, on every halt, the rear must run up, to gain the ground it has unnecessarily lost.

Firing, when not in extended order, was to be by single men, each firing as quick as he could, consistent with loading properly, according to the following modes:

FIRING, TWO RANKS KNEELING - PRIMING AND LOADING IN THAT POSITION

At the word ready both ranks sink down smartly on their right knees and throw back their right legs. In the front rank, the left side of the right knees is directly to the rear of the right side of the left foot; but the rear rank carries the right knee about four inches to the right. The left legs of both must be perfectly perpendicular. The front and rear ranks respectively bring their firelocks down to the priming position, as hereafter explained, cock, and replace their right hands on the small of the butt: from the left arm being brought across the body, the left shoulders of both ranks are brought forward in a small degree; but the body must be kept as square to the front as possible, without producing constraint.

PRESENT

Levelling at the particular object and firing without waiting for any word of command; the elbows must on no account be projected.

LOAD

The firelocks of the front rank are in line with the haunches; and those of the rear rank are placed about four inches above the haunches.

The elbows of both ranks must be as close to the body as possible.

The front rank men, after priming, bring round their firelocks to the left side and throw the butts to the rear; so that' the barrels may be close to the left thigh and the muzzles three inches behind the left knees.

The left hand moves the firelock from the right side to the left, and the right hand is brought across the body to accomplish the loading. After loading, the firelock is raised and advanced to the front by the left hand, and the position for making ready is resumed.

The rear rank men, after priming, turn the body to the right in a small degree, lean well to the rear, and throw the butts to the front, so that the firelocks may be in contact with the right thighs of the front rank men and the muzzle in line with the hip bone.

They then resume their original position for making ready.

On the signal to cease firing, the ranks resume their standing position and shoulder.

FIRING ON THE SPOT

Each man selecting his particular object and firing.

FIRING IN EXTENDED ORDER

It is a standing rule that two men of the same file are never unloaded together. As soon as the front rank man has fired, he is to slip round the left of the rear rank man, who will make a short pace

An original Baker rifle on display at the Royal Green Jackets Museum, Winchester forward, and put himself in the other's place, whom he is to protect while loading.

FIRING ADVANCING

In extended order, the signal to march given, then the signal to commence firing where the rear rank moves briskly six paces before the front rank, each man having passed to the right of his file leader, makes ready, takes his aim and fires; and as soon as he has loaded again, trails his arms, each rank continues advancing and firing alternately. At the signal to cease firing not a shot must be heard.

FIRING RETREATING

The first rank begins to fire upon the signal to retreat, goes right-about, marching 12 paces in the rear of the second rank, fronts and loads. The Sergeant on the flank whistles when he sees the first rank formed and loading, whereupon the second rank fires, thus alternately, each rank retires, supporting each.

FIRING UNDER COVER

In firing from behind trees, large stones, etc. Light

Infantry men are to present, to the right of the object which covers them; and in changing places with the other man of the file, after firing, they will step back and to the left, so that the rear rank man may step forward without being exposed.

Similar instructions were outlined for other circumstances including:

TO FIRE ADVANCING IN EXTENDED
ORDER, AND COVERING EACH
OTHER
DEFILE FIRING.
FIRING AGAINST CAVALRY
FIRING OF TWO RANKS BY
INDEPENDENT FILES, WHEN
FORMED THREE DEEP

Once fully instructed in the firings and manoeuvrings, the recruits were next instructed in skirmishing which included:

FORMING CHAINS
EXTENSION OF FILES
ESCOURTING OF CONVOYS
MASKING THE MANOEUVRES OF
REGIMENTS
COVERING THE RETREAT OF
BATTALIONS
FORMING THE ADVANCED GUARD
OF AN ARMY
KEEPING UP COMMUNICATION
SKIRMISHING BEHIND HEDGES
FORMING SQUARE OR ORB

A chain was a line of men extended ten paces away from each other and 50 paces in advance of the company. Men in groups of three would fire alternately and fall back to load as the next man advanced. All in all, experienced officers knew that keeping such precise distances in the field was seldom practised, being very inconvenient, though the principle was practised: in general, the distances were regulated according to the ground and circumstances.

Success, however, ultimately depended 'upon the coolness, and presence of mind, of the commanding officer, and the silence and obedience of the men, fully

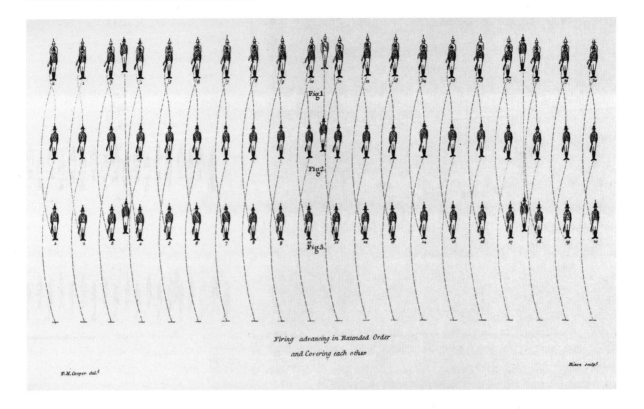

Fig.1

Fig.2

Fig.3

Firing advancing in Extended Order
and Covering each other

T.H. Cooper delt.

Hixon sculpt.

as much as upon their bravery.' Coolness was the test of Light Infantry caught in the field by charging cavalry. Armed with the national weapon, the bayonet, they formed a square or an orb, which was a round mass, six deep, disposing the soldiers in a circular form of defence in the mode of Caesar and the Gauls. In this situation, when confronting the thunderous sound of the horses charging, they had only to present the bayonet to the horses' nostrils and steadily wait for the charge.

All in all, the numerous movements of Light Infantry may be reduced to the following:

Marching in file;
Marching in column;
Marching in line;
Changing front;
Changing order or disposition;
Forming the square and oblong.

Finally, the recruit learned the 40 plus bugle and whistle signals of the Light Infantry used in the field, 14 while in the barracks and those of the drum used by the line Infantry, all intended to induce the hundreds of movements.

THE UNIQUENESS OF THE RIFLEMEN:

Though Riflemen were included in the Light Infantry, there was a very real difference between them, that went well beyond the colour of their jackets: their weapon. The Light Infantry carried a lighter and slightly shorter version of the Brown Bess, a smoothbore musket or fusil. Riflemen in England, however, were issued for the first time in the history of the British Army, a rifled musket – a sharpshooter's gun – called the Baker Rifle. There was nothing new about rifling the barrel of a musket by making a series of grooves inside the bore of the barrel so the ball would come out spinning. Rifled firearms were in use as early as the mid 15th century, and shoulder rifles from 1563. The Flintlock Pennsylvania/Kentucky Rifle dates back to 1750. Rifles had been used by colonial and continental armies during the 17th and 18th centuries. In 1800, however, the smoothbore musket was the standard infantry weapon. It followed that Riflemen would focus their training on marksmanship – aiming and shooting the guns with live ammunition and related tactics.

THE BAKER RIFLE:

Until the formation of the Experimental Rifle Corps in 1800, no indigenous British regulars were supplied with a rifled musket as standard army issue, even though rifles were well known and had in fact been in use for sport and hunting for hundreds of years.

To select the first rifle for standard issue, the Board of Ordnance ordered field trials to be held at Woolwich Arsenal in February 1800. All of the major rifles of the day were tested and in the end, the rifle submitted by Ezekiel Baker of Whitechapel, London, maker of sporting and military weapons, was selected because of its superior performance and the fact that its rugged construction could withstand the rigours of the battlefield. Baker had discovered that the rifling, or the

A portrait of Lt Col William Humbley.

degree of twist of the grooves cut inside the barrel, only needed ¼ turn (most rifles had a ¾ turn), making it precise from 200 to 300 yards. His gun also had a barrel that was only 30 inches long instead of the normal 36 to 40 inches. During the trials, 11 shots out of 12 were placed in a six-foot circular target at 300 yards, outperforming rifles of American and Continental manufacture. In Baker's own tests using a man-sized target at 100 and 200 yards, his 34 shots and 24 shots respectively were all hits. In the hands of a semi-skilled soldier, the Baker Rifle could be deadly accurate at three times the distance it took for standard muskets to even hit a mark.

Manufactured by a number of munitions suppliers, the Baker Rifle had a plain or twisted barrel rifled with seven 4 millimetre rectangular grooves. These grooves were almost equal in width to the lands or surfaces between grooves, making a ¼ turn in the length of the barrel. It was retained by the standard three flat keys and an upper swivel screw.

THE RIFLED AND SMOOTHBORE MUSKET COMPARED

Baker Rifle

Barrel:	30 – 30.5 inches
	Rifled
Caliber:	.615 – .70
	20/bag
Bayonet:	24 inches
Weight:	9 lb. 6 oz
Ignition:	Flintlock
Rate of Fire:	1-2/min
Accuracy:	300 yards
Expert:	>300 yards
Sights:	Two

Brown Bess

Barrel:	39 – 42 inches
	Smoothbore
Caliber:	.753
	14/bag
Bayonet:	17 inches
Weight:	9 lb. 11 oz

Ignition:	Flintlock
Rate of Fire:	3–5/min
Accuracy:	75–80 yards
Expert:	<100 yards
Sights:	None (There was a clip at the end of

the muzzle that could serve as a sight, but it was used to fix the bayonet to the musket and was obscured whenever the bayonet was attached.)

The muskets were measured in terms of barrel length. To determine the full length, add approximately 16 inches for the stock. The Baker Rifle, issued between 1806 and 1815, was .625 calibre and used a .615 calibre ball (20 to a pound bag). The ball was encased in a greased leather patch which lodged it in an airtight passage giving it a spin as it exited the gun and, as a bonus, also served to clean the barrel. This combination of ball and patch might take as much as a minute to fully seat because of the very tight fit in the barrel. However, this tightness, coupled with the rifling, made the Baker extremely accurate at ranges far out of reach of standard smoothbore muskets. Although mallets were issued, the men discarded them, relying on brute strength to pound the ball home. The .615 ball and leather patch could be replaced with a ball used without a patch to gain speed in reloading. The butt could be jogged on the ground to seat the ball and shake the powder through to the pan. However this practice seriously clogged the rifling in the barrel, rendering the gun useless as a rifle until it could be completely cleaned. Later special ball ammunition cartridges were specifically designed for the Baker Rifle. The rifle, which Ezekiel Baker suggested should have a trigger draw of 15 to 20 pounds, could be fired twice per minute by an experienced semi-skilled rifleman loading under battlefield conditions. It tended to misfire once every 6.5 firings.

The Baker came with a single steel ramrod and, unlike the smoothbore musket, which had no sights at all, had a backsight (which was dovetailed into the barrel) and a foresight, which was a thick, low blade integral with the base. The lock had a flat bevelled-edge ring-neck cock with a brass sideplate and raised semi-waterproof pan. The lockplate measures 5¼ inches. The brass cover of the butt-trap is typical of the Baker, and varied in size over time. The preferred stock was walnut, though that was not always available. The overall length of the Baker was 46¼ inches with a barrel length of 30¼ inches.

The British gunsmiths had limited experience and technical expertise in the manufacture of military rifles which meant that production was slow and costly – the price of one Baker rifle would buy three regular smoothbore muskets. From 1800 to the end of the war in 1815, over 30,000 Baker Rifles were manufactured.

For those issued a rifle, the original accoutrements included: two powder horns, one carrying especially fine grain to prime the flash pan, 60 balls (later 60 cartridges), leather patches stored in the brass butt-trap in the stock and a small toolbag including a turnscrew, ballpuller, worm and tommy bar and new flints.

The Baker had a distinctive brass trigger guard and to ensure that the reach of the rifle would be equal to that of a standard musket, each man was issued a 24 inch brass handled sword-bayonet that was attached to the barrel by a spring socket. However, since the rifle could not be so easily fired with the bayonet attached, the bayonet was rarely used in battle. The barrel of the Baker Rifle was 'browned' so that it would not reflect the glint of the sun giving away the position of the rifleman. Shooting positions included prone, standing, sitting and kneeling. Riflemen took pride in being able to reload and shoot lying on their backs with the muzzle tucked between their feet and the sling wrapped around the ball of their foot.

The Baker Rifle was a precision weapon which did not need a volley of fire from massed troops to be effective. Rather it invested a new kind of power in the individual or small teams of soldiers now able to advance ahead of the columns. The challenge to the Rifle Corps, therefore, was to command the hidden potential of both rifle and rifleman.

Recruits started firing at 50 yards resting their rifle on a "horse" used as a machine to assist when taking aim. Each man, practised daily with live ammunition, shooting about six times, so that he came to know his weapon's sound and kick, becoming fully proficient in shooting as well as cleaning and taking care of his gun. As soon as a company returned from practice, every man carefully cleaned their rifles and oiled their lock and cap.

The care of rifled arms is of such serious importance, both from the expense of the workmanship, and the superior nicety of their construction. No arms or accoutrements are ever to be changed from man to man. As Riflemen are supposed to be Soldiers of the greatest attention toward arms, no lenity will be shewn to those who injure or spoil them.

There were four ranges on the practice field: 90 yards for recruits and bad shots; 140 yards, 200 yards and 300 yards.

There were generally two kinds of targets used: the first was the familiar round target painted in alternate black and white circles. The second target was a figure or screen made of canvas stretched on a wooden frame which was 7 feet high, 3 feet wide, with a 6 feet high and 2 feet wide representation of a figure. The figure was

10

TRAIL ARMS, (FROM SHOULDER.)

THE left hand seizes the Rifle even with the shoulder, (see fig. 1, plate 5,) without the Rifle being raised as at the 'Present,' and 'Order;' the right hand then seizes it about four inches above the lock, (see fig. 2, plate 5,) the left hand then quits it, and falls back to the left thigh, and the right trails it on the right side at arm's-length. (See fig. 3, plate 5.

N. B. Fig. 3, plate 5, is turned, merely to shew the right hand in a side view.

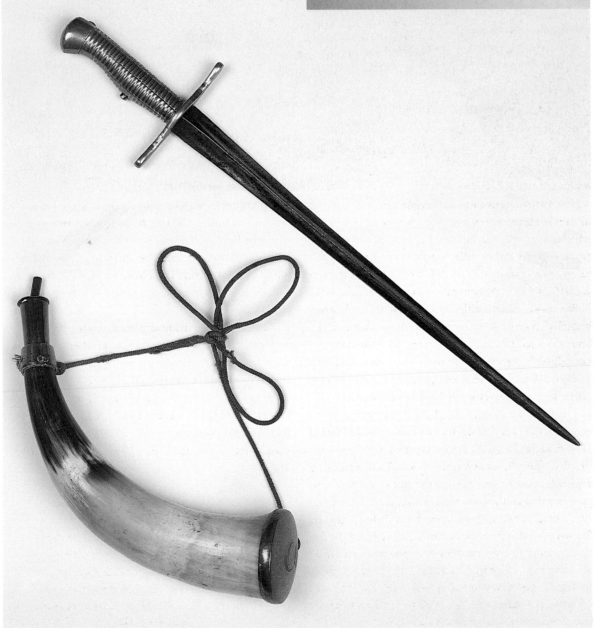

dressed so that each 'wound' could be clearly seen to grasp the effect. Every man was issued a target-book to record his skill.

In all target practice, the ground cannot be too much varied: woods, heights, hollows, plains, brushwood, water and every other description of surface, should be fired over occasionally. Also, the bodies of old trees, or other substances, to be fired at sometimes, in lieu of the regular targets.

On occasions, when the men were shooting blank cartridges, the Buglers or those who were unoccupied, were to move about at any given distance in front, to be levelled at during this exercise.

To further emphasise marksmanship, every company captain was encouraged to offer prizes for the best shots in his command. A first class (the lowest or 'awkward' class), was a soldier who could put five shots out of six into a target at 100 yards, firing from the shoulder, for two out of three consecutive days. To qualify as a second class ('the tolerably good'), a rifleman's abilities were tested further:

A portrait of Lt Gen. Sir Harry Smith, Bart, GCB.

Two shots in the round target, or two in the body of the man at the 2nd range (140 yards) and upwards, out of the six, for two days firing out of three, for the period, will be ranked in the 2nd class, and wear the small white cockade.

Contests to become Marksmen required shooting at ranges of 200-300 yards, often at moving targets, and the winners were rewarded with a gold 'medal.'

Any Rifleman who puts four shots in the round target, or three in the body of the man in the canvas one, out of six, at the 3rd range (200 yards) or upwards, but not at a less distance, for two days practice out of three, for two months after the receipt of the new rifle, will be ranked in the class of marksman, and wear the green cockade.

Exceptional marksmen wore a distinctive white armband. Captains were to keep a firing book containing the monthly roles and the daily work of the target. If a Rifleman failed to maintain his level for two months in a row, he was reduced to the lower rank. If he had not attained sufficient proficiency when the regiment sailed, he was not permitted to embark.

Sergeants were to fire four rounds once a week, but were not to fire with their company. However, officers were to practice with them on occasion to enter into the spirit. No books were to be kept on the subject.

The Riflemen loved to show off their daring and skill. An Irish officer, Major Hamlet Wade, later promoted to Colonel, and various Privates would hold the target for each other at the distance of 150 or 200 yards, while the other fired at it. So steady and accurate was their shooting they left the old Earl of Chatham, who had requested the display, in extreme agitation and horror, to which Major Wade replied, 'Oh, we all do it!' while proceeding to switch places so that he could hold the target.

LIGHT INFANTRY OFFICER TRAINING:

All Officers on joining the rifle corps will learn the manual and platoon exercises with the rifle and the sword exercise. When the Officers are fully

REGULATIONS

FOR THE

RIFLE CORPS,

FORMED AT

BLATCHINTON BARRACKS,

UNDER THE COMMAND

OF

COLONEL MANNINGHAM

August 25th, 1800.

LONDON:

PRINTED FOR T. EGERTON, AT THE MILITARY LIBRARY,

NEAR WHITEHALL,

By C. Roworth, Hudson's Court, Strand.

1801.

instructed in these three exercises of arms, they will be exercised by the Major; nor will they do any regimental duty whatever until reported by that Officer to the Commanding Officer as fully acquainted with the whole.

The Rifle Corps and the Light Infantry regiments were based on the principle that in subordination real discipline implied obedience and respect, where command, exerted with steadiness founded on good common sense and propriety, inspired obedience which was prompt and cheerful. Every officer, before he could exercise any responsibilities within the Regiment, had to demonstrate his competence, understanding, suitability and his ability to keep pace with operations in the field. Contrary to normal army practice, it was the rule of the Light Infantry and the Riflemen that all young officers must be drilled for six months in the ranks with the men before being allowed to do duty as an officer. Those who refused, or who failed to measure up to the standards of military merit and suitability to the service were rejected.

FIELD EXERCISES:

'No officer or soldier, be he ever so zealous, can be formed without much and constant practice.' Marksmanship was not seen as a free-floating skill, but rather, was treated as an integral element of successful field tactics. Thus, marksmanship was to be acquired in its total context and a six month program of field exercises (boot camp or basic training) was devised for both officers and regular soldiers – officers being given the same standing as the men.

To be as realistic as possible, these exercises involved living off the land, fluid skirmishing tactics, expertise in penetrating the enemy lines, hit and run raids, swift preparation of ambushes and ruses, surprise in taking outposts, the ability to act as reliable advance and rearguards and competency in the evolutions and manoeuvres prescribed by Dundas. Riflemen were taught to march at ease, to move swiftly (120 paces a minute compared to the normal 70), to use all available cover, never to waste a shot and to shoot to kill.

However, here, as everywhere, precision of tactics and scientific dexterity was secondary to the perfection of the discipline of mind inherent in the military character of light infantry. 'Bravery without discipline, and without long preparation of the mind for the dreadful trade of war, will not avail.'

As part of this regime of training, full regimental field exercises were held regularly, much like the one carried out one August day for the benefit of the Duke of York. Over 5,000 men, including the 4th Regiment of Foot, the 52nd, the 43rd, the 59th and the 95th, met on the cliffs above Shorncliffe looking out over British ships in the Roads towards Napoleon. The action was described by an eyewitness:

> **There were no cavalry. Exactly at 7 o'clock the Duke of York came on the ground. The ships of war in the Roads, each saluted him, which had something of the appearance of an assault, and the Artillery on the ground of review saluted him about the same time; the firing had a very fine**

effect, as the situation of the camp, a fine extensive level on the top of a cliff, is a beautiful one. The bands of each regiment saluted the Duke as he passed along the line; the regiments then passed in quick and slow time and marched admirably. They formed in column, and went through several manoeuvres, one of which was very picturesque. The Rifles and Artillery advanced to the brow of the hill, that overlooks the sea, and covered the advance of the troops marching against a supposed enemy landing. The rifles next retired behind the line, and covered the retreat of the main body. After a few manoeuvres, the brigade formed on the brow of some steep hills hanging over a valley, through which a small brook runs, hills rising on the opposite side. The Rifles lined the hedges, and fired through at the supposed enemy, while the Artillery played from the heights. Under this cover the brigade in line advanced down the hill, the Rifles retired into the rear, and the brigade made the grand attack. After firing for some time the brigade retired, the Rifles again advancing to cover the retreat up the hill. When at the top of hill the brigade made a stand and fired generally, the Artillery fired very briskly. The whole of the troops then returned to their original ground in front of the camp, when after the usual salutes the Duke of York took his leave.

A portrait of Lt Col James Fullerton.

hours in the canteens and alehouses. Officers were encouraged to be frequent participants in all of these endeavours.

EDUCATION:

Unlike their red coated comrades of the line, Riflemen and Light Infantry were expected to be thinking, fighting soldiers, capable of acting independently in the field. Consequently, a regimental school was established

for the instruction of those who wish to fit themselves for the situation of Non-commissioned Officers in reading, writing, and the four first rules of arithmetic. The knowledge of these will also be much in favour of promoting the private Riflemen.

Teaching these basic skills was to be a source of real use and instruction, using a combination of theory and

PHYSICAL EXERCISE:

Exercises were not only for skill, safety and success in the field, but were also devised to promote the health and amusement of the men. All those who served in the Light Corps were to know how to swim for military reasons and for good health and cleanliness, and daily athletics included vigorous games of cricket, hand or football, leap-frog, quoits, vaulting, foot races and dancing. Dancing was not only thought to be good exercise, it also helped to prevent men from passing

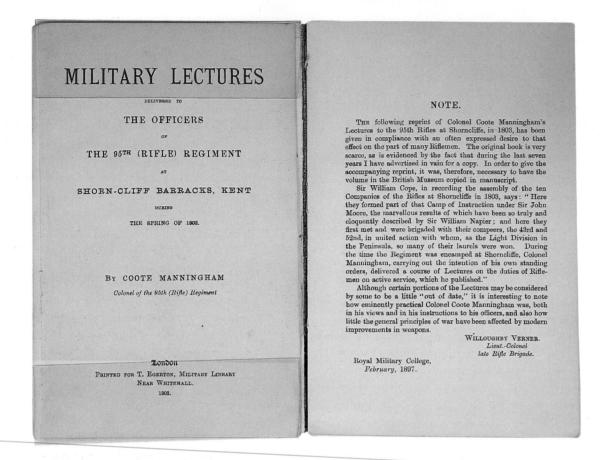

MILITARY LECTURES

DELIVERED TO

THE OFFICERS

OF

THE 95TH (RIFLE) REGIMENT

AT

SHORN-CLIFF BARRACKS, KENT

DURING

THE SPRING OF 1803.

BY COOTE MANNINGHAM

Colonel of the 95th (Rifle) Regiment

London

PRINTED FOR T. EGERTON, MILITARY LIBRARY
NEAR WHITEHALL.
1803.

NOTE.

THE following reprint of Colonel Coote Manningham's Lectures to the 95th Rifles at Shorncliffe, in 1803, has been given in compliance with an often expressed desire to that effect on the part of many Riflemen. The original book is very scarce, as is evidenced by the fact that during the last seven years I have advertised in vain for a copy. In order to give the accompanying reprint, it was, therefore, necessary to have the volume in the British Museum copied in manuscript.

Sir William Cope, in recording the assembly of the ten Companies of the Rifles at Shorncliffe in 1803, says: "Here they formed part of that Camp of Instruction under Sir John Moore, the marvellous results of which have been so truly and eloquently described by Sir William Napier; and here they first met and were brigaded with their compeers, the 43rd and 52nd, in united action with whom, as the Light Division in the Peninsula, so many of their laurels were won. During the time the Regiment was encamped at Shorncliffe, Colonel Manningham, carrying out the intention of his own standing orders, delivered a course of Lectures on the duties of Riflemen on active service, which he published."

Although certain portions of the Lectures may be considered by some to be a little "out of date," it is interesting to note how eminently practical Colonel Coote Manningham was, both in his views and in his instructions to his officers, and also how little the general principles of war have been affected by modern improvements in weapons.

WILLOUGHBY VERNER.
Lieut.-Colonel
late Rifle Brigade.

Royal Military College,
February, 1897.

information with practice. Experts were brought to Shorncliffe to lecture on military subjects such as the duties of patrols, pickets, the conduct of advanced and rearguards, small-scale manoeuvres, tricks and stratagems, marksmanship, etc. There was also a library where scholars could read books on military subjects or other instructive publications where many of the military lectures were subsequently published. The following books were required for the regimental collection:

A copy-book of all Public Letters received and answered;
A copy-book of all General Orders;
All Monthly Return and Muster-books;
A Daily Orderly-book;
A General Casualty-book;
A Journal-book of all marches, field days, and campaigns of the corps;
A book of Court-martials or black book;
A book of Merit, or distinguished soldiers;

A Target-roll, or Marksmen List book;
The Rifle Corps Exercise book;
Dundas's System for Cavalry and Infantry;
The Standing Regulations of the Regiment, ditto of the army, by the Commander in Chief;
The annual Army List;
Adye and Tytler on Court-martials.

All Officers were to purchase copies of:

The Articles of War
The Standing Regulations of the Regiment
The Exercise Book of the Rifle Service

Though open to all who wanted to attend (students paid a small fee based on their rank), non-commissioned officers were required to attend the school if they were not masters of the essential skills required for their duties. Sergeants were expected to be able to read, write and master basic mathematics. The men were encouraged to learn all the skills that would help in their promotion as well as make them more effective in the field.

In the school, which was held daily except Sunday and Saturday evenings, there were three classes: one for those learning to read, one for those able to read but were learning to write and one for those who could read and write, but were learning arithmetic. Additional classes in practical geometry, vulgar fractions, the rule of three and advanced mathematics were also available. Examinations took place every two months and the schoolmaster was a Sergeant.

Rifleman were issued a copy of Regulations for the Exercise of Riflemen and Light Infantry by Baron Francis de Rottenburg and Colonel Coote Manningham's treatise, Regulations for The Rifle Corps formed at Blatchington Barracks under the command of Colonel Manningham (although Manningham is the author of record, it is generally agreed by scholars of the time that William Stewart probably wrote the manuscript, devising most of the activities and regulations included and essentially commanded the Corps as Manningham was away a great deal of the time serving the King). The driving idea behind the institution of the school and the library was:

It is only by the theory and just reading, that the first principles of all professional subjects are in general attained by the majority of mankind. The practical parts may be afterwards successfully pursued.

ORGANISATION:

Discipline was integral to the thinking of the British Army, although it was to be achieved by different means, in the Light Infantry and Rifle Corps — one of these being the 'Company System'. Authority was given to a captain commanding a company and discipline was to be inculcated by officers who knew their duties thoroughly and were always in touch with their men — not by the lash.

Each company was made up of small teams or squads called a Mess, composed of ten men working in teams of two or three based on battlefield tactics, with one man firing, the second loading and the third standing watch. The Mess was the basic living unit and included an

officer and a corporal – a Chosen Man – who was to take responsibility when the officer was absent. Daily duties were to be shared out. Every man was required to cook, in turn, breakfast and dinner, being punctually ready at the appointed hours or to act as the Fatigue or Orderly Man – excepting corporals (for cooking), Buglers and the Chosen Man. This duty was for a 24 hour period and commenced at sunset every evening. The Orderly Man equipped with the brooms, brushes and Mess-utensils necessary for ordering and sweeping the barrack room twice a day, was held responsible for any damage done or necessaries plundered, belonging to the company while the company was on parade.

Quarters were to be kept clean and regular, because:

Not only good health follows cleanliness, but good order in the disposal of all articles of clothing, bedding, arms and necessaries of a Rifleman in his barrack room is of essential consequence to his being ready and alert for service at the shortest warning.

A place for everything, and everything in its place.

Every man's bedding is to be neatly folded against the wall, the mattress doubled, and the blankets and sheets laid fourfold on it; his pack, with all necessaries in, is to be hung above the bedding; his clothes, i.e. his regimental or undress suit, are never to be put on the pack whilst in the barrack room, but to be neatly folded, and laid on the top of the bedding; his cap to be hung on a nail above the pack, and his accoutrements on the right side of the cap; his rifle to be fixed in the stand, barrel outwards, cock let down, and lock cap always on, loosely tied.

In addition, each squad was to be composed of 'comrades', a tent-fellow and a comrade-in-arms, two men who selected each other and whose officer was never to replace either man without the permission of his captain. These comrades always had the same berth in quarters and were separated as little as possible. This system was founded on a standing order that these squads were not to be broken up or added to in the field without an extraordinary reason and without the express order of the Battalion or Company Commander or consent of the men.

Riflemen, being liable to act very independently of each other, and in numerous small detachments in the field, will feel the comfort and utility of their own officer, non-commissioned officers, and comrades with them, and the service will be benefited by the tie of friendship, which will more naturally subsist between them.

Paperwork recorded every task and obligation, each company having a chest dedicated to its stationary and books. Though given to the charge of the Sergeant Major, every Captain had as his responsibility:

A Monthly Account-book;
A Day-ledger;
A Monthly, Fortnight, and Weekly State-book;
A Target Roll;
A Target Practice-book;
A Company's Articles of War;
A Company's Copy of the Standing Orders;
A Daily Orderly-book.

The Officer's Mess belonged to the Regimental Officer's Mess, stimulating the good order and economy of the regiment by providing comfort and unanimity at meals – a source of friendship and good understanding.

All Sergeants messed together and on no occasion whatever with the rank and file and Buglers.

Messes were to be supplied with bread, meat and a plentiful supply of vegetables. Washing was to be paid for by the Mess at an agreed rate. All soldiers were to be completed in every article of regimental necessaries and to pay for all repairs of damage committed upon arms and accoutrements.

THE SCHEDULE IN TRAINING CAMP:

The uniform system of daily duty was highly regular, even to a minute degree of nicety. Throwing a degree of variety and recreation into the whole, was thought to create good order, discipline and comfort, as it was the Colonel's wish that duty should be done with cheerfulness and inclination and not from mere command and the necessity of obeying.

Times were regulated by the seasons, the following sequence being followed in general, but varying during winter and summer:

Dawn	Reveille sounded by two Buglers (Sunday a half hour later)
5:30 AM	Men stand to their berth as the roll is called
	Windows thrown open, beds neatly made, berths swept out
	Wash hands, feet, face, comb hair, dress
	Orderly sweeps the room and lays out breakfast tables
6 AM	Drill bugle — one company to parade for exercise under arms
	Awkward men or recruits parade
6:30	Subaltern orderly officers make rounds to barracks and cook house
	Breakfast bugle
9 AM	Sergeants report to the Orderly Room
9:15	Parade bugle warning
9:45	Parade bugle — parade to form in open columns of companies
10 AM	General morning parade
	Inspection of the regiment, manual and platoon exercise, or field exercise and movements.

(12 PM Sundays, Thursdays, and Holidays — dress parade only with side arms)

Mid-day	Dinner bugle

Afternoons left to discretion of regiment

5:45	Parade bugle warning
6 PM	Parade bugle — parade to form in open columns of companies
6:30	General evening parade Inspection of the regiment, manual and platoon exercise, or field exercise and movements.

Sunset minus 30 minutes — Buglers call

Sunset -	Buglers sound retreat
8 PM	Buglers sound taptoo
	Roll called

9 PM	Buglers sound curfew/setting of the watch/all lights out.

THE WORTHY GOOSE:

Even the Regimental Goose followed the schedule and stood its watch:

Among the other novelties of the aforesaid guard-house on that memorable night, I got acquainted with a very worthy goose, whose services in the Rifle Brigade well merit a chapter in its history. If any one imagines that a goose is a goose he is very much mistaken: and I am happy in having the power of undeceiving him, for I am about to show that my (or rather our regimental) goose was shrewd, active, and intelligent, it was a faithful public servant, a social companion, and an attached friend, (I wish that every biped could say but half so much). Its death, or its manner of departure from this world, is still clouded in mystery; but while my book lives, the goose's memory shall not die.

It had attached itself to the guard-house several years prior to my appearance there, and all its doings had been as steady as a sentry-box: its post was with the sentry over the guard; in fine weather it accompanied him in his walk, and in bad, it stood alongside of him in his box. It marched with the officer of the guard in all his visiting rounds, and it was the first on all occasions to give notice of the approach of any one in authority, keeping a particularly sharp lookout for the captain and field-officer of the day, whether by day or night. The guard might sleep, the sentry might sleep, but the goose was ever wide awake. It never considered itself relieved from duty, except during the breakfast and dinner-hours, when it invariably stepped into the guard-house, and partook of the soldiers' cheer, for they were so devotedly attached to it that it was at all times bountifully supplied, and it was not a little amusing, on those occasions, to see how the fellow cackled whenever the soldiers laughed, as if it understood and enjoyed the joke as much as they did.

COMMAND AND OBEDIENCE:

In the British Army at the beginning of the century the primary mode of discipline was to flog, but among the founders of the Rifle Corps, flogging bore a stamp of infamy.

The frequent infliction of corporal punishment, in our armies, tends strongly to debase the minds, and destroy the high spirit of the soldiery; It deprives discipline of the influence of honour, and destroys the subordination of the heart, which can alone add voluntary zeal to the cold obligations of duty. The perpetual recurrence to the infliction of infamy on a soldier by the punishment of flogging, is one of the most mistaken modes, for enforcing discipline, which can be conceived.

The most effectual and just mode of securing discipline in a regiment, in the first instance, was to be accomplished through establishing exact responsibility. An attitude and practice of civility and a strict chain of command was the mode of operation within the Rifle Corps, since order was essential within the chaos of battle. That achievement depended on the gradation of responsibility, from the highest field officer to the corporal who directed a squad, so every individual entrusted with command knew his precise station and what was required of him. This was an invariable rule so that in the absence of a superior, the responsibility would devolve upon the next man in rank. Superiors were forbidden to:

Receive or transmit reports, returns, or other official communications through any other than the regular channel of rank, upon any consideration whatever, except in the event of necessity, or for urgent reasons.

As important to the chain of command, was the balanced quality of its practice. Every Superior was directed to,

Give his orders in the language of moderation, and of regard to the feelings of the individual under his command; abuse, bad language, or blows, being positively forbid in the regiment.

PUNISHMENT:

Discipline was not bereft of punishment, but flogging was a last resort for the incorrigibles – the 'bad men'. Prevention was worth ten corrections:

A full acquaintance of the soldiers' characters by their officers, a strong example of good conduct on their parts, and a steady unchangeable mode of authority towards those who are under their orders, is certainly the best plan for maintaining discipline; this mode prevents evil being done.

Punishment, when necessary, was proportional to the gravity of the crime – there being two kinds of punishment, private and public. The private mode was preferred, but could only be issued after formal inquiry, and could include confinement to barracks, turned coats, fines for the benefit of the Messes and cobbing.

Cobbing involved striking the offender a certain number of times on the breech with a flat piece of wood called the cobbing-board, or a pipe staff.

Public punishment pertained to cases of public injury, either to the service, or the corps in general, and included confinement to barracks or quarters, a turned coat or disgrace, confinement in the black-hole (never more than 8 days), punishment at the triangles or flogging.

Non-commissioned officers could also be reduced in rank.

Disgrace involved the letter 'C' was to be sewn on the right arm of a man's turned coat (turned inside out) for which the soldier was to be charged the cost. Confinement or a turned coat, however, did not relieve the soldier of the responsibility of carrying out his duties.

Corporal punishment was never to be administered without a court martial of no less than five members and no officer who had been with the regiment less than three months could serve on a court martial. Where a 'good man' was involved, he was issued a warning and, where feasible, the sentence was waived. A rigorous sentence was to be given to 'bad soldiers'. All corporal sentences were to be executed promptly and in the presence of the evening parade.

Quite unlike their red coated compatriots in the regular army, the regimen of Riflemen and Light Infantry at Shorncliffe was to be a family under its captain, the whole being cemented together by honour, comradeship, mutual confidence and affection.

To The Front

Though every soldier was a pedestrian on land, the only way to get to the war was by sea.

Readiness:

As regiments came into a high state of discipline and military order, every preparation was made to be ready whenever they were called for their services. Kits, arms and accoutrements were frequently inspected to ensure that they were in excellent condition and complete, as orders for immediate departure could come at a moment, with not a minute to be lost.

The contents of a soldier's kit were tightly regulated, varying only slightly between heavy, light and rifle regiments. The regulation 'Heavy Marching Kit' of a Rifleman included:

1 knapsack and straps
1 great coat
2 shirts
1 blanket
2 pair of stockings
1 powder flask, (filled)
1 pair of shoes
1 ball-bag for 30 loose balls
1 pair of spare soles and heels
1 small mallet (to hammer ball into muzzle of the rifle)
3 brushes
1 box of blacking
1 belt and pouch for 50 rounds of ammunition
1 razor, 1 soap box and strop
1 extra pair of trowsers
1 sword-belt and sword
1 mess-tin, centre-tin and lid
1 rifle
1 haversack
1 canteen (used as a water-bottle)
Also sundries at all times required by a Service soldier

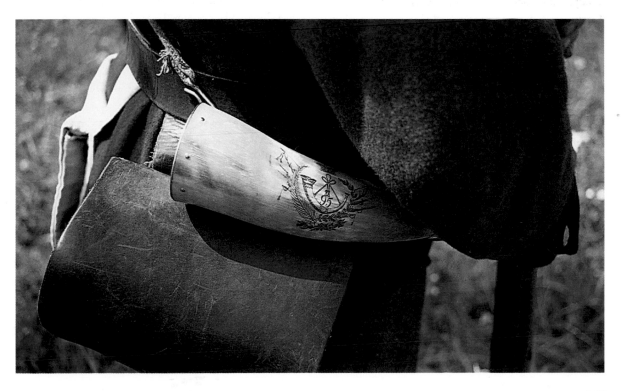

All in all, the regulation kit carried by every man weighed between 70 and 80 pounds, not counting water in the canteen which added an additional 2½ pounds.

OFFICER'S KIT:

Being a young officer presented a different problem. Although they had some advance notice that their regiment was to be called up for Foreign Service, they were responsible for determining and assembling their own kit. Letters were sent home and many fretted that the government embarkation allowances would not be enough:

> *My living at Plymouth until we go on board quite alarms me, lest we should be detained any time there, and then there is sea stock to provide for the voyage, which must be sufficient to last a month or more in case of contrary winds. We must lay in pigs, poultry, tea, sugar, etc from our own purses, and different things to be bought where we land. Nor can we rough it, as we must unavoidably all mess together, and officers of superior rank of other Regiments won't confine themselves to short commons, nor sit down to a poor table.*

New officers followed the advice of the old soldiers in their midst making selections from their wardrobes of articles that would last the longest and filling up canteens with tea, sugar and other luxuries. One subaltern offered the following advice :

> **I myself packed up in two small portmanteaus, so formed as to be an equal**

balance to each other, when slung across the back of a mule; and as my kit was not remarkable, either for its bulk or its scantiness. In one of these portmanteaus, then, I deposited a regimental jacket, with all its appendages of wings, lace, etc.; two grey pair of trousers; sundry waistcoats, white, coloured and flannel; a few changes of flannel drawers; half a dozen pairs of worsted stockings, and as many of cotton. In the other were placed six shirts, two or three cravats, a dressing-case competently filled, one undress pelisse, three pairs of boots, two pairs of shoes, with night-caps, pocket-handkerchiefs, etc, etc. in proportion. Thus, whilst I was not encumbered by any useless quantity of apparel, I carried with me quite enough to load a mule, and to ensure myself against the danger of falling short, for at least a couple of years to come.

A man of higher rank would carry much more:

A pelisse with black lace lined with fur or something warm;
A blue great coat;
A blue cashmir waistcoat and another of buff;
Two pairs of blue or grey loose trousers, they are cool for summer and in cold weather you can wear any number of drawers you like under them;
Two pairs of boots, either laced or strapped;
One pair of shoes;
Six changes of linen, if you are in the habit of wearing flannel, of course you will continue it;
Instead of neckcloths I should recommend a black stock of velour or leather;
A cocked hat, rather low than otherwise;
A cap for common use from Bicknell, the corner of Bond Street and Piccadilly;
A sword, with black belt and sabretache;
A brace of pistols;
Two English saddles, one for yourself with holsters and a small military valise fitted behind. Recollect that nothing will plague you so much as sore backs, therefore take care that your saddles are well stuffed, strong and very high over the withers so as

not to press on any horse's shoulders. The pad which supports the valise should be large, forming one with the pommel of the saddle. The valise should on no account be stiff but made of cloth and be flexible; a small piece of oil skin will keep it dry. Your other saddle should be contrived to carry a common-sized pair of saddle bags behind;

Two military bridles;

Two good blankets to put under your saddles when travelling and to sleep in at night;

A large cloak made of cloth and lined with baize to come well up about your throat and cover your feet when riding;

A small dressing case, rolling up, holding two razors, a penknife, a pair of scissors, a corkscrew and your tooth brushes;

A similar rolling case holding a knife, fork, spoon and teaspoon to go always in your sabretache;

A small canteen to sling on your shoulder holding about a pint or a pint and a half;

another for your servant holding somewhat more;

Two or three small tins to fit one into the other in which you may boil tea or coffee or make a stew, to be tied to the side of your servant's mule;

A small frying pan, a silver cup for yourself, holding near half a pint;

This cup, your dressing case and two changes of linen and your shoes, you had better always carry in your own valise behind you, together with your cap, which will serve as a night cap;

A servant who could also serve as a groom.

Some officers brought their own horses, but many bought horses and mules once they arrived in Lisbon.

ORDERS TO SAIL:

The anticipated directions from London, so impatiently desired, arrived. We were ordered instantly to prepare for foreign service; and never, I verily believe, was an invitation to a feast more readily obeyed.

'The route came upon us all of a heap, in the midst of fun and frolic, to march for Portsmouth, and embark for Portugal, and away we went, thoughtless jolly dogs.' In

high spirits, marching into towns and villages 'swords drawn, and our drum and fife playing marital music' and bugle-horns playing as 'all the little boys and girls were pressing into the ranks to hear the band and see the soldiers'. Inhabitants cheered, old women toddled to the wayside crying out, "There goes a few more lambs to the slaughter, poor things!" though 'in general the women seemed sorry to see us depart.'

Battalions embarked upon the vast range of transports.

When we arrived at the waterside, the boats were ready to receive us. We then embarked by companies: the men were in high spirits, and gave three cheers as they left the shore, the bugles and band playing.

But, oh! what an affecting scene took place between the married men and their families. It was truly distressing to see the anguish of the poor women at parting, some of whom were nearly frantic, others fainting away, and their children crying by their sides or in their arms, so that the hardest heart must have been moved at the sight. Many of these pitiable creatures never saw their husbands more; and even before six weeks had passed over numbers of them were widows, and their children orphans. On this occasion my feelings nearly overcame me, and I really could not help rejoicing that I was a single man.

The ships held until the convoy, which could include over a hundred ships, collected and weighed anchor. Officers with means waited on shore, while those in penury slept aboard. The wait for fair weather could be days, weeks or months. The soldiers, except for some ingenious Riflemen required to practice on land every day, bobbed up and down at anchor.

'The conveyance of troops on board transports in those days was anything but luxurious, rapid, or even safe.' Every kind of transport was requisitioned and converted to carry soldiers, horses, cattle, baggage, fruit, food, timber and the objects of war. Commanding officers found themselves in cabins the size of a coffin, while a dozen commissioned officers messed and slept in a 'cuddy' or sort of dog kennel.

The warships, those which had been in action at Trafalgar, had Nelson's signal, 'England Expects Every Man to Do His Duty' emblazoned in bold gold letters on the afterpart of the quarter deck. The guns were removed from the lower deck to accommodate the troops, sometimes over 1,500 men, the ship's company and the manger with its complement of animals.

All was darkness, and the deck completely covered with the troops. There was nothing but living bodies to walk on. I had contrived to get the length and breadth of my person on the deck where I lay 'til morning.

But the best is to come. The decks had been newly caulked, the heat of so many bodies had drawn the pitch and tar, so that we were stuck fast in the morning. It was the most ludicrous sight imaginable, some were fast by the head, others had got an arm secured, those who had laid on their backs were completely fast, some who were wrapped in their blankets came off best, but their blankets were completely spoiled. It was a fine treat for the blue jackets to see all the lobsters stuck fast to the decks.

A voyage could be remarkably pleasant, landing at the 'desired haven without danger or loss' or quite the opposite: 'Imaginations were sobered by bad weather and boisterous seas; realities are very unsentimental, and sea-sickness is a sad undignified disorder.'

The voyage could take a week or a month and through disease or disaster some never arrived.

ON FOREIGN STRANDS

We were close off the coast of Portugal. Every heart elate, we continued our course southward, now steering direct for the theatre of actual war; and the true martial spirit glowed in the breast of every true soldier.

The army came to the grim labours of the tented field either by way of the crowded quays of the City of Lisbon or through the pounding surf and sand of the coastal beaches. No matter which, it seemed as if they 'had fallen into another world.'

LISBON:

Men on their way up the Tagus River, to anchor at the quay at Black Horse Square thought it a joyful day as they were soon to be free of their floating prisons. The scenery all around was very beautiful:

On awakening next morning, and looking around me, the scene appeared one of enchantment. The world was basking in a blaze of golden light, such as I had never before witnessed. Lisbon sate queen-like, enthroned upon her hills, surveying her beauty in the Tagus – calm and majestic.

Boats laden with fruits and provisions swarmed round our vessel; – the dusky natives – the peculiarities of their dress and gestures, and the Babel confusion of their unknown tongue, were all themes of wonder and delight; – but never was the promise of hope more cruelly disappointed than on the day that I entered Lisbon.

However, what first seemed beautiful became disgusting in detail on approach. Stuccoed walls crumbled to pieces in narrow streets choked up with 'filth of the most horrid kind' amid a thousand symptoms of indolence and squalor – there had been far more gratification from the expectation than afterward realised.

Once landed, the men were sent to monasteries, by night sleeping on the cool flagstone floors in the corridors; by day shipping and unshipping, arranging accoutrements and waiting. Officers spent their time providing for the many things needed before taking to the field: horses, mules, and donkeys were to be purchased; blankets and camp-kettles had to be secured along with the many little things that went into laying in a little stock of provisions for the excursion.

For many this was the first time they had set foot on foreign strands and speaking not three words of the Portuese lingo, they spent their free time on rambles, alternately repelled and amazed:

above: A campaign medal of a rifleman of the Peninsular War

The strange figures, the uncouth noises, the appearance of representatives of every country in their native dress, congregated in one dense crowd, was fairly bewildering, till our sensations, agog as they were for novelty, required a double portion of the usual facilities, visual and auricular, to see and comprehend what passed before us.

Evenings, however, saw them at dinners, balls and the theatre and could all be very gay:

The military and naval uniforms of our own country mingled with those of Portugal and Spain; the dark eyes and expressive countenances of the Lisbon ladies, contrasted with the fair faces of our countrywomen.

Leaving the ball, they encountered armies of half-wild dogs in the streets, in conjunction with pigs, the sole scavengers of Lisbon, feeding on its filth and if interrupted at their orgies, bold enough to attack foot-passengers conning the unfamiliar way back to local billets in the darkness.

> 'My life resembles a magic lantern, in which bright and gloomy pictures follow each other in quick succession.'

THE BEACHES:

> 'We had been for upward of four months cooped up in miserable little transports. The men had scarcely the use of their limbs.'

There was a teaming multitude on the 300 yards of sandy beach enclosed by a lofty chain of rocks. The breakers, 50 deep, with terrible roaring and thundering, raised their heads houses high, pressing forward in walls of water, then sweeping in a roaring storm of foam far over the beach. 20 or 30 British sailors dashed into the surf, casting a rope to the boats, the men clinging frantically to the gunnels and their seats, then running at top speed through the advancing breakers and with a loud hurrah, dragged the loaded boats to stick fast on the beach. Horses, dashed helter-skelter out of the reeling vessels into the surf. Confined for months in the stuffy hold of the ships they were suddenly thrust into the light of day and once they reached the shore, they galloped wildly along it, to and fro, snorting, panting, neighing and biting and kicking one another, to the great danger of all those gathered on the beach, and then they would roll over on the sand. Dragoons were busy catching and saddling their horses. But the latter, owing to their long sojourn in the ship, had lost the use of their legs and the moment a trooper mounted one of them, the horse folded up his back legs like a dog, or rather dropped his hind quarters to the ground.

There were soldiers, sailors, officers shouting, guns, wagons, mountains of ships' bisquets, haversacks, trusses of hay, barrels of meat and rum, tents. The rocks and the sand were burning with the heat and neither fresh nor spring water was not to be had, so all suffered terribly from thirst.

Whether battalions and divisions were formed and marched days, weeks or months depended on the progress of the war, the seasons of the year, the sufficiency of the columns to depart, the location of the troops on the frontier or a million small matters of logistics and supply. Some marched out straight away into the 'storm of war', some arriving only to retreat, others standing down to wait.

> With all my earthly belongings, I stood with wide-open eyes on Portuguese soil, on the sand shore of the Bay of Maceira, hale and hearty, and muttered to myself;
>
> Here I am, now what next?
> God help me!
> Amen!
> Then my splendid life began.

JOHNNY NEWCOMES:

No matter when or how their march commenced, troops arriving from England, those 'rosy-cheeked, chubbed youths' looking as 'delicate as women', often joined the Army at an unhappy period. The marches were often harassing and severe and the company that had just arrived struggled to keep pace with the old campaigners. Marching, especially if the enemy were near, turned into 'a sort of military academy' and 'a youngster (if he did not stop a bullet by the way) might commence his studies in such a place with nothing but the soft down peeping through the white skin'. The home drill had not prepared them for their real duty.

Though near the battlefield, these soldiers were 'Johny Newcomes, Johnny-raws' again, recruits to be drilled into a new form of Peninsular discipline.

The first and most important duties to be taught to the new soldier, now on active service, were to learn how to take care of himself, how to obey orders, to have arms and ammunition in proper order at all times, to prevent straggling, to discipline the inclination to languor and fatigue, to find shelter, sustenance, and warmth and to get to the end of the day's work with the least delay.

> On service as every where else, there is a time for all things, but the time there being limited and very uncertain, the difficulty is to learn how to make the most of it.

It was a severe school:

Frequently, have I been awakened through the night by the sobs of those around me in the tent; more especially the young soldiers, who had not been long from their mothers' fire-sides. They often spent the darkness of the night in tears.

OFFICER NEWCOMES:

On entering this new stage in their profession, the young officers – gentlemen who had been campaigning in London, Brighton, Hampton Court and Weymouth – became for a time the butt of the old hands.

Our first and most uncharitable aim was to discover the weak points of every fresh arrival, and to attack him through them. If he had redeeming qualities, he, of course, came out scatheless, but if not, he was dealt with most unmercifully.

When officers from home came out to us, we found them too frequently impregnated with all the punctilios enforced by the Horse Guards clock; with ideas redolent of hair-powder and blank cartridge; stiff in stocks, starched in frills, with Dundas's eighteen manoeuvres or commandments. All this had to be changed. A normal school for real soldiers was undergoing the process of formation; the newcomers at first thought they had tumbled amongst a strange, loose set of half-wild men, little in accordance with their preconceived opinions. At length they began to discover how the art was carried on, and found that they had much to unlearn, as well as much to acquire, before they could make themselves useful.

THE TENTED FIELD

For the first time in my life I was treated with a bivouac. Hungry, wet, and cold, and without any covering, we lay down by the side of the river. I put one hand in my pocket and the other in my bosom, and lay shivering, and thinking of the glorious life of a soldier, until I fell fast asleep. We fell in at daylight. I found the dew had wet me through, but the sun soon made his appearance and dried me.

While campaigning, about half of the time, all, or part of the Army 'bivouacked'. They slept on the bare ground in an open field, wrapped in their cloak or blanket with a piece of green sod and a smooth stone for a pillow. One officer notes that in six years, he spent about half the time 'under the canopy of heaven.' Even Sir Arthur, on a number of occasions, slept on the open ground wrapped in his cloak or snug in his 'wigwam.'

SELECTING AND PREPARING THE LOCATIONS FOR A BIVOUAC:

The regimental frame of mind was assiduous in picking out and preparing a bivouac. Almost every phase of this task was defined and organised, working with precision most of the time, yet collapsing utterly on others.

To start, the 'Orders for Movement' were written by the Duke of Wellington, Commander of the Forces, for each day's march. These were then passed to his Quarter Master General who distributed them to the General Officers' commanding divisions, who in turn, gave them over to their own Assistant Quarter Master General.

The divisional Assistant Quarter Master Generals appointed guides and distributed the orders to the battalion officers. He then left for the station in order to make arrangements with the local magistrates and select the ground for the bivouac.

24 hours before the columns were to march, each battalion sent out one officer who was to go ahead to the planned station, which, if circumstances allowed, was located on the edge of some wood and near a river or stream. He met with the Divisional Assistant Quarter Master and prepared the bivouac by marking off the brigade alarm-posts or parade (the primary assembly points). Then if there was a local village, he marked off any quarters to be assigned including officers quarters, staff accommodations, an orderly room, guardroom and

a place for the Quarter-Master's stores.

In the meantime, the Brigade Generals, who had also arrived early, selected what each considered the most favourable ground. The General also designated where the piquets should be posted, to be in constant communication with the outposts of the cavalry in front and to cover all the approaches with piquets and sentries for no-one to be able to arrive without being seen and stopped. He decided on the signals that would be used such as setting fire to beacons, a specific number of musket shots, for example, to communicate an alarm as quickly as possible. The Assistant Quarter Master General turned these decisions over to the first advance battalion officer.

The first battalion officer waited for the second battalion officer who had been ordered to march the same day as the columns set out, but who left early enough to arrive before they came upon the ground. The second officer travelled with ten camp-colour men from each company. It was his task to take over the quarters, prepare the alarm-posts, implement any orders from the Assistant Quarter Master General and get ready to accompany the battalion into the area when it arrived.

When everything was ready, the first officer would proceed to the next bivouac station and the second battalion officer would wait for the columns to arrive.

MANNING THE BIVOUAC:

Arrival of the columns did not mean immediate rest.

As soon as the division was escorted to its alarm-post, the outlying piquets were immediately marched off to their posts. The temporary division hospital and the Commissariat magazines were pointed out to their respective officers. The brigades and battalions were then allowed to proceed to their respective company alarm-posts and the ground set aside for them. The inlaying piquet, quarter and rear guards were mounted, to be relieved in two hours by fresh troops.

FATIGUE PARTIES:

After piling arms, doffing their heavy kits, setting the guards and piquets, the first order of business was the assignment of fatigue parties for rations and shelter.

ISSUING RATIONS:

Fatigue parties of two or three men per company, under a corporal, were 'told off' for rations of bread, meat and spirits, as well as for building huts or erecting tents.

In this army,

> no opportunity should be allowed to escape in inculcating the habit of order and regularity in whatever is done by the soldier; and, however simple the act, it should be impressed on his mind, that what is ordered is the easiest, and that what is his duty is his interest.

Issuing rations was a fine example of 'inculcating the habit of order and regularity' as even this mundane chore was etched in routine:

> The issue of rations was regulated by the Quarter Master and Commissariat, agreeably to the instructions of the General commanding the division or brigade, communicated in orders to the battalions, and was done regimentally by individuals from all the companies, and not by the company on general fatigue. On the issue of any article, such as bread, meat, wine, or forage, the fatigue parties from each company, as before described, were summoned from the quarter guard by the Quarter Master, who called out the watch in the lines of each company; those previously warned for each article turned out under their respective non-commissioned officers, and assembled under the officer of the inlying piquet named in the orders at the quarter guard. He then proceeded with the Quarter Master or Quarter Master Sergeant to the place of issue; after the delivery he returned to the quarter guard, reported to the Captain of the Day, who was the captain of the inlying piquet, the regularity or irregularity of the particular issue under his superintendence, and then dismissed the parties under their several non-

commissioned officers to their respective companies, where the delivery was immediately made under the orderly Officer of each company.

As the supplies were gathered and set, the Commanding Officers reported through the Major of Brigade that their respective battalions had received their bread, meat, spirits and forage, specifying the number of days for each, how many companies they had marched and what their strength was (for the outlying piquets and other guard duties). They also ensured that they knew where to find them.

BUILDING HUTS AND ERECTING TENTS:

If the division had tents, the tent mules, which always immediately followed the column were unloaded and the job of erecting the camp commenced. If there were no tents, then the bill-hooks came out and regular squads were formed, some for cutting branches, some for drawing them to the lines and others to act as architects for constructing officers' huts. Relieved of their heavy packs, accoutrements, haversacks and other encumbrances and the piling of arms re-invigorated the men who took pride in constructing the finest of huts for their officers.

TAKING POSSESSION:

This business done, the men reassembled in columns of companies at full, half or quarter distance from each other, depending on the space available. No matter how tired, as soon as the familiar order was given 'to make themselves comfortable', the older and more experienced troops rushed to find the best places for the night. Each individual knew his place and took possession accordingly. A sprinkling of trees afforded shelter from the sun by day and the dews by night and was, therefore, a much sought-after spot. It also served as a sort of home or signpost for groups of officers denoting the best place of entertainment. They indulge, according to their various humours, in a complete state of gypsyfication.

COOKING ON BIVOUAC:

THE STANDARD DAILY RATION:

1 lb of meat (travelling on the hoof)
1 lb of 'biscuit' or 1½ lbs of bread or rice
1 pint of wine or ⅓ pt of spirit

To cook this fare, up until 1813, the English had large 'Flanders camp-kettles' made of iron, one for every ten men, carried on the back of a single mule (although in 1813, the Flanders Iron Kettles were replaced by lighter tin kettles carried by the men and the mule carried a Bell tent). Getting the kettle to boil took one full tree or at least one church door. In this receptacle (or the later tin kettle, serving six), the men cooked one of 'but two dishes seen in a camp, namely soup or bouillie, or an Irish stew, which, with some 'rice, pumpkin, tomatoes, and a bottle of good country wine, left a moderate man little to wish for." Dinner hour, for fear of accidents, was always the hour when dinner could be 'got ready.' They dined at two o'clock and other times at ten at night.

Whenever the camp remained stationary a week or more,

> the sutlers who followed the army overtook and opened their temporary shops in the towns near us, or in our very camps; and thus we were often well, though dearly (300% profit was not uncommon), supplied with many comforts, such as tea, sugar, brandies, wines, segars, etc.

These comforts were often supplemented from the villages with local bread, corn, wheat, meat and luxuries such as butter and milk, paid for in coin or by promise. Wellington did not abide plundering the villages and death waited the man caught doing so.

Officers on bivouac were obliged to manage for themselves and generally divided themselves into mess-parties of twos and threes. The more fortunate who had servants to cook and a large entourage of mules for transport fared better, but the bit of beef and the ration of biscuit was frequent fare for perhaps two-thirds of the officers, with the allowance of ration, rum or wine (generally execrable stuff). When the cook of a French general strayed into the British lines, he was immediately bundled off as a present to headquarters.

On rainy and cold outpost duty, an officer could, at times, have his servant prepare a breakfast of four eggs, roast fowl and plenty of tea.

RATIONS FROM THE REAR:

The army drew nearly all their rations from the rear and what they got from the countryside, they paid for in ready money or receipts given. The whole of the transport was paid for and they never required any contributions.

> The system of supplying an army by means of mules in Spain and Portugal is brought to the greatest perfection. There are about sixty mules to every cavalry regiment, for the purpose of supplying bread to the men and corn to the horses. Each mule is hired at the rate of a dollar a day, and the

muleteers have each a dollar per diem. There is one muleteer to every five or six mules. Reckoning about 60 mules and ten muleteers—in all 70. There were never less than ten regiments of cavalry. The difficulty of procuring dollars was so great that the army was always six months, and frequently eight months, in arrears, and the muleteers two years and sometimes longer. There were, besides the mules for the cavalry, a certain number to each division of infantry, and a large train attached to the commissary-general, headquarters, etc. Oats and hay from England, were brought, at an enormous expense, in vessels to the Tagus, and then transported up the country by means of mules or bullock cars. The hay from England did not come out in any quantity, being only used for the horses at headquarters and some stationed at Lisbon, etc.

In the first instance, it was difficult to get any muleteers to serve the army. They were all Spaniards, and probably a large sum was requisite to induce them to enter the service. If any amount could have been raised to pay them up within six months, I have no doubt much more reasonable terms might have been obtained. A dollar per diem for each mule was an immense allowance. They, however, were quite requisite to the army, and any disturbance with them would have deprived us of supplies and consequently crippled our operations. The system, though expensive, was excellent, and the army continued its operations in countries where there was nothing to be had, and where any other army without mules would not have remained. Our advance from the lines in 1811, through a country completely exhausted, was most wonderful. The enemy were quite astonished how we got on.

EATING LOCAL FOODS:

Although happy to eat local staples of bread, mutton, beef, fowls, turkey, coffee, potatoes, figs, milk or butter, the British soldier, either by superstition, habit or true incompatibility, avoided locally cooked and seasoned dishes unless terribly short of rations. When they broke this stricture, the outcome could be far from pleasant. Honey was plentiful, but left many a strong man with dysentery.

> We called it the furnace camp, and were here about six weeks, during which time we suffered dreadfully for want of rations, and from the oppressive heat of the weather.
>
> While we were at Reguengo, Tom Crawley imagined himself poisoned. He gorged himself on some pork and caravanqes (a pulse like peas or beans), and was suddenly seized with violent paroxysms of pain. Old Doctor Burke was sent for. He found Crawley on the ground groaning most piteously. He had swelled to an enormous size, and two of his comrades were busy rubbing the lower part of his belly. The Doctor, who fancied that two years in Spain had brought Tom's stomach to suit the convenience of the commissary, commenced a volley of abuse: 'You cannibal, what garbage have you been swallowing to leave you in this condition!' 'Oh murther, do you hear him, boys,' roared Tom, as he turned his eyes towards his tormentor. 'By the mother of God, sir, this infernal country will kill us all. May a curse fall on it. When I came into it I had a stomach like any other Christian, but now? Oh God, have mercy on me poor stomach! For want of Christian food, it is turning into a scavenger's cart, obliged to take in every rubbish.' The Doctor, who seldom did anything by halves, gave him an emetic sufficient to physic a dromedary. Crawley, who never feared death on the field, hesitated meeting him in quarters

and so, between the groans he uttered, he made the most vehement promises, if spared, to mend.

CARRYING THE WINE:

The men usually carried their wine in a calabash, but the local transport was generally animal skins.

> Wine in this country is carried in pigskins, dried and stripped of their hair but retaining their original strength. The mouth is sewed up and the liquor generally drawn by one of the ears or a foot. The prudence of not putting *new wine into old skins* is exemplified for the new wine sometimes ferments and then the skins, unless they are very strong, burst. Old skins are the best as they never give the wine taste, which unseasoned ones always do.

When they moved about, they had mules and an ass to carry provisions, carrying the wine in deer skins. The skin of a large buck amounted to at least 70 bottles of wine.

THE QUALITY OF RATIONS:

Army 'bisquit' was either rock-hard (at least one British officer saved his life by stuffing his jacket with biscuit and thus turning a musket-ball), or alive – full of maggots.

Sometimes rations arrived so slowly that

> the biscuit, when it did arrive, was in such a state, owing to the long carriage, and being exposed to all kinds of weather, that no human being (such as we were) could make use of it. For it actually stank, and when emptied out of the bags it smoked equal to a dunghill at a stable door. The beef was at all times most miserable. There were more shins served out to the men than came to the share of one bullock, for good cuts were not fit for a private soldier.

Days when the rations did not arrive at all, men in the ranks ate whatever they could find, even going so far as eating acorns for several days. Acorns that came from the holm oak were sweet and pleasant to the taste, however other kinds could be hard and bitter.

TOBACCO:

A further bulwark against hunger and cold was that friend-in-need, the pipe. A pound of tobacco and its companion a pipe sold for 6/6, though there were ingenious substitutes for the pipe, such as a wooden pipe whose bowl was made from a tailor's thimble:

> For let our hardships be ever so great, if we could muster a pipe of tobacco it proved a sovereign remedy, and though you might as well part with your blood as the ration of liquor, yet it would be cheerfully done to obtain a few pipefuls.

In fact, tobacco was the only thing that had the fascinating power of causing a soldier to part with his liquor for a few pipefuls, it being considered a luxury:

> 'I smoke a great deal when out all night as I think it prevents cold, spends the time and encourages meditation.'

WARM AND UNDER COVER:

BLANKETS:

Each soldier was issued a blanket and a greatcoat to hold off the cold, dew and rain. The soldiers – those who had the luxury of having two blankets – quickly found that if they stitched the sides of their blanket together, they had a sack in which to sleep.

> My usual bed was two blankets stitched together and made into the shape of a sack, into which I crawled, and if I rolled about, the clothes never left me until I took a fancy to crawl out again.

Some officers had 'oiled cloth' they used as a cover on top of the blanket or if there was a lot of thick clayey mud that could be smeared on an old blanket, to help keep the rain from soaking through.

GREATCOATS:

The winter clothing issued to the infantry was a grey pepper-and-salt coloured great coat of very thick cloth, with a cape reaching down to nearly the elbow, so as to give a double thickness of protection to the shoulders.

Since greatcoats weighed about 5.5 pounds, the rank and file did not normally carry both a greatcoat and a blanket at the same time – it was only one, the other being back in the stores.

The greatcoat, though warm, was not a perfect substitute for a blanket. Its drawback lay in the fact that legs and feet were exposed during the night. To overcome that disadvantage, the men simply inverted it, thrusting their legs into the sleeves and wrapping the coat around their body. They pulled their forage cap over their ears and used their knapsack as a pillow, claiming to be quite comfortable and fairly rainproof.

If they could procure them, officers and men preferred the naval boat cloak to the army greatcoat as it was thicker, had a baize lining and was better at repelling rain and water.

Cavalry, of course, could carry both, using the blanket under the saddle, with their greatcoat strapped down behind it. Officers, when they had access to their baggage, would also have both blanket and greatcoat or boat-cloak, if not a bear skin or even a camp bed.

BLANKET TENTS:

Some men used blankets to build a simple tent, easy to pitch and to pack up. Based on a Portuguese idea, two to 4 men made a tent consisting of two blankets, two firelocks and four bayonets. A hole, similar to a buttonhole, was worked at each corner and in the centre of the blanket. Firelocks at each end served as poles. The bayonet of these firelocks passed through the corner holes of both blankets, a ramrod secured the top and a bayonet at each end fastened in the ground completed the tent. Wellington ordered that all the men were to have blankets made with leather reinforced holes so that

they would not tear away with hard use. When four men crowded themselves into these improvised tents, they were left with only two blankets to use for warmth and cover, more than likely their heavy greatcoat far away with the stores.

CHESTNUT TREES:

Anything that could provide cover, did. Chestnut trees could reach extraordinarily large sizes and were often hollow, sometimes accommodating up to ten men.

> We halted one night at the village of Soito, where there are a great many chestnut trees of very extraordinary dimensions; the outside of the trunk keeps growing as the inside decays. I was one of a party of four persons who dined inside of one, and I saw two or three horses put up in several others.

Hutting was the step above simple blanket tents: it was in wide use throughout the regiments, including the Duke of Wellington and his staff, who often preferred sleeping in huts or wigwams rather than local flea infested houses. Huts were canopies or lean-tos built with tree branches covered with straw, fern and sometimes tarpaulins or blankets. They created shade during the heat of the day and held off the dew, rain and snow at night. They ranged from very simple to quite elaborate. The more intricate hut was constructed with two upright posts about seven feet high, with forked ends planted in the ground approximately 15 feet apart. A ridge-pole or roof-tree was placed on these posts, against which other poles were fitted on each side in a slanting position, so as to form the frame of a roof. It was then completely covered with pine branches, heath, broom or straw. One end was closed up with poles placed very closely together and the joins were stuffed with grass or moss. The other end, which was left open at the entrance, had a movable screen of wicker for a door. In these thick bowers, where beds could be made of heath, a large smooth slate could serve as a table and a bench of cork as a seat; men could live comfortably and contentedly. Some of these hut camps served as homes for up to a month, with the entire encampment taking on the look of a small village.

The British, however, were outdone in the construction of huts. After a number of battles, British soldiers advanced into the abandoned camps of the French and found neat well-built huts in regular lines, arranged with 'comfort and taste'. They sported windows, furniture and other special contrivances to make day-to-day life easier. At Televera, the French huts were made with sturdy walls of corn still in the ear and roofs thatched with ripe wheat that they had found standing in the fields. Even more, with the boughs of trees they had made an immense 'salle de spectacle' and leading up to it, they had made an avenue of some length, formed by cutting down the largest olive trees and sticking their ends into the ground. John Bull was not opposed to moving into Johnny Crapard's little homes. Sometimes Johnny's corpse greeted them as they entered.

Neither huts nor sleeping sacks were respected by the native inhabitants of the fields, who kept their ways unperturbed. To them, it did not matter that the soldier's

ears are assailed by a million mouths of chattering locusts; no matter that the scorpion is lurking beneath his pillow, the snake winding his slimy way by his side, and the lizard galloping over his face, wiping his eyes with its long cold tail.

In fact, on one occasion, a soldier had swallowed a lizard.

He knew not when or how, and the first hint he had of the tenement being so occupied, was in being troubled with internal pains and the spitting of blood, which continued for many months, in spite of all of the remedies that were administered. But a powerful emetic eventually caused him to be delivered of as ugly a child of the kind as one would wish to look at, about three inches long.

Some parts abounded with lizards of various sorts, some of which the men thought to be quite beautiful. There was one which the men called 'Goannas' after lizards they had seen in India. When a man lay down,

several of them will come round him, always keeping at a humble distance; they will raise themselves on their fore feet and stretch up their necks and watch him; if he moves they will scamper away in all directions.

They were thought to be harmless.

Men pushed their feet into boots only to crush a scorpion or turned over a rock to find one of the same. At times the campgrounds abounded with a variety of venomous reptiles, luckily, they rarely injured the soldiers.

BELL TENTS:

Tents for officers were commonly used throughout the Peninsular War, varying in size and availability depending on the rank of the officer and access to the baggage train. However, it was also the case that many lower order officers were completely without tents, using huts or sleeping under the stars until tents were introduced for the rank and file in 1813. They were conical 'Bell' tents which had a nine foot centre pole and weighed 43 pounds. Wellington retired the old and heavy iron kettles carried one to a mule and substituted them for a lighter tin kettle (one kettle to six men), which the men alternated in carrying on top of their knapsack, allowing the Bell tent to be carried on the mule. Companies (at strength about 100 men) received four Bell tents with one tent set aside for the officers. Quite popular and a great respite from the effects of the weather, the tents, designed to house 12 men, usually had 20 crowded together, heads to the rim and feet pointing to the centre pole. This arrangement, of course, had its lighter side as no one could turn without general consent!

> Our canvas tents rise in a moment. A minute before nothing was to be seen but the soldiers, now the whole camp was studded with several hundred bell tents as white as snow.

Beautiful as the views may have been, the men were advised to pitch their tents out of sight of the enemy so it would not be possible to make an easy count of the troop strength. This, of course, eliminated many of the safe places that would be furthest from the cascading torrents of rain.

SLEEPING 'UNDER ARMS:'

When the enemy was near, the men slept 'under arms,' fully dressed, horses saddled, muskets loaded, ready to respond to an alarm in minutes. In fact, many went weeks or months without changing their clothes or taking off their boots.

> Riflemen seldom pile arms and, as was our usual custom, each man's rifle was loaded and leaning on his arm, close to his breast. It was hugged with the affection a fond lover would use to press to his bosom the girl of his heart, or in marital wedlock, each folding to his breast his better half – his musket.

SOUNDS OF THE BIVOUAC:

With the men fast asleep, one could be tempted to imagine the camp as a quite place. This was rarely the case:

> The whinny of mules is between the bray of an ass and the neigh of a horse, more unharmonious than either. The whole camp could be as still as the grave, with nothing to disturb the soldiers' repose but a million mouths of chattering locusts. Or some villainous donkey, who every half hour pitches a bray note, which as a congregation of presbyterians follow their clerk, is instantly taken up by every mule and donkey in the army and sent echoing from regiment to regiment, over hill and valley – until it dies away in the distance. A little further some drunken Portuguese have got some music and are singing, playing and huzzaing, much to their satisfaction.

VICISSITUDES OF BIVOUACING:

The smoothly-working regularity and planning of the system devised for bivouacs did not always work in practice. There were marches when the plan could not be carried out either because of the need to hurry, unexpected changes in direction, and/or the vagaries of the weather. If there was some sudden movement by the

French, Wellington was forced to throw his army onto a route that had not been arranged which meant the elaborate provisions made by his officers as harbingers could not be carried out. When the men halted very late at night and sometimes at an unforeseen destination, there could be no selection of billets or erection of huts. The baggage and rations might not arrive at all. Everything had to be done haphazardly in the dark.

And then there was the weather:

> In the camp or bivouac in fine weather, all went on merrily, but there came moments which the iron frame of the most hardy could not always resist. Deluges of rain not only drenched the earth, but unfortunately all that rested or tried to rest upon it; the draining through the hut from the above by some ill-placed sticks in the roof, like lightning conductors, conveyed the subtle fluid where it was the least wanted; while the floods coursing under, drove away all possibility of sleep: repose was, of course, out of the question, when even the worms would come out of the earth, it being far too wet for them.

Even if the weather was fine during the day, men often woke up either soaked in dew, drenched in rain or crackling with ice. Sometimes their blankets, cloaks and hair were frozen to the ground. They might find the water making a gutter on both sides of their body, or if they slept in a nice green hollow they could wake up to find themselves floating away as the snug harbour turned into a cascading watercourse fed by descending torrents of rain: 'We have made a raw and rainy beginning of our campaign, how did you sleep?' to which the answer was, 'Slept like a fish. I believe they sleep best in water.'

When the men finally arrived at a bivouac, the ground, perfectly flat, might be flooded more than ankle deep with water. One Highlander used the following tactic to pass his nights in the rain and cold:

> I placed my canteen upon the ground, put my knapsack above, and sat upon it, supporting my head upon my hands; my musket between my knees, resting upon

my shoulder, and my blanket over all, ready to start in a moment, at the least alarm.

Unfortunately, came the morning, he could not stand, his legs numbed to the knees.

If the field happened to have been recently ploughed, the rains also brought mud. Sanguine as ever, one wit remarked that if 'inclined to sleep we were obliged to repose like so many turkeys, on the branches of trees, to keep us out of the water and mud.'

> Marched and bivouacked in a wood near Cilleros. Very ill off for provisions, every step I was up to the knees in mud. Small rills, which it was necessary during the day's march to cross, frequently became rivulets from the continued rain.
>
> When we reached our halting-ground for the night, our prospect was most desolate for we were wet to the skin, and without fire or shelter. The first thing I did

was take off my jacket and shirt and wring out about half a gallon of water. I placed them upon my back to dry as they might. Most of our men cut down boughs of trees to keep themselves out of the mud, but it was some hours before we could obtain that greatest of luxuries, a good fire. It had been a fatiguing day, and although possessed of a ravenous appetite, we had nothing to satisfy it. We had not a morsel to eat, no rations having been issued, so our men suffered from pangs of cold, and hunger.

Hunger, incessant duty, and fatigue were the disagreeable things attendant upon our life in the Peninsula, and I am convinced that it was these sufferings that so often rendered our men callous to death. At different periods during the war, some men, from the privations they endured, wished to be shot, and exposed themselves in action for that purpose.

On one occasion,

the 16th went about a mile to its rear, and encamped in an olive grove up to the horses' knees in mud; it raining incessantly the whole night, most of the officers got into a wine vault. One of the men of the Royals, in getting some wine out of the vat, fell in. The grapes were just pressed, and left in that state. In this state the men drank it. The dragoon got into it in the night, was half smothered, and caused great confusion. He, or some other, stole a ham from Colonel Archer, which when the colonel perceived, he made a great row; and what with loss of ham, and dragoon in the vat, we had not a very tranquil night.

Life in a tent was also subject to the vagaries of the weather, especially the ubiquitous mud, where wind often tore the pegs out of liquid ground, causing the tent to billow down upon its soldier – the object of wild mirth as others shouted out 'Boat-a-hoy', adding to the

misery of those scrambling to get out from the clammy winding-sheets. Just staying under the folds of a downed tent could be preferable to whatever was outside.

In an effort to bring his tent to the heights of English comfort, one officer decided to build a fireplace that would take the smoke underneath the walls and up a turf chimney that he built outside.

It went exceeding well. I was not a little vain of the invention. However, it came on to rain very hard while I was dining at a neighbouring tent, and on my return to my own, I found the fire not only extinguished, but a fountain playing from the same place up to the roof, watering my bed and baggage and all sides of it most refreshingly. This showed me, at the expense of my night's repose, that the rain

It was a most excellent camp, the trees affording capital shade; and from the length of time we had been there, each man had a good hut, and the encampment wore the appearance of a small village. We were much safer from any sudden attack; the men and horses both continued healthy from having plenty to eat and something to employ themselves with. The men got as much rye-bread, mutton, potatoes, and wheat flour from the adjacent mills as they wanted, and the horses as much rye in the ear and thrashed as they could eat, and now and then some wheat nearly ripe. We had nothing with us but a change of linen, a pot to boil potatoes, and the same to make coffee in, with a frying pan, which were carried on his led horse. We never wanted for a single article excepting wheat-bread, which failed us occasionally, and with a person not accustomed to rye, it does not agree. We could always march in five minutes, never slept out of our clothes, and never enjoyed better health; half-past two in the morning was the hour we got up.

oozed through the thin spongy surface of the earth and the rock which it covered, and any incision in the former was sure to produce a fountain.

A bivouac was at its best when the men were safe from attack, the daily rations of food and spirits were prompt, complete, and wholesome, the baggage came up, the ground hospitable, and the weather was fine.

Here we are a distance from the enemy, we get our rations regular and we can purchase every eatable very cheap, wine is both good and cheap, so is tobacco. We have in our power to make ourselves comfortable.

In another's words:

BILLETS:

When a village was nearby, billets or quarters within homes, churches, monasteries or barns were assigned to officers and men by rank. However, these could vary greatly in comfort.

The rank and file were often lodged in convents or castles where they might occupy only the corridors, into which straw was generally put by the authorities of the place, the men lying close to each other to keep warm.

As the war progressed, the men, stuck in these conditions, had little esteem for quarters other than a respite or refuge:

What the English soldier cannot see any purpose in does not interest him. Everywhere bayonets and nails were stuck into the crevices of precious columns, or into the beautifully decorated walls, and knapsacks and a cartridge boxes were hung upon them. In the large fireplaces, decorated with marble, there burned huge fires, kept alive with broken pieces of antique furniture, either gilt or artistically carved; and the same thing was going on in the courtyard, where the walls were all black with smoke. A good deal was wantonly destroyed, and every corner was scoured for hidden treasure. The officers, who were residing in various parts of the castle, enraged by their men's lust of destruction and desecration, seemed crushed with grief, and did all in their power to limit the damage as far as possible.

Officers were given the best quarters, with quality diminishing and crowding increasing down the line.

In these early marches the villa, the monastery, and the cottage were thrown open at the approach of our troops; the best apartments, the neatest cells, the humble billet apartment, hung with the richest crimson damask, filled with heavy antique furniture...

Junior officers, consequently, were left with the last choice of quarters, which too frequently was a dirty floor with a only blanket – wretched hovels barely as good as an English pig-sty.

At times, the conditions were so bad, some men preferred to stay in the camps.

They provided us with only uncomfortable and unwholesome quarters, and the houses all around were uninhabited and had been left in a filthy condition by the troops passing through, we preferred to camp out in huts in a fine field not far from the church, where we kept our store of straw.

The reason lay in the company, for though the bed might look tolerably clean, before the morning a man could be

nearly eat up in it; so surrounded they were with the 'myriads of fleas' who, play at a perpetual hop, skip, and jump, or 'hush'd in grim repose, expect their evening prey.'

Striving to have the advantages of a roof and walls, but at the same time to avoid the pervasive cold and the vermin of every kind that lurked within the habitations of many peasants, led some soldiers to create unique and fastidious accommodations as the order of their day:

In one corner of the room I have collected a quantity of dry fern, this forms my bed, it being necessary to strip to keep free from vermin. Every night the contents of my haversack are transferred to my knapsack. This forms my pillow, at the same time secures my kit and provisions from midnight marauders. The haversack is then converted into a night cap. Being stripped, my legs are thrust into the sleeves of an old watch coat, carefully tied at the cuffs to keep out the cold. The other part of the coat wrapped round my body served for under blanket and sheet. Next my trousers are drawn on my legs over the sleeves of the coat, my red jacket has the distinguished place covering my seat of honour and lastly my blanket covers all. In this manner I have slept as comfortable as a prince.

Not far away, another officer found the homes had a sitting apartment in the centre, with sleeping-cabins branching off from it.

Each (was) illuminated by a port-hole about a foot square. The air circulated freely, and mild it came, and pure, and fragrant, as if it had just stolen over a bed of roses. The outside of my sleeping-cabin was interwoven with ivy and honeysuckle, and among the branches a nightingale had established itself and sung sweetly, night after night.

Sometimes the men were lucky. Billets in established

cities like Madrid, Salamanca, or Vittoria could be very comfortable, indeed maybe even described as luxurious. If anything, they offered the advantage of being dry most of the year

> My bed is made up of the finest muslins with rich damask curtains, the pillows such as you would admire very much, edged with lace, with rosettes of crimson ribbons.

…or from the depths…

The Witch of Endor

At last I reached the bridge at Salamanca in the moonlight, after a very long march. It was ten o'clock at night. I watered my mule in the river, and rode through the gate of the town, where, after exhaustive inquiries, I at length found a man who showed me the house of the assistant quartermaster-general, who allotted billets. This officer was most comfortably installed beside a brasero in a magnificent room, and was reading a book, while at his side there stood a bottle of wine and a dish of roast chestnuts. I asked him for a good billet. 'You must take your chance, sir,' was his reply, and dipping his hand into a bag of billets as if we were at a lottery, drew mine forth in a perfectly haphazard manner. It turned out to be a bad draw, for the house, from basement to attics, was full of soldiers. There was only one smoky attic kitchen free, and this was on the fourth story and occupied by an old woman not unlike the witch of Endor. I took possession of this place. At first the old dragon who lived in this inferno spat fire and flames ; when, however, she saw my money, she grew more tame ; and by the time I had put some wine and a cigar between her jaws, she became quite friendly and talkative. My usual food in these parts, consisting of chocolate, ham, roast pork—the loin—and onions, was procured and prepared for me at the cost of great pains— for it was midnight—by the witch herself; whereupon wrapping myself in my cloak, I laid myself down on the bare floor close to the fire, and in

spite of the fleas and bugs, and the cries of the old woman, who was singing a litany to the Virgin Mary, I was so tired that I was soon asleep.

November 20th, 1808.

IN QUARTERS:

A soldier only meets his enemy thrice or four or, at the most, a dozen times a year.

Billets were temporary lodging for the army on the move. The rest of the time (sometimes over 60% of the year) the soldiers of the British Army lived in quarters or more lasting cantonments. During the winters, the armies stood down for perhaps five to seven months at a time, sheltering from the cold and the snow; during the summer, escaping the boiling heat or torrential rain. At times, they stayed in towns or small villages or on far flung farms.

Billeted troops, in these semi-permanent quarters (soldiers had no 'permanent' billet), were glad to at least have a roof under which to stay, even if the conditions left somewhat to be desired: 'Comfort is ever comparative; and, after all, if his wishes be moderate, how little does man require.'

The Army took over whole strings of villages stretching out for miles throughout the countryside. Sometimes unenthusiastic inhabitants met them, cold and parched like their environs, while others gave the amiable kindness of a loving family, weeping when their soldier 'son' left to return to the war. Regiments often returned to the same villages year after year, living with the same families over and over, so that these quarters became a home of sorts: 'The people were glad to see us return. We had begun to look upon the villages as our homes.'

British officers when stationed in cold and rainy places, found the smoke from fires made on the ground of peasant houses so intolerable it drove them outside to cough and freeze. The more ingenious ones obtained permission from the reluctant owners to build fireplaces and chimneys, which made the long sojourn more hospitable (nevertheless, most peasants tore them down as the army moved on come spring).

Finding a place for a Regimental Mess was a prerequisite. Circumstances permitting, the Mess sometimes brought food, pipe tobacco, cigars and other luxuries from Lisbon, if not England, sharing the ever-precious newspapers and other news from home.

Wherever the Army was, however, there was work, routine and protocol. Some divisions paraded every day at 11 o'clock and had roll call at five o'clock in the afternoon. Infantrymen had muskets, bayonets and equipment to be kept clean and in working order – in some units, 'polished like a razor'. Some drilled, marched or even engaged in target practice. Cavalry and Light Infantry were often on outpost duty and so were in their clothes day and night, ever on the alert and/or had the never ending work of caring for and feeding their horses. Artillery had gun carriages and harnesses to repair and clean, axles to grease, stores to check, packing and distributing to carry out, gun drills and target practice to take part in, mending wheels and making covers. Royal Engineers went out to check roads, repair bridges, make maps, estimate possible billets as well as resources such as water, fuel and provisions that might be on the line of march during the next campaign. But, for

most, these activities did not fill the day, every day. Some commanders tried to keep a tight hand, but once duty was done, mostly the men were left to their own devices.

AMUSEMENTS:

> 'It was those who through fiddling, mathematics and dancing, in a word 'sense and nonsense', hwo got through the business pretty well.'

Being at ease, or retired for rest and recreation for these long periods of time, soldiers became idle either because of confinement and isolation, or from dearth of the spark to play. For some, not being under test was a greater burden than being in daily danger from the French.

Not being regimental, 'sense and nonsense' was left to ingenuity and was as varied in its appearances and presence as the men who were in the Peninsula during the war. Often young men left to themselves with little to do were bound to get into mischief.

> In every interval between our active services we indulged in all manner of childish trick and amusement, with an avidity and delight of which it is impossible to convey an adequate idea. We lived united, as men always are who are daily staring death in the face on the same side, and who, caring little about it, look upon each new day added to their lives as one more to rejoice in.

Though some men languished, unable to find occupation, most were 'doers' finding or making diversions.

FIELD SPORTS:

Officers had more resources and tried to bring as much of England to the countryside of Spain and Portugal as they could. Therefore, coursing was a widespread and very popular pastime among officers, many owning a brace of greyhounds, a pack of harriers, beagles or foxhounds, or a scratch collections of local dogs. The Duke of Wellington had a huntsman, all properly attired in a long scarlet coat. His own pack of foxhounds, which he exercised two to three times a week, attracting a horde of variously mounted but uniformed men, who followed him about the hills and dales after fox, hare, wolves or wild boars – the pace was a "cracker".

Everyone enjoyed a good run for an hour or so, even though they rarely caught the fox as the country tended to be unfamiliar, rocky and very bad for the feet of horses and dogs alike. One fox, after a two-hour chase, bounded over a shear 150 foot embankment killing five couples and half of the best hounds who were close on its heels. The most forward riders were able to fend off the rest, sobering all to the sport for a while. The other danger was that neither the prey nor the hounds knew anything of wars or boundaries and so at times strayed into enemy lines. Caught though they were, hounds and hunters were politely returned by the bemused French under a flag of truce, while the erstwhile prey was either reduced to 'mask and brush' or got away to run another day. All the same, 'it was one of the most beautiful coursing countries, perhaps, in the world.'

This sport, however, was not open to all. A man had to be well mounted to even consider the chase. For the officer who only had one horse, his duty had to take precedence over sport for poor forage and hard work often left his charger ill conditioned, and such amusement could cost too dearly.

In a variation of the excitement of the hunt, riflemen, whilst marching to the river to bathe (dressed in fatigues and carrying only a stick), extended into one single line across the plain and thus in skirmishing order. Backed by officers with greyhounds and fowling-pieces, they took to startling the hares, rabbits and partridges, who were

then easy prey for the dogs. Once the men were bathed and dressed, the same happy scene took place on the return march, and everyone arrived back in high spirits, looking forward to a fine feast.

With no hounds, other groups of officers, sometimes calling themselves 'Trigger Clubs', went out with carbines to shoot game and make themselves a good meal. After their hunt, all gathered at the house of the club member whose turn it was to cook and entertain that day. The ultimate in simplicity, members of 'Walking Clubs', set out to their dinners, long poles in hand, walking over 20 miles each way. More serious, were the Wolf-hunts. Pressed by hunger, wolves were numerous and dangerous, sometimes being so bold as to kill animals as large as an ass or a mule standing close to homes or barns. Armed men stationed themselves at the passes in the wood, while drivers went amongst the trees, scouring in line, driving everything before them. The wolves, coming upon the armed men, were shot (if the men didn't run) and a prize was given for every wolf's head.

Officers walking or riding out of their encampments went armed with fowling-pieces or carbines and would shoot at anything they saw. They often went after wood-pigeons, doves, quails, wild duck, teal, grouse, stone curlews, red-legged partridges, snipe, woodcocks, bustards (which could weigh 20 pounds measuring six feet from the tip of one wing to another and tasted like turkey) and partridge. It followed that shooting at eagles or vultures, circling high overhead, was a common practice. Game was not the only target. Quartered in a large sized town where cats were prone to roam free,

making dreadful noises at night, a group of officers would station themselves in an open window with their pistols ready and shoot the offending cats as they crept along the rooftops.

Fish were abundant, but this was a quiet and mostly solitary activity. Those who had not brought tackle from home complained about the local versions – clumsy hooks poorly built. Some, the entrepreneurs, went hookless to outsmart the fish. Rafts were built of small empty rum casks. The fishermen then sprinkled smutted corn over the surface of the water stupefying the fish and making them rise to the surface, rolling about as if they were drunk. Another way to ensure a catch, was to have good tackle sent from England and lovers of the sport who did that, found grand variety in the rivers of the Peninsula including trout, mullet, dace, salmon, barbel and rock-fish. Innocent, hungry enthusiasts who fished for carp, easily caught but tasting horrid, soon abandoned the sport. Next to catching fish, watching from a bridge as salmon struggled upstream helped pass the day.

Taking long rambles riding through the countryside was good enough for many and the outing was spiced up if there were shaggy wild ponies to chase. However, a good horse race was better and a race with an angle was a favourite. Without hounds or prey, officers delighted in an outrageous steeple chase. Two officers had to ride through a district not very well known to them and across which in the distance a predominating feature, such as a church tower, could be seen. One bet the other that he could reach the church tower in question on horseback in a given time, by following an absolutely straight path and going out of the way neither for swamps, rivers, clefts, walls nor farmhouses, in fact, that he would either walk through or climb over all obstacles. The other officer, reckoning on the certainty of some impracticable obstacle, bet him that he would not. Then off they would go. A whole concourse of officers would accompany the one who had accepted the bet, in order to enjoy his embarrassment when he had to ride through a swamp or climb over a house. These bets always provided an enormous amount of fun.

Betting was another favourite occupation. A few jockey clubs sprang up which measured out a reasonable one mile course. They appointed stewards, arranged for judges, a clerk of the course, weighed the jockeys and posted the winner's bag of dollars in a large olive tree. There were Derby days, sweepstakes, divisional race meetings, ample punch and donkey races with every Jock sitting with his face to the tail, a smart fellow running in front with a bunch of carrots. After the divisional races attended by large crowds and many officers, the officers would sit down to a fine dinner and then attend a grand ball.

HandBill

Seventh Division Race Meetings, 1813

'Major Roberts' bay mare, *Countess*, beat Captain Kelly's chestnut horse, *Slyboots*; one mile heat, *Countess* the favourite. Surgeon Reid's Portuguese horse, *Lancer*, beat Captain Byrne's grey horse, *Dashaway*; one-mile heat, *Dashaway* the favourite but having bolted, was distanced. Major Roberts' *Brown Bob* beat the Assistant Commissary's grey horse, *Wagtail* – odds five to four on *Brown Bob*.

Sweepstakes of Country Horses – all ages

Captain Smellie's *Bonny Robin*	1
Lieutenant Jones' *Corsair*	2
Lieutenant Simpson's *Doctor*	3
Captain Douglas' *Rockaway*	4

'Hard running between *Bonny Robin* and *Corsair*.'

A Silver Cup for Mules.

Paymaster Gibbs' *Money-Bag*	1

'A hard race and showed much sport.'

Naturally, the men also played cricket.

> We amuse ourselves in this place chiefly at
> Cricket. From the Spirit with which the
> Officers in general enter into this game
> one would hardly suppose there was an
> Enemy within an hundred Leagues of us.

In addition to the occasional field day, every conceivable game was played, with every imaginable homemade device for equipment. Artillery and Highlanders liked to play football. Infantry and Dragoons played fives. Rackets was popular and was played with wooden bats against the sidewall or tower of the village churches. Men made balls out of worsted stockings. Battledore, marbles, and shuttlecock were played indoors when there was unremitting bad weather. Men also made up games of their own. Some subalterns, high in the Pyrenees mountains, devised ways of loosening huge rocks and letting them roll down the French side of the mountain creating tremendous noise as limbs and branches were torn from the forest trees by the crashing boulders. These activities were supplemented by leaping, running, jumping, wrestling, cuffing, casting the stone and chasing the greasy pig.

All of these games were used to help divert and amuse the men, allowing them every possible indulgence compatible with the discipline of the battalion so as to keep them cheerful until the day of trial arrived.

SIGHTSEEING:

When lucky enough to be quartered in or near a large town or city, the ever curious Englishmen, both officers and rank and file, flocked to visit the sights and Spain and Portugal being inhabited from ancient times offered much to see. The Romans had built roads, bridges and public and private buildings which still held grandeur and purpose. The acoustics at the Roman theatre at Merida still rang true and strong; the aqueducts still brought water from the mountains and bridges with their ancient temples intact, still spanned huge roiling rivers. The Christians and Moors had built castles, forts, churches, mosques, monasteries, colleges, hospitals, fountains and villas throughout the land – many filled with art and treasures. Madrid had public walks, botanical gardens and museums with collections of art, silver, mosaics, ancient marbles, statues, shells, fossils, stuffed birds, beasts and fish. Steeped in the history of those times, the well-read especially appreciated the famous people who had set foot on those stones. They were keenly interested in the ancient battlegrounds as well as those on

which their own war had been fought (though mostly they visited the sites where other regiments had bled and died). British soldiers would come and stand on the very spot where Wellington had stood to conduct the operations – while an officer who had taken part in the battle took to explaining the action in detail.

After doing the rounds of everything worth seeing, it was the custom of some officers to finish their rambles with a visit to the nunneries and convents. These being very numerous, they never failed to meet with some pleasant adventure, either in carousing with the jolly fat friars or in holding soft parlance with the nuns from noble families. After arriving, the officers, usually two or three, were left in the reception chamber to amuse themselves as best they might, assured that a few of the sisters would be sent to their comfort.

The entrance of three as fair penitents as ever took the veil broke on the tenor of our contemplation's. I am quite sure there was no sincerity in their vows, for the mischief that lurked beneath the most beautifully-pencilled eyebrows and sparkling eyes I ever saw, betrayed another tale. They smiled benevolently as they took their seat beside the 'grating'– alas, for the villainous grating!' and said the world had done with them: but they now were guarded from the world, and all its vain pursuits, by this their friendly grating. The nuns, who, by way of rewarding us for our affecting stories, played on the spinet, singing in accompaniment with plaintive sweetness, that made us almost forget the past and all its cares. Presently, they served us with cakes, liquors, and sweetmeats, passed to us through the revolving shelves. During the repast, the nuns became more animated; when, after a round of lively conversation, the approach of midnight, and the tolling of the convent bells, reminded us that time was hastening on, and that our regiment was to march the following morning.

Where they could, shopping helped enhance the table, providing materials to mend tattered clothing, even supplying books for the multilingual, though often this simple pleasure was severely hampered for most soldiers by a dearth of money since pay was mostly months and months in arrears. For those with ample funds, very serious shoppers sent home livestock, dogs,

Spanish chestnuts, broom seed, Portuguese laurel berries, cork tree acorns, etc., all to enhance the great estates of the English countryside.

Bullfights, however, were not so popular. Local magistrates staged bullfights as celebrations when the French retreated or as a fiesta in honour of their British defenders. However, the British guests saw the fight as bad sport: the torment and death of a poor animal and the ghastly spectacle of horses gored by the beast in its excited rage, was a barbarous amusement (the Spaniards were often described as having an inate love of cruelty). It would seem the only thing drawing some of the soldiers to the bullfights were the Spanish girls who laughed at them and persuaded them to go again.

Weather permitting and once the sight-seeing was over, wandering about the town cracking jokes or flirting with the local beauties, waiting for the evenings to begin, was as good an occupation as any.

I remember that, in passing the house of the sexton one evening, I saw his daughter baking a loaf of bread. Falling desperately in love with both her and the loaf I carried the one to the ball and the other to my quarters. A woman was a woman in those days, and every officer made it a point of duty to marshal as many as he could to the general assembly, no matter whether they were countesses or sextonesses. In consequence, we frequently incurred the most indelible disgrace among the better orders for our indiscriminate collection, some of whom would retire in disgust; yet as a sufficient number generally remained for our evening's amusement, and we were only birds of passage, it was a matter of the most perfect indifference to us what they thought. We followed the same course wherever we went.

EVENING ACTIVITIES:

Evening amusements were greatly influenced by the locale. In a city or fairly large town where there was a social class

including the wealthy and influential, British officers were quickly incorporated, attending and giving dinners, balls, dances, frequenting clubs or coffee houses where they would play cards, converse and smoke.

Whether in town or city, the regimental mess was ever present answering for dinner and the evening – sometimes being the only amusement available.

There we had the best of things that this part of the country could produce; it was a means of passing away the dreary winter nights pleasantly around a fire, drinking mulled wine, eating roast chestnuts, and smoking cigars.

The city, however, offered sophisticated attractions. In Lisbon there were faro tables to attract, sometimes addict and often impoverish the card player with its giddying high stakes games. In smaller towns officers were invited to local card parties where a bit of tea or coffee was served (you were expected to find your own dinner) before the players turned to whist, casino, or a 'rub of cribbage'. Stakes were small and the evening also

sometimes included music and a hot supper. Rank and file were also keen on card games and the accompanying gambling, but they played in their own circumstances.

The 'tertulia' was an open, informal reception held in cities and towns where four or five wealthy and distinguished women opened their homes to the best of the local society, providing a place for conversation, music, dancing and playing cards. The lady acting as hostess simply issued an invitation and starting about 9 or 10 o'clock in the evening, people of her class including the British officers, would come and go as they chose. There might be 10 to 12 in a room at a time. Since it was assumed that everyone had eaten dinner, little if any food was served with water the major beverage, though sometimes there was tea or a bottle of wine standing on the table. The lively atmosphere and 'indelicate' stories that were related before ladies, who were not in the least shocked, along with the sharing of half smoked cigars and constant spitting on the floors left some officers a bit put off by this amusement.

Dinner parties were not regular nightly affairs, but any occasion could be used to justify assembling food and company in celebration. These parties ranged from large and sumptuous dos, often given by the local gentry, the Duke or his Generals, down to the simple fare served by a Lieutenant for this comrades in honour of a birthday. Christmas dinners were served to each Mess in a Division, the Commissariat providing lean roast beef, poultry, plum pudding with whatever else the men could add. The King's German Legion came up with punch and a Christmas tree decorated with lights and oranges.

The dinner parties given by the Duke and his Generals might frequently have as many as 500 guests. Or as was more often the case, ten to 30 officers came together in their best uniforms and orders to enjoy the food, the wine and the lively talks. Although everyone did not always find it a relaxing evening when the Duke was present: the party might be so intimidated by the presence of such a high personage as his Lordship, affable and good humoured though he invariably was throughout, they would sit unmoved for up to eight hours, no one leaving the table until he himself had arisen.

An individual officer might choose to invite his own General and perhaps four other guests going to great trouble to set a fine table in crystal, china and silver, with delicacies sent from home. The menu might have looked something like this:

First Course:

Salt fish and potatoes (i.e. 'chowder')
Removes

Roast saddle of mutton
Stewed beef, roast potatoes
Steaks
Broiled chicken
Soup removed
Ham

Second Course:

Roast partridges
Apple stewed
Rice Pudding
Tart
Mushrooms
Omelette

Dessert:

Grapes

It was however, very possible to spend a large amount of money on entertaining. Goods such as tea, sugar, spices, peppers, mustards, pickles, curries, vinegars, wines and hampers of cheese were brought from England. First rate cooks and cosmopolitan servants were also used and some men had to leave their regiment because of the debt they incurred. As reported by one man: 'He and his friends had literally eaten up his little fortune.'

Regimental dinners were momentous affairs. With the large contingent of Irishmen in the army, St. Patrick's Day was a roaring favourite, commanding bands marching through the streets playing Irish and English favourites, and constant rounds of toasts and cheers.

With as many as 50 officers sitting at the table, toasts would go on and on:

St Patrick (three times three)
(Tune: 'St Patrick's day in the morning')
Shelah, St Patrick's wife
The King
(Tune: 'God Save the King')
The Prince Regent of England
(Tune: 'The Prince and Old England for Ever')
The Duke of York and the Army
(Tune: 'The Duke of York's March')
The Wooden Walls of Old England
(Tune: 'Rule Britannia')
The Marquis of Wellington, and success to the next campaign
(Tune : 'The Downfall of Paris')
General Picton and the 3rd Division
(Tune: 'Britons strike home')
General Pakenham and the Battle of Salamanca.
(Tune: 'See the conquering Hero come')
Colonel Keane and the light brigade (three times three)
(Tune: 'British Grenadiers')
St Patrick, the Shamrock and the Land of Potatoes
St George, the Rose and Prosperity to England
St Andrew, the Thistle, and the Land of Cakes ...
And on and on...

Hailed far and wide was the first Regimental Dinner of the 95th Rifles, isolated high in the Pyrenees:

The 25th August, being our regimental anniversary, was observed by the officers of our three battalions with all due conviviality. Two trenches, calculated to accommodate 70 gentlemen's legs, were dug in the green sward; the earth between them stood for a table, and behind was our seat, and though the table could not boast of all the delicacies of a civic entertainment, yet the earth almost quaked with the weight of the feast, and the enemy certainly did from the noise of it. For so many fellows holding such precarious tenures of their lives could not meet together in commemoration of such an event without indulging in an occasional cheer – not a whispering cheer, but one that echoed far and wide into the French lines, and as it was a sound that had often pierced them before, and never yet boded them any good, we heard afterwards that they were kept standing at their arms the greater part of the night in consequence. Neither vocal nor instrumental music was wanting after the feast, and with the aid of cigars and blackstrap, we enjoyed the most extraordinary 'fête champêtre' I ever witnessed.

Grand Balls were often combined with the dinner parties and they were especially glittering when held in the ballrooms of the large cities possessing fine food, wine, crystal, servants and professional musicians. In Madrid, there was a ball at least twice a week.

There being no ballrooms in the country villages, determined officers would fix up barns by hanging tapestries and colourful silks or constructing their own outdoor ballroom:

A very pretty bower of leaves, lighted up with paper lamps, and wreathed round with flowers; the English colours formed an ornament at the upper end, or place of honour, of this temporary apartment; a band from the German Legion set the swimming dance in motion; we had waltzes, boleros, and fandangos, dark eyes, favourable glances, agreeable smiles, white teeth, charming figures, and graceful movement. We actually began to feel a little humanised; in short, to us it was 'una tierra de los duendes (a Fairyland).' They even extracted (although in the enemy's keeping) many sweetmeats and domas hermosas, to adorn our bower and deck our table.

Dancing on a much smaller scale than the ball was a popular local activity as it brought the ladies into the circle. 'The soothing influence exercised by the presence of many pretty Spanish women softened all rude or contentious feelings or recollections.'

On Sundays, in some villages in the country, everybody in the neighbourhood put on their best and cleanest clothes and in the afternoon danced the fandango or the bolero in one of the open spaces in the village. In other villages, the evenings were spent dancing with the village girls, who sometimes tried to teach Spanish dancing in return for instruction in English country dances, Scottish reels and Irish jigs. Though no matter how hard they tried, many officers attempted in vain to learn these dances and others came

away considering these local dances, especially the fandango, scarcely decent.

To supply the music clarinets, octaves and tambourines were borrowed from some neighbouring infantry regiment. The truly lucky drew on their own regimental bands and if that was not possible, they would rely on local talents and instruments.

The one downside to these happy gatherings was the gradual loss of novelty for the officers, which made these events only half as exciting as they had once been.

Our village belles, as already stated, made themselves perfectly at home in our society, and we, too, should have enjoyed theirs for a season; but when month after month, and year after year, continued to roll along, without producing any change, we found that the cherry cheek and sparkling eye of rustic beauty furnished but a very poor apology for the illuminated portion of Nature's fairest works, and ardently longed for an opportunity of once more feasting our eyes on a lady.

Moreover, the culture and cuisine of some areas of the Peninsula left many a soldier equally astonished by their very presence in the room: 'These delicate ladies feed so grossly and eat so much garlic, that it is enough to suffocate a person being in the room with 20 or 30 of them.'

Sometimes officers liked to try their hands at private theatricals or amateur dramatics, putting on many plays ranging from the stolid Shakespearean military, Henry IV, a current tragedy by Edward Young, The Revenge (which in practice was transformed, unintentionally, into comedy), to Sheridan's comedy, The Rivals, which was a great hit. Chapels, barns or whatever was available, were transformed into theatres; scenery and costumes improvised and the regimental bands provided the orchestra.

Many of the officers acted extremely well, and I saw one infantry subaltern in particular who as regards costume, mimicry, dancing and singing, impersonated a prima donna with such

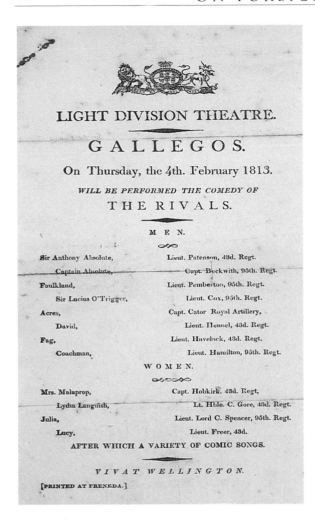

LIGHT DIVISION THEATRE.

GALLEGOS.

On Thursday, the 4th. February 1813.

WILL BE PERFORMED THE COMEDY OF

THE RIVALS.

MEN.

Sir Anthony Absolute,	Lieut. Patenson, 43d. Regt.
Captain Absolute,	Capt. Beckwith, 95th. Regt.
Faulkland,	Lieut. Pemberton, 95th. Regt.
Sir Lucius O'Trigger,	Lieut. Cox, 95th. Regt.
Acres,	Capt. Cator Royal Artillery,
David,	Lieut. Hennel, 43d. Regt.
Fag,	Lieut. Havelock, 43d. Regt.
Coachman,	Lieut. Hamilton, 95th. Regt.

WOMEN.

Mrs. Malaprop,	Capt. Hobkirk. 43d. Regt,
Lydia Languish,	Lt. Hble. C. Gore, 43d. Regt.
Julia,	Lieut. Lord C. Spencer, 95th. Regt.
Lucy,	Lieut. Freer, 43d.

AFTER WHICH A VARIETY OF COMIC SONGS.

VIVAT WELLINGTON.

[PRINTED AT FRENEDA.]

LIGHT DIVISION THEATRE

GALLEGOS

on Thursday the 4 February 1813
Will be performed the COMEDY of
THE RIVALS

MEN

Sir ANTHONY ABSOLUTE
Lieut. TYLDEN-PATTENSON, 43rd Regt
Capt. ABSOLUTE
Capt. BECKWITH, 95th Regt.
FAULKLAND
Lieut. PEMBERTON, 95th Regt
Sir LUCIUS O'TRIGGER
Lieut. COX, 95th Regt
ACRES   Capt. CATOR, Royal Artillery
DAVID   Lieut. HENNEL, 43rd Regt
FAG   Lieut. HAVELOCK, 43rd Regt
COACHMAN
Lieut. HAMILTON, 95th Regt.

WOMEN

Mrs. MALAPROP
Capt. HOBKIRK, 43rd Regt
LYDIA LANGUISH
Lieut. Honble C. GORE, 43rd Regt
JULIA
Lieut. Lord C. SPENCER, 95th Regt
LUCY
Lieut. FREER, 43rd Regt

After which a Variety of Comic Songs

VIVAT WELLINGTON

Printed at Freneda

Quotes from The Rivals

Mrs. Malaprop: Illiterate him, I say, quite from
your memory.

inimitable skill and comicality that he might without fear have appeared on any stage.

These plays, though, had such a double entendre within the community of men serving together in the War that there was always an undertone of humour, if not hilarity.

It is impossible to imagine anything more truly ludicrous than to see Lydia Languish and Julia (which characters were performed by two young and good-looking men, dressed uncommonly well, and looking somewhat feminine on the stage), drinking punch and smoking cigars behind the scenes at a furious rate, between the acts.

Wellington was a frequent patron of these arts and often rode the 20 or so miles from his headquarters to see the performances, and then would ride back again that same night.

'Tis safest in matrimony to begin with a little aversion.

He is the very pineapple of politeness!

If I reprehend anything in this world, it is the use of my oracular tongue, and a nice derangement of epitaphs!

My valour is certainly going! it is sneaking off! I feel it oozing out, as it were, at the palm of my hands!

Absolute: take care — you know I am compliance itself — when I am not thwarted; — no one more easily led — when I have my own way; — but don't put me in a frenzy.

Sir Lucius: you may be assured my love shall never be miscellaneous.

Among other things, officers who were Freemasons had established lodges and Freemasonry went on until Wellington put an end to it by a general order. He pointed out that the Spanish priesthood not only felt greatly affronted by it, but had also raised a protest against it out of fear lest they should infect Spain with this devilry, as they called it.

With nothing on the social calendar, the 'Idle Clubs' (an assembly of officers off duty) sat about smoking and talking about everything: from shop to socialites, nit-picking comrades, political motives at home, speculations about Napoleon to analyses of Wellington, complaints about pay to hopes about promotion; from the past to the future. They speculated, postured, complained, joked, reminisced, argued, pondered and listened: 'You would laugh if you could hear our conversation here, one moment spherical case and round shot, the next tea or shoes or Russian ducks.'

Much conversation was triggered by the arrival of newspapers from home. There were subscriptions to The Times, The Globe, the Courier, the Morning Post, the Day, the London Chronicle and many, many others, all avidly read and amply shared around so that all could be alternately incensed and buoyed by the representations of the escapades of the Army. They contained old news of events in the Peninsula, and endless speculative opinions on the result of the war according to the author's political views and interests: 'With one we were all glorious and successful, with another Lord Wellington was an ignoramus and we were all going to a place not to be named in print.'

Many wrote Letters to the Editor from the front, often politically inclined, written by ignorant or discontented officers — at times the truth and just as often erroneous. These letters proved a boon to the enemy as they often listed dispositions of the Army, plans for military action and essentially important military intelligence which the enemy would have never known about, were it not for this voluntary and public offering provided by the press. The Duke tried to stop these security leaks as well as the widespread public 'croaking' by his officers with a General Order forbidding such sensitive communications and many officers warned their families not to circulate their letters. Nevertheless, the press was persistent, publishing the truth with the grudge; the public probably believed it all, while the Ministry and the French treated it as intelligence, acting on the shreds of information, true or false.

Greatly anticipated were the lists of promotions, gazettes, obituaries and articles covering military subjects; accounts of Napoleon's victories and defeats on the Continent and in Russia — all topics of lively conversation.

Given the tedium vitae, the arrival of letters from England was a great event.

A mail, — ay, news from England — dear old England! — a bundle of friendly letters awaited my arrival. No one but those who have experienced long delay and doubtful silence can sufficiently appreciate the pleasure derived from receiving in a distant land letters from home; circumstances at other times of small import then appear matters of deep interest; the slight indisposition of a friend, or the death of some favourite old dog, casts a deeper regret, — the success, health, or happiness, of those you love, bestows a greater pleasure. In distance and uncertain

absence the thoughtful minds and kind hearts whose affections guide their pens, afford invaluable testimonials to the longing recipients of them, particularly when one calculates the chance that they come from friends you ne'er may see again.

Next to reading newspapers and letters, books were a dependable though hard to obtain, solace.

As there were no libraries in Portugal or Spain, there was little for those who could read to read, other than a bible belonging to a rifle sergeant and carried in the mess-kettle of a comrade, a novel carried in the pocket of an officer, or the newspapers which occasionally reached them from England.

Books brought from England were limited to a chest or so and had to be left in storage once the campaign started so men were pressed to select some small few to carry. Bibles resting in coat pockets stopped musket rounds as well as inspiring life or informing death. For those in quarters who did not have books of their own or friends with a supply, only the lucky ones who could read French, Spanish, Portuguese or Latin were likely to find material to read. At times, the men were able to borrow books from priests or monks who had a library or from their host in the billet. A real treasure was an abandoned cache of books left behind by the French or a bookseller who had stocked but not sold a trove of books he hoped the French invader would buy.

Officers interested in understanding more about Spain and its people sent home for travel guides and read Cervantes' novel, Don Quixote, or the story by Lesage, Gil Blas, also a popular choice:

He that has not Seville seen
Never has a traveller been.

Some officers frequently wrote home asking for more books to be sent out to the Peninsula and some managed to assemble notable collections such as this one:

de Saxe: Revêries
Essai General de Fortification
Jomini: Traité de la Grande Tactique
Memoirs of Prince Eugene
Lloyd: History of the Seven Years War
Tempelhoff: translation of above

Mémoires sur la guerre des Pyrenées par M.B
Treatise de la Guerre de Vendée par M. Bouchon
Histoire de Cartes dernière compagnie de M. de Turenne
Hassell's Statistique Européenne
Stuart: Elements of Philosophy of the Human Mind
St Pierre: Theory of the Tides
Blair's Sermons and his Lectures
Bonaparte: The Secret Cabinet
Rousseau: Nouvelle Eloise
Ferguson: Lectures
Adye: pocket Bombardier
Caesar's Commentaries
Walton: History of English Poetry
Percy: Ancient Ballards
Milford: Grecian History
Dulles: Mathematics
Spenser: Fairy Queen
Milton: Paradise Lost
Campbell, Thomas: Gertrude of Wyoming
Defoe: Robinson Crusoe
Hammond: Love Elegies
Scott: The Lady of the Lake and Sir Roderick's Vision

Allison: On Taste
Rational Recreations, including Experiments in
Pneumatics,
Hydrology & Pyrotechnics
St Evremond
Tacitus
Vergil
Shakespeare
Pope

Out on the frontier, isolated and recovering from wounds, officers read aloud the poems of Robert Burns deep into the night.

Though a few men from the ranks had well-thumbed copies of the Bible, Horace or Gil Blas in their pockets, most passed the evenings playing cards, throwing dice or just talking and singing. Staying in a deserted farm, with eight officers living in the farm itself and 200 men quartered in the barn, the evenings were passed with jests, tales and songs.

The early part of the evening was generally spent in witticisms and tales; and, in conclusion, by way of a lullaby, some long-winded fellow would commence one of those everlasting ditties in which soldiers and sailors delight so much – they are all to the same tune, and the subject, (if one may judge by the tenor of the first ninety-eight verses,) was battle, murder, or sudden death. Sometimes a fresh arrival from England would endeavour to astonish their unpolished ears with 'the white blossomed sloe', or some such refined melody, but it was invariably coughed down as instantaneously as if it had been the sole voice of a conservative amidst a select meeting of radicals. The wit and the humour of the rascals were amusing beyond any thing.

THE DRINK:

The strength of three pints of strong beer was awesome. It could make a fellow's insides like a shaking bog – and as rotten; but barleycorn, such as would put the souls of three butchers into one weaver. Ale that would flare like turpentine good, unsophisticated, John Bull stuff – stark! – that would stand on end – punch that would make a cat speak.

The Duke was once quoted to have said that the British Army was composed of 'the scum of the earth … fellows who have enlisted for drink. That is the plain fact – they have all enlisted for drink.'

Though this was not universally true, it was nevertheless a predominant phenomenon. With little to do in the evenings, many turned to alcohol.

In fact, an enormous consumption of alcohol was not uncommon within the society as a whole and hard drinking was equally present among officers: drunk from an evening's entertainment, men would loose their way on the trek home in the dark; some, finding huge wine vats (some were so large they held over 3000 gallons) brimming full, fell in to drown and sinking to the bottom, left themselves to spice the vintage.

Drinking inevitably led some men to committing offences and the penalty for misbehaviour was heavy: Men were flogged for small offences and for graver crimes flogged to death – a thousand lashes were often awarded by courts-martial.

I have seen men suffer 500 to 700 lashes before taken down, the blood running down into their shoes, and their backs flayed like raw red chopped sausages.

Some men bore such punishment without flinching for 200 or 300 lashes, chewing a musket-ball or a bit of leather to prevent or stifle the cry of agony.

The frequency of these punishments was not always high: one battalion, for instance, witnessed only six floggings in a period of six years whilst serving in the Peninsula. The rare occurrence of corporal punishment in some battalions was usually the result of officers allowing the men to determine the type of punishment required.

Deserters, some claiming in palliation of their heinous crime that they were forced to desert for want of food or clothing, were to 'atone with their lives for one of the greatest crimes known in the criminal code of the army'.

The division was formed into three sides square, on a plain in front of the village, the graves of the hapless beings occupying a

part of the fourth face of the square. When all was ready, and a firing party from each regiment had been formed in the centre, the provost-marshal went to the guard-tent, where the prisoners were in waiting, to conduct them to the place of execution. They soon after appeared, poor wretches, moving towards the square, with faces pale and wan, and with all the dejection such a situation is calculated to produce. Their arms had been pinioned one by one as they came out from the guard-tent, and all being ready, the melancholy procession advanced towards the centre of the square. The proceedings of the court which tried them, together with the sentence was read in the hearing of the whole division; which concluded, the prisoners were marched round in front of every regiment, that all might see and avoid their unhappy fate. They were then moved towards their graves and when they reached the bank of earth in front of each, they were made to kneel down with their faces fronting the square, and then being one after another blindfolded, and left for a few moments to their own reflections or their prayers, the provost-marshal proceeded to the firing party, who had been previously loaded, and directing the men of each regiment to fire at their own prisoner, he advanced them to within about ten or 12 paces of the wretched men, and giving the signals by motion for their making ready and firing, the whole fired at once, and plunged the unhappy criminals into eternity; and in such of the others as they perceived life still remaining, they also immediately put an end to their sufferings, by placing their muskets close to their body, and firing into them. One poor man, when he received his death wound, sprung to a considerable height, and giving a loud shriek, he fell, and instantly expired.

When all was finished, the division was formed into column, and marched round in front of the bodies,

where each soldier might distinctly perceive the sad and melancholy effects of such a fatal dereliction of duty. They were then, without more ado, thrown into their graves, which were filled up without delay, and the division separating, each regiment marched to its quarters.

I cannot describe the uncomfortable feelings this spectacle produced in my mind, nay, not only there, but in my body also—for I felt sick at heart. Death in the hundred shapes it assumes on the field of battle seems honourable, and not near so revolting to the feelings, and withal comes suddenly; but to witness the slow and melancholy preparations for an execution such as this, is productive, in any heart that can feel, of the most unpleasant sensations, I think, imaginable.

IDLENESS:

If not given to drink, those not employed often succumbed to idleness:

I am heartily tired of this idle life. We have

been five months in snug winter quarters. Our situation here was pleasant in the extreme, as we had little duty to perform. I was quartered, with my comrade, on a miller, about a mile and a half from the village. Although we were so pleasantly situated here, we began to get tired of the monotony, and there was a restlessness, and an anxiety to know what the French were about, and how soon our services would be required.

Idleness, monotony and inactivity. Some officers observed that when a soldier became prey to *ennui* it was all over for him. He was first sorrowful and then sick. A man would always get *ennui* unless he had the power to amuse himself. It was worse when a young man was left by himself without much duty as sometimes happened, or landed amongst strangers. On these occasions, especially the new hands from England gave the matter up, went to bed and reported themselves sick.

SICKNESS:

Above half our men are in hospital, and from the number of deaths our burying ground begins to have the appearance of a ploughed field.

The number of sick being uncommonly high, the army in quarters, was often reduced to half its effective strength, the total amount of ineffective men at one point, not less than 20,000 men. Wellington, at times, curtailed operations because of this.

The prevailing disorders were fever and dysentery, aggravated by weather, rations, drunkenness and the environment. The Spanish had a saying: 'Where oleanders thrive, fever thrives also.'

The finest oleanders prospered in the flat country enriched with lively rivers – choice spots that leave a "harlequin of plague."

It was true that very fine huts had been built in these cantonments, but the men lived as the saying goes, 'with snakes amid roses'. For the banks of the river and the morasses beyond, which were flooded in winter, were exposed to a grilling heat in summer, which dried up the

rivers leaving a nasty damp place. The exhalations from the vegetable matter, which was decaying from the heat of the sun and the half-dried swamps that were swarming with vermin, laid the foundation of disease amongst the men. The unwholesome vapours, which arose from the beds of the many stagnant pools scattered over the surface of the plains always dried up by the summer heats, were said to produce this evil. Be this as it may, this insidious enemy found his way into the tranquil quarters, crowded the hospitals with sick and filled the chapel vaults with victims, gloomily and sullenly mourned.

During this time a dreadful mortality took place.. The flux and brain fever reigned to a frightful extent. The epidemic was so virulent that some men died from it in 24 hours. One very healthy-looking gunner of the legion came back to his hut one day and said that he was ill. After he had been examined and told to go to the hospital, he left his hut and the doctor said : 'That apparently robust man, who does not, after all, look so very ill, will be a corpse the day after to-morrow.'

There was great mortality amongst the troops, fever and ague prevailing. There was no cure. All the charms the doctors got from the medical department at home was some rotten old bark intended to be mixed with some country wine, to dose the

soldiers. Some fusty sawdust would have had the same effect! Lives were held cheap, but they cost money, nobody cared: 'things will last my time', and the national debt will probably last a while longer!

Such calamity would have been resigned in the field of battle, perhaps, with a sigh, yet not without some proud feeling of consolation; but here, to see the cheek blanched and the arm unnerved by disease, was a constant source of affliction and despondency. There was nothing about which Englishmen were so generally incredulous, or to which they appeared so indifferent, as any report touching the danger of a season or a climate, and the approach of sickness and mortality. For this very reason, when once an alarming disease appeared among them, they were overcome with surprise, they lost all elasticity of spirit, hope forsook them and they sunk unresistingly to the grave. The sickness prevailed in the army to an alarming extent, of which the number the deaths was most afflicting.

> I think it probable notwithstanding the warlike appearance of every thing that in the course of the next six Months we shall lose more men by Sickness than by the Sword.

Those surviving the initial onslaught devised a diverse course of treatments for cures and relief.

> Our doctor used a very singular expedient, which was this: we were ordered, when off duty, to sit up with the sick in our turns, and about midnight to take each one out of bed – they all lay without shirts – lead them to a flight of steps, and pour two buckets of cold water on each. They were so deranged they knew nothing about it. I would put my finger into their hand, when they would jump out of bed, follow me, and sit quietly while we poured the contents of the buckets over them, and would be led by the finger back again to bed, and never uttered one word. It was thought by the officers and doctors, that this mode of treatment had a good effect.

Another variation:

> Had the ague daily, and kept my bed from its debilitating influence. I took bark in very large doses, combined with opium, and placed a hot stone on my bosom and two at the soles of my feet as soon as there was any appearance of the cold fit. From treating myself in this way I soon dislodged this insidious enemy from my body and gradually recovered.

Convalescents were frequently required to see the dead interred:

> This was a horrible office, which obliged us to attend at the hospital to receive the bodies, which were conveyed away, cartloads at a time, to the ground appropriated for their burial. This lay outside the town beneath the ramparts, and was so small that we had to get large, deep, oblong holes excavated. Two stout Portuguese were employed packing the bodies, heads and heels together, into these to save room. For this duty these two brutes seemed to have been born, for never before did I see two such ruffianly looking fellows.
>
> It was revolting to witness how the pair handed the bodies from the hospital to the cart. Each carried a skin of vinegar, with which they first soused themselves over the neck and face, then, with one jerk they jilted a single corpse, naked as it was born, across their shoulders and bolted off to the cart, into which it was pitched as if it had been a log of wood. Although the women who fell victims to the epidemic were generally sewed in a wrapper of calico, or some such thing, they partook of the same hole as the opposite sex, and otherwise were as little privileged. Many were the scores of my poor comrades I thus saw committed to their first parent, and many were the coarse jests the gravediggers made over their obsequies.

The most sickly seasons were October and December, and the January and February following, were the most healthy, the climate of the country during the hot months in autumn considered as little less unhealthy than that of the West Indies. While the army was in motion, sickness to a great extent seldom prevailed, but within a limited time after halting, diseases broke out, exacerbated by the weather.

For many who survived, the evil continued to inhibit those on duty as the fever persisted latent on a fiendish schedule.

I was all right and ready for the road, barring the ague, which left me prostrate every second day. The 7th of July was one of my very worst ague days. I was lying under an apple-tree in the beautiful valley, hors-de-combat, in a hot fit, my head splitting open, as I thought, with pain. The day was extremely hot, which only aggravated the malady, and increased my sufferings. All of a sudden the drums beat to arms, the bugles sounded the assembly, and the men hastened to the alarm post, and the order of march was – up the mountain as fast as we could go. I joined my company, and dragged myself along with difficulty, faint and weary with pain and debility. There was in those days a chivalry, an esprit de corps amongst officers and men never to be absent if possible when there was a chance of a brush with the enemy. It was a point of honour not to be detained by any trifling illness, and so I stuck to my trade as usual.

The trip to the hospitals was harrowing and conditions, once there, were lamentable:

I had an attack of Dysentery; this was succeeded by Fever. A large blister was put on my back and one on each instep. I think my head was also shaved, but being a long time insensible, I remember little.

The sick were removed on cars. Nothing can exceed these abominable vehicles for jolting and intolerable noise. Each rubbishly car is drawn by two bullocks, at a pace sufficiently slow and unpleasant to wear out the patience of any healthy man, even if the roads were good.

This removal and jolting I could not bear. A violent bleeding from the nose came on, and continued till I tied some small cord tightly round my little fingers; this stopped the bleeding. To make things worse it rained. I do not think that I was quite conscious of what passed on the first day's march.

Next day, which was also wet, we arrived. Not being able to walk without support, I remained on the car till nearly night, and was then helped up the steps of a convent. The sick not being then disposed of, I was laid down on the cold flags at the stair head, and left there till removed by order of a surgeon. A relapse of fever and insensibility was the consequence. I was afterwards carried into a corridor among perhaps 200 sick and dying men. My case was really pitiable; my appetite and hearing gone; feet and legs like ice; the three blisters on my back and feet unhealed and undressed; my shirt sticking in the wounds caused by the blisters; my knapsack and necessaries lost ; and worst of all, no one to care a straw for me. One day a woman belonging our regiment passed my bed. I called her, and asked her to bring me a little tea. I had several small loaves that I could not eat, under my pillow. These I gave her, but she forgot to bring the tea, though she often went by my couch of dried fern.

Some days after, we were removed to a Bomb proof barracks. No ventilation, 20 sick men in the room, of whom about 18 died. In this place there were one door, and one chimney, but no windows. Relapse again; deaf as a post; shirt unchanged and sticking to my sore back; ears running stinking matter; a man lying close on my right hand with both his legs mortified nearly to the knees, and dying. A little sympathy would have soothed, but sympathy there was none. The orderlies (men who acted as nurses to the sick,) were brutes. In a little time my strength and appetite began to return, consequently I asked the doctor for more bread, etc. He kindly allowed me an increase of it, and a pint of wine per day. I now got rapidly better.

While sitting on my bed one day, I was gladdened by the sound of bells ringing. No one can imagine the pleasure I felt, on being again favoured with the sense of hearing. I was afraid that it had gone for ever.

Several of us were now collected and marched up the steep streets to a large building capable of holding 1,700 or 1,800 men. I think there might then be more than 1,000 in it. Here the pavement was our bed. Some straw, once long but now short enough, was carried out and laid in the street every morning to air, and brought in at night by the nimblest. The slow footed got none. Our daily allowance was, 1 lb. of Biscuit, lb. of Salt Pork, and a pint of Wine. I was still very weak and deaf.

Every night I buttoned up closely, and waited till someone beckoned me to take a share of his blanket and pavement couch. But deliverance came at last; an order arrived for all the convalescents who could travel, to join the army, which had marched to the other extremity of Portugal. In the detachment were men of nearly all the regiments in the Peninsula. Truly we were a motley group.

After arriving I had another severe relapse of fever and immediately sent off to hospital; but the place being crowded, I was placed in the dead house all night. The infection was dreadful: nearly all in the room where I was were at one time insensible, bawling out the most incoherent jabber. I had my turn of that also. Although there were about 12 of us in two small rooms, there was not a single chamber utensil. A blanket was spread on the floor instead. Some made use of a window for every purpose. I saw neither basin, soap, nor towel. Such was the place, and such our condition. However, having a good constitution, I soon recovered.

Far more soldiers died from fever than from wounds received in battle. At one point, Wellington said that 700 of 1,400 officers were sick, their constitutions probably broken. 50 men a day were dying of disease. 'The sickness which prevails is dreadful, and the mortality melancholy… We are an army of convalescents.'

In the spring, the army broke up from its winter quarters, coming together, and the sight afforded a great deal of amusement.

There is not only the greeting of long-parted friends and acquaintances in the same walks of life, but, among the different divisions which the nature of the service generally threw a good deal together, there was not so much as a mule or a donkey that was not known to each individual and its absence noticed; nor a scamp of a boy, or a common Portuguese trull, who was not as particularly inquired after, as if the fate of the campaign depended on their presence. All was summer and sunshine. 'The dismal swamps had now become verdant meadows; we had plenty in the camp, vigour in our limbs, and hope in our bosoms.'

ON THE MARCH

Marching in a column of fifteen thousand men is beyond description.

Roused from sleep before daylight by the bugle, the soldiers were usually on their feet like lightening – planting themselves on their alarm posts. The army stands to arms for an hour, shivering and anxious in the early chill of a drizzly morning until a grey horse could be seen a mile off, which is the military criterion by which daylight is acknowledged and the hour of surprise is past. Unharnessing, they indulged in such luxuries as toilet and table afforded, then rolled blankets, packed, equipped, loaded, sent the baggage to the rear and assembled in squads and companies at the designated alarm-posts/place of parade.

THE COLUMN:

An hour and a half after the first bugle, the report of 'All Present' was made in succession by the Brigade Majors up to the Assistant Adjutant General, and the General commanding the column ordered the soldiers to march in sections of three. The advanced guard, composed of one company of varying strength, often from the Light troops, formed and marched out preceding the entire force. With band and bugles playing martial music, the rest moved out in close column, in complete silence, in step, arms sloped, in well regulated intervals of the greatest precision and regularity. Flankers and skirmishers moved on the eminences to the sides of the line of march, keeping an eager look out. Following the troops was the baggage train in the following general order:

> *Wheeled carriages drawn by horses or mules*
> *Mules with ammunition*
> *Horses or mules with baggage for staff*
> *Mules with camp kettles or tents*
> *Horses or mules with baggage for regimental officers*
> *Commissariat mules*

A number of slaughter oxen to provide food also moved with the baggage train. The women sometimes preceded the column, but generally moved in detached parties with the baggage along with the servants, sutlers and other camp followers. The Assistant Provost Marshal with his guard and delinquents brought up the rear, followed by the rearguard under an officer who took up the stragglers and men with their tickets that had obtained permission to fall out.

The army travelled in three or four parallel columns on different roads, each given a specific route to points or towns marked in the orders issued by the Deputy Quartermaster General. Each column was composed of Infantry, Cavalry, Artillery, Staff, and the Commissariat in divisions in varying proportion. On July 13th for instance, three columns proceeded as follows:

13 July 1812

Left Column
11th Light Dragoons
3rd Division
Maj. Gen LeMarchant's Brigade Of Cavalry
Brig. Gen. Bradford's Brigade
Portuguese Infantry
Brig. Gen. Pack's Division

Centre Column
1st Hussars
Light Division
12th and 16th Light Dragoons
5th Division
4th Division
Gen. Bock's Brigade of Cavalry
Reserve Ammunition

Right Column
14th Light Dragoons
1st Division
6th Division
7th Division

THE BAGGAGE TRAIN:

At the rear of the column came the baggage, carrying all of the impedimenta of the army – spirits and bisquit for 10 days, slaughter-beef, tents, cooking utensils, engineering equipment, trunks of papers and records, local specie, ammunition, tools, medical chests, the coats, blankets and supplies of the regiments, all of the silver, clothing, wine, books, rugs, camp cots, stools, tents, forage, candles, etc., of the officers' personal effects. All baggage was to be transported on mules or horses as a general order. This was because bullock carts were found to glut the roads and slow the columns from their march, an embarrassment of obstacles and obstruction to the body of troops on the march, especially on narrow roads. They were relegated to convoy duty – forbidden in the line of march.

Anything that anyone required had to be carried, as the country could not support such a vast horde and lacked the amenities and requirements of an British army on the march. A scale was used to determine the number of mules and horses allotted to officers of varying rank, regiments and companies, including a

sufficient ration of forage to support the animals themselves, though it seems there were often more animals than those for which the rule would account. In a column of 15,000 men, there could be over 3,500 commissariat mules with their mule drivers carrying baggage, servants, the sick and stragglers, wives and slaughter bullocks that would walk, and usually then be slaughtered and cooked within a short time. Along with this horde, there was a huge number of additional mules and horses, for the attending wives, sutlers, adventurers, reporters, women camp-followers, rogues, thieves and other opportunists – numbers beyond count.

All three columns numbered about 46,767 troops, staff and wagon train drivers, to which must be added the wives, other camp followers, up to 5,000 horses, some 10,000 commissariat mules and the slaughter-bullocks – all stretching out for miles and further than the eye could see.

To look at the mass of impedimenta and camp followers trailing behind the British, you would think you were beholding the army of Darius.

THE WOMEN:

The women (six wives were chosen by lot to accompany each company – though there were many local women who followed the men) were often described as sticking to the army like bricks. All of women were expected to accompany the baggage in the rear, following the column through rivers and across mountains, which they did even in defiance of general orders to the contrary. But they were known to impede progression. In spite of general orders issued for their own guidance, the women blocked up narrow passages and checked the advance of the army with their donkeys. After repeated orders requiring them to follow in the rear, they were warned their donkeys would be shot.

'I'd like to see the man that wud shoot my donkey,' says Mrs. Biddy Flyn, *'faith I'll be too early away for any of 'em to catch me. Will you come wid me, girls?'* And away they all started at early dawn, cracking their jokes about division orders, Wellington, commanding officers, and their next bivouac.

Mrs. Skiddy led the way on her

celebrated donkey called the 'Queen of Spain.' A squat little Irishwoman, and broad as a big turtle, she cried out:

'Dhrive on, girls, and we'll bate them to the end ov this day, at any rate.

'An' the morrow, too' says Mrs Flyn.

'An, the day after,' cried Betty Wheel, and then a chorus of laughter by the whole brigade.

Alas! The Provost Marshall was in advance – a man in authority, and a terror to all evil-doers, waiting here in a narrow turn of the road for the ladies with an advance guard, all loaded. He gave orders to fire at once on the donkeys, killing and wounding two or three, 'pour example.' More weeping and lamentation than one generally hears at an Irish funeral, with sundry prayers for the vagabond that murdered the lives of these poor, darling, innocent 'crathers!'

'Oh, bad luck to his ugly face – the spy of our camp – may he nivver see home till the vultures pick his eyes out, the born varmint.'

They gathered up what they could carry, and marched on along with the troops, crying and lamenting their bitter fate. It was wonderful what they endured; but, in spite of all this warning, Mother Skiddy was foremost on the line of march next morning, as she said,

'We must risk something to be in before the men, to have the fire an' a dhrop of tay ready for the poor crathers after their load an' their labor.'

Faced with a particularly difficult river crossing, Mother Skiddy, the 'Brigadier-General of the Amazons' so-called, addressed the meeting of women:

'I have the weest donkey of you all, an' I'll take the wather if I'm to swim for it, and let me see who's to stop me, Bridget Skiddy, who thravelled from Lisbon here into France. If Dan falls, who's to bury him. God save us! Divil a vulture will ever dig a claw into him while there's life in Biddy, his laful wife. Now, girls, you may go or stay.' And so she began to saddle her ass.

my firelock, while I'm a soger.' 'Dogs then,' sis I, 'you 'ont live long, for the French are comin' up quick upon us.' The poor crather hadn't power to stir a lim'. So I draws him up on the bank and coaxed him to get on me back, for, sis I, 'the French will have ye in half an hour, an' me too, the pagans.' In truth I was just thinkin' they had hould av us both, when I draws him up on me back, knapsack an' all. 'Throw away your gun,' sis I. 'I won't,' says he. 'Biddy, I'll shoot the first vagabone lays hould av your tail,' says he. He was always a conthrary crather when any one invaded his firelock. 'Well, sir, I went away wid him on me back, knapsack, firelock, and all, as strong as Sampson, for the fear I was in. An' fegs, I carried him half a league after the regiment into the bivwack. Me back was bruck entirely from that time to this, an' it'll never gel strait till I go to the Holy Well in Ireland, and have Father McShane's blessin', an' his hand laid over me! The curse av the crows be on his fire-finger that shot the donkeys.'

They shared all of the privations of life on campaign, caring for their husbands, and foraging, cooking, washing and darning for some officers – for which some were reluctant to take any payment, saying: '0, sir sure you always belonged to me own company, an' you're welcome to the bit av washing.' When their husbands died, they married again, within a few days – some having had as many as five husbands. With their children, even bearing children on the road, they marched even in the worst dregs of retreat, suffering grievously, many dying.

'We were all kilt and destroyed on the long march last winter, and the French at our heels, an' all our men droppin' and dyin' on the roadside, waitin' to be killed over agin by them vagabones comin' after us. Well, I don't know if you seed him, sir, but down drops poor Dan, to be murdered like all the rest. Says he, 'Biddy dear, I can't go on furder one yard to save me life.' '0, Dan jewel,' sis I, 'I'll help you on a bit; tak' a hould av me, an' throw away your knapsack.' 'I'll niver part wid my knapsack,' says he, 'nor

Officer's wives travelling with the column shared the vicissitudes of the roads and weather as much as the wives of enlisted men:

Cold and shivery as she was, she laughed. We had nothing to eat that night, as our mules were sent on, and there was this young and delicate creature, in the month of November in the north of Spain, wet as a drowned rat, with nothing to eat, no cover from the falling deluge.

The soldiers, who were generally averse to having horses interfere with their line of march, liked many of the officers wives, and were 'ever delighted to get her to ride with their company'.

THE CONVOY:

Transport was the 'great lever of the Commissariat', for everything required by an army on the march – munitions, hospitals, depôts, canons, bullets, clothing, beef, bisquet, fodder, gunpowder and shoes, supplied from the ends of the earth (England, Morocco, Turkey, and America) – had to be managed in all their details. Then received, conveyed, and distributed hundreds of miles from the storage bases near the sea, across rough country, to the army at the front in the interior. For the most part, however difficult the task, the Commissariat did do its duty and the French envied the length of time for which the British Army could keep concentrated. The French were living on the country and were forced to disperse whenever they had exhausted the resources of the particular region – in a matter of days.

The convoys left the coastal areas every few days and plied their way independently of the marching columns to resupply the army during the campaign and the long season in cantonments. Bullocks, mules and horses provided the power to move these masses of stores; the bullocks being relegated to convoys, movement of the sick and wounded and artillery transport. Modern wheeled traffic could not pass on the roads to the interior, although local bullock carts did so admirably, being expressly made to transverse the local roads and being so simple in construction that they could easily be repaired by peasant drivers.

Primitive Portuguese bullock-carts consisted of wicker sides with little more than rough planks nailed to a massive pole or shaft, riding on two blocks of fixed semi-rounded wood with a hole in the centre, through which an axle was fitted. This was a live axle firmly fixed to the wheels, never greased, which made a loud squeaking and creaking noise. The wheels were solid, massive and had no spokes. They were most skillfully designed for resisting the terrible shocks and jerks they got, as the wagons went over the stones and rocks. The bullocks were harnessed by means of a wooden yoke which was fastened behind their horns and attached to the axle by leather straps, there being a peg in the front of the axle for that purpose. They were shod with a kind of iron shoe, to enable them to drag a load of about a half a ton up hill and down dale along the roughest mountain roads with the greatest of ease. The driver walked alongside carrying a long pole with a spike, using this to goad the bullocks on by striking them over their shoulders.

A bullock travelled about a mile or two an hour, with two bullocks drawing a cart of wounded men, and 16 bullocks (8 pairs) hauled a 24 Pound cannon. Generally slow but sure, bullocks could take it into their heads to run away, carts and all, stopping when they finally ran out of breath, or refusing to follow their brothers into the river for a swim, repeatedly making their way back to the bank until ferried across. The wild or slaughter bullocks, killed for their meat, were generally shut up in pens surrounded with a wall 5 feet high. Although often they 'nevertheless used sometimes to jump this height like stags, and charging into the bivouacs, would send the tents, the huts, the sentry boxes and camp kettles all flying.'

Owing to the horrific conditions of roads in the Peninsula, mules formed the basis of transport operations, requiring over 10,000 for basic commissariat convoy duty, supplying 53,000 men. The mules were adorned with bells and their tails tied up in a bunch with red or other coloured binding, the men would sit on their backs singing boisterously or plaintively, accompanied by a light guitar. Each mule carried 200 pounds of public supply and 30 pounds of his own food for six days. An artillery brigade of perhaps 100 men working 5 nine-pounders and one howitzer required 245 mules for the guns and supplies and 83 mules to carry the corn, bread and spirits for men and beasts for six days – a total of 328 mules. 6 twenty-four pound howitzers required 640 mules. There were 60 mules for every Cavalry regiment for the purpose of supplying bread to the men and corn to the horses and most officers had about two mules to carry their personal baggage, though some had many more.

Mule drivers, locals, were given a dollar a day for each beast along with their rations and were described as the 'very life and sustenance of the Peninsular war'. They were generally years in arrears for their pay so their fraud and carelessness was tolerated, and the fear of losing their debt kept them with the soldiers. The greater part of them carried long knives in their breeches or short carbines, being notorious thieves and murderers, and they tended to drink the liquors entrusted to their conveyance and fill up the vacancy with salt water – a nauseous beverage.

The column usually marched for a half an hour and then halted to give stragglers or those who had fallen out a chance to rejoin. Arms were piled and the men had a chance to eat a bit of bread or cold meat, arrange accoutrements, their knapsack, haversack, canteen so they would 'sit well', and trade jokes until the call for 'Fall-in'. Halts were called either every hour or every

three or four miles and lasted five or ten minutes. The column then marched out again in step, with sloped arms and music playing just as in a perfect field day. When the order 'March at ease' was given, ranks were opened and files loosened; men could carry their arms at the trail (horizontally), cradled or slung over their shoulders, talk, light up their pipes and sing, 'though every man had to remain exactly in his place'.

> The men were generally cheerful and full of mirth for the first few leagues, some passing by as merry as larks, singing and cracking their jokes.

Marching was an art mainly to be acquired by habit and experienced soldiers had a round-shouldered gait to keep the pace, marching in the easiest manner which, according to the Commander-in-Chief, would never pass muster back on the parade grounds of England.

From the long perspective, this army on the march appeared:

> like glittering scarlet threads in the fine mountainous scenery, where long lines of bayonets suddenly jet up from gorge and glen—flash their light upon the eye, and then as suddenly disappear, as if swallowed up by the earth; a countless army, glittering steel as far as the eye could stretch, inexorably moving across golden plains of waving wheat, part of an immense sea undulating with the wind as the waves in the ocean punctuated by incongruous picturesque vignettes such as the English Captain riding on a very fine horse and warding off the sun with a parasol: behind him came his wife very prettily dressed, with a small straw hat, riding on a mule and carrying not only a parasol, but a little black and tan dog on her knee, while she led by a cord a she-goat, to supply her with milk. Beside Madame walked her Irish nurse, carrying in a green silk rapper a baby, the hope of the family. A grenadier, the Captain's servant, came behind and occasionally poked up the long-eared

steed of his mistress with a staff. Last in the procession came a donkey loaded with much miscellaneous baggage, which included a tea-kettle and a cage of canaries; it was guarded by an English servant in livery, mounted on a sturdy cob and carrying a long posting-whip, with which he occasionally made the donkey mend its pace.

In fine weather and under normal conditions, the columns marched three to six leagues a day, which translating 2.63 leagues to the mile was about 8 to 15 miles a day. It might take eight hours or more.

We call four leagues a long march.

When all was summer and sunshine and the swamps had become verdant meadows it seemed a pleasant task to march. The air is impregnated with odours from the soil, clothed with myrtles and aromatic shrubs, such as strawberries, rock-rose, thyme, sage, rosemary, lavender, woodbine, dog-rose and lovely blossoming brambles of all kinds, together with poppies and buttercups – a perfect paradise when the whole heath is in bloom, a sheet of flowers as far as the eye can see.

Some of the officers, as a favourite amusement during the long marches played a bit of a joke that they called 'hunt a Caçadore'.

Portuguese officers as well as our own were always mounted, and when their corps happened to be marching in our front, any officer who stopped behind (which they frequently had occasion to do) invariably, in returning to rejoin his regiment, passed ours at a full gallop; and on those occasions he had no sooner passed our first company than the officers of it were hard at his heels, the others following in succession as he cleared them, so that by the time he had reached the head of the regiment the whole of our officers had been in full chace. We never carried the joke too far, but made it a point of etiquette to stop short of our Commanding Officer (who was not

supposed to see what was going on) and then fell quietly back to our respective places.

I have often seen the hunted devil look round in astonishment, but I do not think he ever saw the wit of the thing, but it was nevertheless amusing to us; and not without its use, for the soldiers enjoyed the joke, which, though trifling, helped to keep up that larking spirit among them, which contributed so much towards the superiority and the glory of our arms.

Marches, though unmolested, could be long, dreary and provoking. With no inns or resthouses the only thing that kept them marching was the knowledge that there was a town to be reached in the distance. The army on the move was inexorable. Any stop was to be avoided at all costs as it would have thrown the whole column into confusion.

Moving such a large column of men and animals up to 15 miles a day required the greatest discipline and calculations. Demonstrating true mathematical principles, pauses were abhorred as disorderly, because a man stopping to drink delayed the one behind him and so on. Given all of the obstacles usually encountered on a day's march, such delays could make a difference of many hours in arrival. Thus, if indulged, the men were that much longer labouring under their load of arms, ammunition and necessaries, besides bringing them to their bivouac in darkness and discomfort. In extreme conditions, the discrepancy might mean life or death, a battle won or lost.

To expedite movement, General and Divisional Standing Orders prescribed regulations to govern movements on the march to be enforced by the Generals of Division.

EXCERPTS FROM THE ORDERS TO MARCH

Preparations for the March
The first horn sounds one hour and a half before the time of marching, during which the squads dress, accoutre and pack the baggage, both regimental and private, loading it on the horses and mules.

The second horn, or rouse, sounds one hour after the first, upon which the companies turn out on their respective parades.

The third horn, or assembly, sounds a quarter of an hour after the second, upon which companies are marched to the regimental parades, baggage is sent back.

The fourth horn, or advance, sounds a quarter of an hour after the third, where the battalions march off to the place of assembly of the brigade.

Of the March

Marching out, the battalions are to march off by word of command with music (unless particularly ordered to the contrary.)

The men must be perfectly silent, dress, slope their arms and keep the step, just the same as when manoeuvring on a field day, until the word March at Ease is given.

When marching at ease, the ranks may be opened and the files loosened; but each rank, section, or division, must be kept perfectly distinct and every man must remain exactly in his place.

When the brigade is marching independently of any other, the officer commanding the leading regiment will sound the Halt half an hour after it marches off, and afterwards once an hour; each halt to last at least five minutes after arms are piled.

Defiling to be prevented, or executed by word of command

No battalion, company, or section is at any time to defile, or diminish its front, or attempt in any way to avoid any bad spot in the road, unless the preceding battalion has done so.

Any man who, for the sake of avoiding water or other bad places, or for any other reason presumes to step on one side, or quit his proper place in the ranks, must be confined.

Whenever a stream, ditch, bank, or other obstacle, is to be crossed, it will be generally found, that instead of defiling or diminishing the front, the very contrary should be done, not only by causing the files of each section to extend gradually before they arrived at the ditch, or even by forming sub-divisions or companies.

It is proved that the defiling of one battalion on the march, even if done with as much promptitude as is practicable on such occasions, will cause a delay of 10 minutes; one such obstacle, if not passed without defiling, would therefore delay the brigade half an hour and in the winter, when obstacles of this kind are frequent and the days short, a brigade which is constantly defiling without cause will arrive at its quarters in the dark, whereas, if it had performed the march regularly, it would have got in by good time.

This order respecting defiling, is therefore as much calculated to provide for the personal ease and comfort of the men, as it is essential for the due performance of the movements of an army.

Stragglers

No man is to remain behind, or quit the ranks for any purpose, or on any account whatever, without permission from the Captain, or Officer commanding the company.

Officers are never to give permission to any man to quit the ranks, excepting on account of illness, or for the purpose of easing themselves; or for some other absolutely necessary purpose.

The Officers must be particularly attentive to prevent the men from going out of the ranks for water: when this is required, the battalion or brigade will be halted.

Every man who is obliged to quit the ranks on account of illness, must apply for a ticket or certificate.

Men who obtain permission to fall out for a short time to ease themselves, or for any other cause than illness, are not to receive tickets; but they must invariable leave their pack and arms, to be carried by the section they belong to, until they return.

Every man who quits the ranks without leave, without having received a ticket, or having left his arms and pack with his company, as the case may be, must be brought to a Court Martial, and if not ill, must be done Drum-head, as soon as the regiment arrives, or as the man comes up, and the punishment inflicted forthwith.

Hurry and Stepping out to be prevented

It is of the greatest importance that the men should not on any account be hurried on the march: they are to be instructed that they are never to step out beyond the regular step, still less to run, unless by word of command.

When obstacles which delay the march are frequent, it may be desirable or necessary, in order to avoid loss of time, that each company should march on at the usual rate, without shortening its step: the intervals between companies may be occasionally increased with advantage and without disorder, but unless each company in itself be kept compact, disorder and disorganisation will ensue.

Keeping up this discipline – the relentless pace – was seldom steady or obliging so that the path of the column drove men to march on through whatever obstacles they came upon. Brushwood and briars, rocks or sand, streams or rivers, mud, heat, rain, or snow so that their trousers were literally torn off in shreds and feet bruised upon the roots of the trees. Fatigue and conditions could be dreadful, but the column kept moving despite what was in their path.

The Light Division enforced these orders with implacable sternness.

Into the stream went the light brigade, and Craufurd, as busy as a shepherd with his flock, riding in and out of the water to keep his wearied band from being drowned as they crossed over. Presently he

spied an officer who, to save himself from being wet through, I suppose, and wearing a damp pair of breeches for the remainder of the day, had mounted on the back of one of his men. The sight of such a piece of effeminacy was enough to raise the choler of the General, and in a very short time he was plunging and splashing through the water after them both.

'Put him down, sir! put him down! I desire you to put that officer down instantly!' And the soldier in an instant, I dare say nothing loth, dropping his burden like a hot potato into the stream, continued his progress through. 'Return back, sir,' said Craufurd to the officer, 'and go through the water like the others. I will not allow my officers to ride upon the men's backs through the rivers: all must take their share alike here.'

Any man stepping across a puddle was told to 'Sit down in it, sir! Sit down it!' 'Neither mire nor water' were to 'disturb the order of march with impunity.'

No battalion, company, or section is at any time to defile or diminish its front, or attempt in any way to avoid any bad spot in the road, unless the preceding battalion has done so.

No man was to remain behind or quit the ranks without permission, and it was of the greatest importance that the men should not on any account be hurried on the march; never to step out beyond the regular step, still less to run. Deviators were punished (flogged) almost on the spot, and the Light Division soon held it as their honor to march straight on no matter what obstacles they encountered or how much they suffered. Such control was thought to maintain discipline and concentration – prerequisites of war. Some ease and larking was permitted but only so long as everything went on with a steady, unhalting, unhurrying swing.

Obstacles were inevitable. There were 'shocking roads', 'boisterous weather', a shortage of rations and supply, missing baggage and a destitute ravaged countryside. All of Portugal was a frontier scantily populated and incapable of sustaining a large army even in good times. It had some good roads, as the Artillery Corps keenly noted. However, the war did not always take its direction based on the presence of paved roads and planning a route was made even more difficult; the maps of the Peninsula were so outrageously inaccurate that even the best was considered bad. Cities and towns would have paved roads radiating out from them, but they were only as long or firm as the reflection of their civic importance might make them. The smaller the city or village, the shorter the road, and the worse the state of repair which made travelling from one place to another difficult.

A road paved with large stones might be broad and good, although many roads in the countryside were mere tracks or goat paths – made up of large and small loose stones, often narrow and passing through mountains. Roads made of large round stones or pointed rocks with stones, sticking up in every direction, were impassable to the mules who could scarcely walk on them, or so diabolical that carts overset and wheels were broken up. Others were no more than imprints across plains quickly ploughed up by wheels, cavalry, and baggage animals. In some places, it took 200 men with drag ropes to haul one 9 Pounder cannon across a ridge, as the horses could not stand. 'I had to drag myself forward by the roots of trees: at other times I crept on hands and knees.' Paths through hills and mountains passed over sheets of rock, and were often perpendicular so that carts carrying ammunition or supplies, proved too much for the beasts who could not hold them. With the result that the whole equipage would run backwards and with much scraping, scratching, rumbling, and bellowing, plunge headlong into the abyss.

Soldiers in work parties, as with the Roman legions of old who had passed these same paths, were constantly employed in mending, widening and levelling the roads and opening new roads where the old were bad. Often having no foundation of either stone or wood, many roads were built on sand, sandy soil, deep clay, or a deep rich loam. Men sank ankle-deep in the sand strewn with stones and cut by deep ruts in the shifting soil.

> Getting a quantity of sand in one's shoes also made me a complete cripple. I was so lame that I could not keep up with the regiment. I walked with the greatest pain and trouble to myself, having frequently to take off my shoes and walk barefoot.

The enemy cut trenches across the roads, both deep and wide, to impede the march and render the road impracticable. These were generally 8 ft wide and 6 ft deep, and one Company Commander setting the example, cried out as he made the plunge, 'Come men, dash,' no sooner said than in he floundered and was completely covered with red mud.' (He was ever after known as 'Dash').

The route of march could go through dreary regions of solid rock, bearing an abundant crop of loose stones without a particle of soil or vegetation visible to the naked eye in any direction, everyone as lively as stones. But five minutes later the view could be one of the richest, loveliest, and romantic spots to beheld, and in a moment:

> we were all fruits and flowers and many a pair of legs that one would have thought had not a kick left in them were, in five minutes after, seen dancing across the bridge, to the tune of 'the downfall of Paris,' which struck up from the bands of the different regiments.

All soldiers were pedestrians alternately experiencing grandeur and gloom – all joy and elasticity – and the next one of misery!

Stopping to halt in great plains of long dry grass, by some accident the whole might catch fire and a breeze springing up:

> the fire ran along with the rapidity of gunpowder, while clouds of insects, flying to escape, through quick on the wing, perished. The men were in as great haste to protect their ammunition, several pouches of which were blown up.

Most disconcerting, it was not an unknown thing marching on a road to cross an old battlefield, meeting with skeletons bleaching in the wind, or molding there, terrible to contemplate.

When the heavy pre-winter rains began, roads ceased to be roads instead becoming ponds, seas, even oceans of mud and mire, a vast ankle, if not knee-deep quagmire, passing through the comfortless and slobbery gorges. Dips in the ground became dangerous precipices. The cavalry was unable to advance on the slippery, sodden, and slimy soil.

> Village streets, or rather roads, in Portugal are at all times bad. The centre of the road from house to house down the long straggling village was like a brook of mud with deep holes, some deep enough to swallow up a mule. The footpaths were of rough stones some three or four feet high; consequently, to move from place to place was not without danger, and required the precaution used by the inhabitants, who carried a stick about seven feet long with an iron spike at the end.

The tenacious mud tore the shoes from off the soldier's feet. We were now walking nearly knee-deep in a stiff mud into which no man could thrust his foot with the certainty of having a shoe at the end of it when he pulled it out again. More of the Regiment were not complete with shoes. As for my own part I had lost the right foot shoe early in the day and had to plod through thick and thin in that state, and parade in the evening.

On the 16th we moved off, it being a fine morning, and soon had to encounter the worst road I ever saw: the whole of our baggage and part of the army, having passed along, had made it like a bog-mire. I have known some of our men sink into the mud and stick as fast as possible: others have gone to their assistance and all have stuck fast together! This was frequently the case: hundreds of the men lost their shoes, and were obliged to walk bare-foot. I had a strap buckled tight over each instep and under each shoe, so that I did not lose mine; but I frequently stuck fast in the mud.

The muddy roads were often strewn with carcases of every description, horses, mules, donkeys and bullocks with abandoned baggage-carts stuck in the deep slough. In fact, some roads were such seas of mud that it was not uncommon to find a mule suddenly disappear in the mire, with naught but a bubble to indicate its grave.

The mud was but a consequence of the rain, which coming in torrents, killed men in its own right.

Our next great annoyance, and I may add suffering, was caused by the inclemency of the weather. On the day upon which we marched into Guarda the 5th Regiment lost five men and the 28th Regiment two men, who actually perished on the road in consequence of heavy rain which incessantly fell during the whole day. A person who has never been out of England can scarcely imagine its violence. Let him fancy himself placed under a shower-bath with the perforations unusually large, the water not propelled divergingly with a light sprinkling, but large globular drops pouring down vertically and descending in such rapid succession as to give the appearance rather of a torrent than a shower; he may then form an idea of the rainy season which drenches Portugal during the autumnal months. Exposed to such rain, we marched many miles to gain the top of the hill.

Dry rivulets became impassable raging waterways. Simple furrows turned into 'purling streams' pouring

down from the hills, with a force destroying bridges, flooding roads, and converting brooks and streams into raging torrents. So extreme was the storm that a young commissary was drowned in attempting to cross a narrow bridge. 'His horse slipped and fell into the river and he was immediately carried down by the violence of the torrent and seen no more. No trace could ever be discovered of his body'. But then again one wit noted that with such rains, it was the only time that some of the corps were ever washed clean!

Men waded for miles in slush and water, the weather so wet that the very shoes were soaked off their feet, which making them extremely tender. Also, not being able to see where to place them, made them hit the stumps of small trees, which gave great pain. The marches were impossible to describe, 'sogers' (soldiers) were wading to the knee in mud and water, most of them barefooted – their shoes having no soles. Those who still had boots dared not take them off knowing that they might not be able to get them on again, The incessant rain made the mountains so slippery that many horses came down and almost prevented the infantry from moving at all. Men and officers went for days, even weeks with no dry clothes, waterproof clothes being 'fudge', the water running 'down my trowsers, into my shoes, and out of them, as though they had been springs or fountains, and in a short time I was almost drowned'.

Coming to rivers engorged by the rain, if there was no bridge the men walked in and over, as if on parade; when pretty deep, they linked together to break the stream, slinging their ammunition on the back of their necks to keep it dry. Cavalry would form in the river above the men to break the force of the stream or provided a hand hold:

I had I know not how many of the poor men hanging about me and my horse. Some were holding by the stirrup, some by the tail, and others by the mane, or wherever they could lay hold, for the stream was so rapid as to nearly sweep them off their legs. Indeed I understand several of those who followed us were actually swept down, and perished.

The heavy rain sometimes saw the heavens 'in a blaze with lightning', hail or heavy thunder:

a soldier of the guards was killed, and four injured by the electrical fluid. Another was struck dead in a second of time by the lightning – his horse was also killed, the hair on his head was scorched, his watch-chain cut in two, and the little steel screws inside were extracted. The glittering arms of so many men, no doubt, was a great conductor for the lightning.

When the temperature dropped, accompanied by a bitter wind, snow and hard frost, a ford across the river resulted in every man who made it across carrying a pair of 'iced breeches'. Roads were too steep and slippery to ride, and it was too cold to sit in the saddle. There was no water to drink: everything was frozen hard.

> The weather was dreadful; we had always either snow or hail, the hail often as large as nuts. We were forced to put our knapsacks on our heads to protect us from its violence. The mules, at these times, used to run crying up and down, hurt by the stones. The frost was most severe, accompanied by high winds. Many of us were frost-bitten and others were found dead at their posts. The 92nd regiment got grey trousers served out to them. They could not live with their kilts; the cold would have killed them.

It was preferable to march through the night than submit to a freezing halt in the deep snow. When the comet appeared in 1811, there were those who wished:

> He would wag his fiery tail a little nearer to may face, for it was so stiff with hoar-frost that I dared neither to laugh nor cry for fear of breaking it.

The Peninsula could be as cold as England and in summer as hot as India. Where there was too much water during the rainy season, there was none to be had in the seasons of 'fire'. Where roads turned to mud in the rain, they became choking dust in the broiling sun, where recorded temperatures could reach 97°, 98° and even 100°. Clay, in fine weather, was firm and passable, but it could also become choking dust.

> The suffering of the men in these dust clouds was dreadful, from the heat, thirst, heavy roads, tight clothing, cross belts, and choking leather stocks. When we came to cross a stream, no halt was allowed; therefore hands or caps were dipped in the water as we went over it.

One morning it was so hot that a hen sitting atop an officer's baggage fell over dead, killed by the heat. The weather so dreadfully hot, scarcely to be borne, proved again the old Spanish proverb that 'whoever lives out September may expect to live another year'.

The British soldiers marched in the heat wearing their usual thick cloth uniforms with leather stocks round their throats and heavy shakos on their heads.

Three times my sight grew dim; my mouth was dry as dust, my lips one continued blister. I had water in my canteen but it tasted bitter as soot, and it was so warm it made me sick. At this time, I first tried a thing which gave me a little relief; I put a small pebble into my mouth, and sucked it.

Almost roasted by the sun's scorching rays, the army would sleep during the day, sometimes awaking to find their lips glued together. Every soldier stuck an olive leaf or a piece of paper on his under lip to prevent it from bursting; their faces were so burnt they could not bear to touch them.

It is a terrible thing to be tanned by the sun. I have been half grilled for the last month, which has cost my nose and lips a great deal of flesh. My nose suffers like a martyr. It has completely spoiled all complections, and made us like hideous creatures.

Marching in the scorching sun caused them to be thirsty. If there was fruit to be had or cold water to drink, men gorged themselves, falling back sick with fever and fluxes. When the rivulets and streams dried up, they could be seen running to any stagnate pond like ducks.

Hunger is bad, and not easily borne, but is nothing in comparison to thirst.

To avoid the burning clime, the soldiers marched out at 2 o'clock in the morning and stopped, on good days, about 10, the column needing to rest during the heat of the day. Moving at night was a mixed blessing, the 'pitchy darkness' could be indescribable and the bad dusty road a nightmare. Although kept on legs during the whole of the night, when daylight broke, the tail of the column had not got a quarter of a mile from their starting post. Staggering among the rocks and stones, men fell into deep holes or stumbled over the roots and boughs of trees, unavoidably tripping up others in their fall. If there were pines, torches were made from the branches, or those with wax candles lighted them so they could march by their light.

Marching in the moonlight, close to the enemy, the men reversed their brass plated shakos, trailed or turned and slung their arms to prevent the enemy seeing their line of march and calculating the numbers, as the barrels were bright in those days and might be seen glistening a long way off by moonlight. Men also unshielded the swords from their scabbards, so as to suppress any rattling.

We marched in close formation and in strict silence, but still a large body moving over the flat face of mother earth might be detected, and the clink of cavalry sabres, the roll of the wheel-of guns, the tramp of horses, and the heavy sounding tread of 13,000 warriors might be wafted through the still night air to a distance, and attract the attentive ears set on watch to warn the approach of coming danger. A dog's bark, a bird's flight, or a hare's course, would create suspicion that some disturbing influence was on foot, and would put on the alert those well versed in outpost duty and war's alarms, thereby betraying the movements of our column. On and on we went, in wearisome darkness and in seemingly interminable space; half-asleep and stumbling, our men blundered against each other, then again resumed their order, giving vent to some grumbling exclamation of discontent.

In one campaign, from January to the end of November, a trooper reckoned the number of miles his regiment had marched was 2,328. Portugal had been walked over from north to south and back again, three times, with much marching and counter-marching across Spain. Over the entire campaign in the Peninsula, only about 500 miles by 600 miles, the army probably marched more than 10,000 miles.

Although four leagues (about 10 miles a day), was 'about right' the reality was often 15, 18 or 20 miles a day, day after day, sunrise to sunset, for weeks at a time. Sometimes in dire circumstances, men went 30 miles or more. In spite of the condition of the weather, the men carried their musket of 13 pounds weight, a knapsack with their whole wardrobe on their back and belly ammunition with 60 rounds of ball cartridges, all weighing 60 to 80 pounds – a moderate load for a good-sized donkey!

So awkwardly was the load born that the men were permanently bent due to the load on their back. Marching 15 or 20 miles a day in broiling heat without water, in torrents of rain sloshing through ankle deep mud, or frost bitten in bitter cold and drifts of snow, men who dropped were so weighted down they could not get up again without a companion assisting. The knapsack, on the roads of the Peninsula became the 'infernal load', a soldier's 'bitterest enemy'.

I felt it press me to the earth almost at times, and more than once felt as if I should die under its deadly embrace.

The kit of a heavy infantry regiment included the following:

1 Musket and Bayonet	14 lbs.
1 Pouch and sixty rounds of ball, etc.	6 lbs
1 Canteen and Belt	1 lbs
1 Mess Tin	1 lbs
1 Knapsack Frame and Belts	3 lbs
1 Blanket	4 lbs
1 Great Coat	4 lbs
1 Dress Coat	3 lbs
1 White Jacket	½ lb
2 Shires and 3 Breasts	2½ lbs
2 Pairs Shoes	3 lbs
1 Pair Trowsers	2 lbs
1 Pair Gaiters	¼ lb
2 Pairs Stockings	1 lb
4 Brushes, Button Stick, Comb	3 lbs
2 Cross Belts	1 lbs
Pen, Ink, and Paper	¼ lb
Pipe Clay, Chalk, etc.	1 lb
2 Tent Pegs	½ lb
Weight of kit without provisions	53 lbs.
Extra weight for marching—	
Three days' bread	3 lbs
Two days' beef	2 lbs
Water in our canteens	3 lbs
	61 lbs

Besides this weight, the orderly serjeant of each company had to carry the orderly book, whose weight was perhaps two pounds; and in turn the regimental colours.

Being so overloaded and suffering from the fatigue and heat '400 of the battalion died a few months after our arrival, without a single shot being fired'. Although after five years, 'I don't think there was a man in the regiment who could show a single shirt, or a pair of shoes, in his knapsack.'

Officers depended entirely on their servants and baggage animals to carry their food and supplies. Although at the beginning of the war, General William Stewart and General Sir John Moore required that officers carry their necessaries with them in a knapsack, weighing about 27 pounds, adding to their comfort, and relieving some 40 effective men to each battalion. Though conducive to the general good, ancient prejudices prevailed and the idea failed overall.

The movements of the British Army in the Peninsula depended entirely upon its convoys of supplies from sea-supplied bases. Unless the Commissariat was good, the army must either retire or be starved, as the country – every year devastated more gravely and completely by the enemy – could give little or nothing. Although the

men marched 15 to 20 miles a day, encumbered by heavy knapsacks; mules only made about eight or nine miles a day and oxen much less, so that frequently the column out-marched its Commissariat and its baggage. Everyone was thus under the necessity of going without what they could not carry – bread, meat, supplies and necessaries – till they could come up. In rapid advance and bitter retreat, the army could go without rations or supplies for days and weeks at a time. The fatigues of the troops and the want of supplies induced the Commander-in-Chief to halt the army on a number of occasions till the supplies could come up. There was a general order against plundering food or goods from the peasantry or the commissary, which was to be punished cruelly with flogging. However, if available and if any money could be had, food could be bought. Pay was almost always vastly in arrears and some men were in the habit of tearing off the buttons from their coats, and after hammering them flat and passing them as English coins in exchange for food and wine. Others found food where they could, officers and troopers included:

There was a mill on the riverside, near the bridge, wherein a number of our men were helping themselves to flour, during the time the others were fording. Our Colonel rode down and forced them out, throwing a handful of flour on each man as he passed out of the mill. When we were drawn up on the heights, he rode along the column, looking for the millers, as we called them. At this moment a hen put her head out of his coat-pocket, and looked first to one side, and then to another. We began to laugh; we could not restrain ourselves. He looked amazed and furious at us, then around. At length the Major rode up to him, and requested him to kill the fowl outright, and put it into his pocket. The Colonel, in his turn, laughed, called his servant, and the millers were no more looked after.

Looking in their haversacks, what the men often found, if anything was generally bad, and thus hunger was added to the privations, fatigue and sufferings of both officers and men on the march.

All of our advances were marked with hunger. Rations grew scarcer, until not a mouthful was to be had for man or beast.

Is it then no privation to be without food – absolutely for 24 to 36 hours? for 24 hours neither bread nor meat was issued when due. Is it no hardship to march 14 hours without food, on the worst of roads in bad weather?

About midnight we received our rum, which revived up; but it made some of our men so exceedingly intoxicated that they could not stand in the ranks. There was no wonder at this, for we had been long without food, at least 48 hours.

The army advanced so fast, that our supplies could not keep up with us, and we began to suffer much. I verily believe I did not receive more than three pounds of bread or biscuit for 12 days. Such now was the rapidity of our movements, that we made no halts. At this period our condition from want of provisions was miserable in the extreme: there were none to be bought for money. I have known hundreds of our men eat bean-tops, or any green herb that could be eaten. When the bullocks were killed, it was a common practice with us to catch the blood, which we boiled until quite sad, and this served as a substitute for bread.

We were very destitute for food, and had been for the last 12 or 14 days; so that we were ready to lay hold of anything that fell in our way, whether living or dead, if eatable; indeed at this time it resembled a famine.

I could not help reflecting on the misery and horrors of war: it was hunger, and that alone, that drove many of us frequently to take what was not our own. Hunger is a sharp thorn, and few would have acted otherwise.

Twas curious to see the men when a halt would happen near where the French cavalry had perhaps been feeding their horses. They went down on their hands and knees, contending for the last grain of Indian corn, like so many hens around a barn door. I saw an officer offer a guinea for a biscuit, and was refused.

It is said that hunger will break through stone walls. Yes, and it will break through stronger than stone walls. For I believe it will break through all the ties of nature.

The British Army moved fast and the privations brought by weather, roads and hunger were exacerbated by the loss of supplies of clothing. The Commander-in-Chief, the Duke of Wellington, cared little about the official dress regulations:

> provided we brought our men into the field well appointed, with their 60 rounds of ammunition each, he never looked to see whether trousers were black, blue or grey; and as to ourselves, we might be rigged out in any colour of the rainbow if we fancied it. The consequence was that no two officers were dressed alike.

This occasioned much surprise and horror to the martinets who arrive from London. However, the rigour of campaigning exacerbated this condition, especially among the ranks, who had been wearing the same uniforms for almost two years, most of the time on actual service and often for five months or more out of doors. Men in the field cried that their clothes were never off their backs, or the shoes off their feet any night during that winter. Never thoroughly dry and going without bathing for days and weeks at a time, the column kept just pressing on. Among many a regiment there was not a rag of a uniform, the men resembling 'an army of sweeps' as each man's coat was so colourful (having being patched with different coloured cloths) it was difficult to tell to what regiment he belonged.

> My poor old tattered trousers and coat were no way improved by these excursions (into the brambles) and in many cases it would have taken no mean judge to determine the original colour; perhaps a piece of stocking covered a few holes on one sleeve while a piece of biscuit bag covered the other. No matter what the colour was, if we were lucky enough to find a piece it found a place very soon on either coat or trousers. The last mentioned indispensables underwent many twinings.

It was difficult to say what they were; some had trousers made of blankets, some wore various pieces of enemy uniforms taken from fallen soldiers and most of them were barefoot.

Shoes and boots were seriously damaged and destroyed on the marches over rocks and through mud, the men having literally marched their shoes off.

> Therefore those plagued and suffering from sore feet, were under the painful necessity (unless totally unable to proceed) of going on until they got well again. I have often seen the blood soaking through the gaiters, and over the heels of the soldiers' hard shoes, whitened with the dust.

Men's feet became so swollen they cut the boots to pieces to get out of them. With no resupply, they went

barefoot or improvised, some wearing the light hempen sandals worn in the mountains, or adopting the system of the Spanish muleteers, whereby they resorted to the raw hides of the fresh-killed bullocks. They placed their foot on the warm hide, cut out a sufficiency to cover this most valuable part of a soldier's person and making a sandal of it marched on with ease. Soon becoming very reluctant to surrender this well-fitting and pliant sandal for the hard and cumbrous leather of captured French or British boots or shoes.

In the distance we descried a cloud of dust rolling towards us, the bright sparkling rays of the sunbeams playing on the soldiers' breastplates, when suddenly the leading regiment of the Light Division burst forth, their bronzed countenances and light knapsacks, and their order of march all united to inspire a conviction that their early discipline had not only been maintained amidst privations, battles and camps, but had become matured by experience. Seven Battalions of Light Infantry and Riflemen defiled before us with their threadbare jackets, their brawny necks loosened from their stocks, their wide and patched trowsers of various colours, and brown-barrelled arms slung over their shoulders or carelessly held in their hands, whilst a joyous buzz ran through the cross-belted ranks as their soldier-like faces glanced towards us to greet many of their old comrades now about to join in their arduous toils after a long separation.

When conditions were bad, great numbers of men were unable to keep up, remaining on the road or in the wet fields. The sick, unable to march were given a 'ticket' permitting them to fall out, but the man had to leave his firelock with the comrades in his section, being now a general burden on them as they had enough to carry their own equipment, let alone add more. Other men felt it shame to complain and some men even dropped down dead, struck by the sun or the frost, overwhelmed by fatigue or hunger.

I, one morning, counted thirteen men dead round one fire, I should say starved to death.

On the first day's march I had the curiosity to number the victims of hunger and hardship that lay unburied along the road – men, horses, bullocks, etc – and they numbered 84; we being obliged in many cases to pass to leeward of the revolting remains of mortality.

Animals on the march took to quarrelling, rearing, and fighting so desperately they suffered injuries, went lame or died. Others, withal rather stubborn, would not, or could not obey the pull of the rein.

The animals were not passive participants. Some horses were great companions, eating acorns and lying down by the fire with their master 'like a Christian'.

FATIMA

The charger I rode during most of the Peninsular War was bought by my father (who was a great judge of horses) at the sale of the King's stud, at three years old, and her name was Fatima. She was of the purest Arabian blood, and perfect symmetry, fifteen hands high, dark brown, a perfect picture, most graceful in all her movements, but very conceited. As she walked along she looked to the right and to the left, as if to see who was admiring her. She was the admiration of the whole army. She was so sagacious that marvellous stories were told of her. She always wore a silken net to protect her from the flies that maddened her when she hadn't it on. She was wounded several times. At Salamanca a shell shattered her stifle or thigh, and I was nearly advised to shoot her as incurable, but the stud groom effected a perfect cure after a long time, only leaving an immense scar and dent. She was twice wounded by sabre-cuts on the head. The last time she actually reared and pawed my antagonists, as if to defend me. She had her head cut open in a dreadful way. She was, though of excellent temper, difficult to ride, from her fiery disposition. In bivouac, when lying down beside me, she would lift up her head to see if I was sleeping, and if she saw I was she would immediately lie down again, for fear of disturbing me. She was particularly fond of raw beef-steaks, and it was difficult to keep the men's rations from her, even if suspended on trees as they usually were, by way of safety.

Simply providing farriers to shoe the horses and mules was a great problem and 'to this I attribute a considerable loss in animals during this service'.

O worra-worra, march the morrow, and not a shoe on me wee donkey. The curse o' the crows be on the French; may they nivver see home.

Horses and mules were so weak some could not carry a load:

The army was terribly off for forage, our mules have had very long marches and more than once nothing to be got when they come in till the next morning. They are all miserable thin and I have had the pleasure of seeing my animals literally starving. Horses became mangy after a few days as there was no kind of forage for them, except what they could pick up in the now completely exhausted fields around us. We had nothing else to give them. The horses often ate the withered grass with so much avidity that they swallowed many of the stones at the roots, and died in consequence.

Nearly half of all of the animals in the Pyrenees died on the march.

APPROACHING THE FIELD:

We had been reinforced by a fresh batch of recruits from England, a number of whom had been drafted into our company. These fellows' rosy cheeks and plump appearance formed a bright relief, and an amusing contrast, to our fierce brown visages, covered with whiskers and mustachios. Their dresses were new, whereas our clothing was patched, and of all colours. They were about to go through the ordeal of fire for the first time, and as it

was such a momentous occasion, Major O'Hare thought proper to give them a few words of advice.

'Recruits to the front!' he commanded.

Some 10 or 12 immediately stepped forward, wondering, no doubt, what they were wanted for.

'Do you see those men on that plain?' said the Major, pointing to the French camp.

'Yes, sir!' several of the men answered.

'Well then,' said Major O'Hare, with a dry laugh, 'those are the French, and our enemies. You must kill them, and not allow them to kill you. You must learn to do as these old birds do,' – here he pointed to us – 'and get cover where you can. And remember: if you don't kill those fellows, they'll kill you.'

'Yes, sir!'

The Major's logic elicited roars of laughter from the old soldiers, but it had a powerful effect on the recruits.

THE STORM OF WAR

THE BATTLEFIELD

Our brigade was marched up a hill, where we had a beautiful view of the armies, threatening each other, like two thunder clouds charged with death.

The enemy lay in dense dark columns

as far as the eye could stretch, the glittering of steel, and clouds of dust raised by cavalry and artillery, proclaimed the march of a countless army; while below their picquets were already posted: thousands of them were already halted in their bivouacks and column too after column, arriving in quick succession, reposed upon the ground allotted to them, and swelled the black and enormous masses. The numbers of the enemy were, at the lowest calculation, seventy-five thousand. The whole country behind them seemed covered with their train, their ambulance and their commissariat. These were the men who, for years, had kept the coast of England in alarm; who had conquered Italy, overrun Austria, shouted victory on the plains of Austerlitz and humbled, in one day, the power, the pride and the martial renown of Prussia on the field of Jena.'

Impressed, perhaps. But the fireside chat of the British soldiers overlooking this vast French army belies any tinge of fear:

The conversation among the men is interspersed with the most horrid oaths declaring what they will do with the fellow they lay hands on. What they intend to get in plunder, hoping they will stand a chance that they may split two at once. Then someone more expert at low wit than his companions draws a ludicrous picture of a Frenchman with a bayonet stuck in him or something of the kind, which raises a loud and general laugh. Others describe what they have achieved in this way. In short, it is more like a fair time than the beginning of a bloody action.

Many jokes are passed on going into battle. There was great hilarity, buoyant spirit, and cheerfulness, a determined resolve to fight to the front, and never say die.

Our men began to fix their flints and examine their powder as we approached.

The weather was fine, everyone jolly, and the Patlanders in particular cracking their jokes.

'*How the d— are we to get over that big sthrame av a river to leather them vagabones out o'that?*' says Paddy Muldoon, for he wasn't kilt yet.

'*0, niver mind,*' says another old cripple, who lost an eye on the Nive, '*that countryman av yours wid the long nose will show you the way when he's riddy.*' '*0, be gar, then, we'll not wait very long, for I seen im over here this morn wid our Farmer Hill, spying them wid his long eye-glass, an' he won't keep us waiting. But there's oceans on 'em down there, so mind that other eye av yours!*'

They were ever laughing and cracking their Irish jokes at the worst of times.

Every officer is more alert than usual and bets fly on the matter of time it will take.

The battle array of a large army is a most noble and imposing sight. To see the hostile lines and columns formed, and prepared for action; to observe their generals and mounted officers riding smartly from point to point, and to mark every now and then, one of their guns opening on your own staff, reconnoitering them, is a scene very animating, and a fine prelude to a general engagement. On your own side, too, the hammering of flints and loosening of cartridges; the rattle of guns and tumbrils, as they come careering up to take their appointed stations; and the swift galloping of aid-de-camps in every

direction, here bringing reports to their generals, there conveying orders to the attacking columns, all speak of peril and death, but also of anticipated victory; and so cheeringly, that a sensation of proud hope swells the bosom, which is equal, if not superior, to the feeling of exultation in the secure moment of pursuit and triumph.

Men show no more concern than on a common field day, they rarely gave a thought to danger, and death was too familiar to be looked on with terror. 'We never thought that the time was short and the soul precious, where the man spared in the battle of today was killed on the morrow.' Fighting was their daily bread – it gave them an appetite.

Will making in the face of the enemy was reckoned a most daring of all daring deeds, for the doer was always considered a doomed man, and so strong the prejudice that many a goodly estate went into forbidden hands. However, there were many presentiments of

death before going into battle, and as many instances of falsification as verification.

The British soldier, English and Irish, had a prepossession that they were superior to every other nation, an invincible confidence, fearing 'neither man nor devil.'

I have said take the world in general, but British soldiers are different from others in their vices and their virtues, their excellencies and their defects. I do not think I am over-partial to my countrymen who have but too many military faults, but I will give them the credit of valour. With a Briton self is everything. He is more afraid of disgracing himself in his own eyes than in those of the world. Everyone else, what ever his merits, is usually an object of contempt, hence he has what few others have, a motive of intrepidity constantly operating. A Briton is very subject to ennui and the spur given to his system by a feeling of danger is, to him, an actual pleasure. If there is a man in the world who likes fighting for fighting's sake, it is a British soldier.

A great stir was observed in the masses of the French solid columns, like black thunder clouds, indicative of a coming storm.

The dawn saw more than 100,000 men standing ready to slay one another. Just as the sun shot his first beams over the mountains on our left, bang went the first gun from the enemy, and bang was the answer from our battery on the hill. Battery after battery now opened, that on our right joining in the fray, and firing over our heads. By and by the cannonading nearly ceased, but it was only a prelude to more serious work. The enemy were massing for attack. The death cloud was gathering blackness, and soon burst with fury.

All this looked very serious, and I began to have a queer feeling of mortal danger stirring my nerves.

The army of the enemy was mustering, thick, ominous and threatening. Several horsemen were seen galloping up the bank and darting out of sight on the other side, where, from the quick firing of artillery, there appeared to be some smart work going on. Now the ground was covered thickly with armed men.

The whole body of the British troops, from one end of the position to the other, started on their feet, snatched up their arms, formed in line with as much regularity and apparent coolness as if they had been exercising on the parade in Hyde Park – as if touched by a magic-wand, full of life and vigour. Now there could be heard a loud hum, and occasionally a jolly shout and many a peal of laughter, with the peculiar sharp 'click-click-click of fixing

bayonets. Their kits, or stock of clothes placed on their shoulders, the army stood perfectly ready to meet the enemy, whose troops, in three immense close columns, by this time were pelting rapidly down the side of the opposite heights. They kept themselves steadily together, looked as dark as the blackest thunder-cloud, and their appearance, on the whole, was the most imposing and formidable thing I recollect to have seen, either before or since.

'Jacques' could see their flags flying. The drums beat to arms and the bugles sounded the assembly, men uncasing their colours, priming the load, columns moving forward, regiments forming up in their long, thin, red lines two deep glittering with bright arms. The stern features of the men were visible as they stood with their eyes fixed unalterably upon the enemy along a front that was miles long. As if at Shorncliffe, swarms of Riflemen were sent out in every direction to act as the shield of the army – ready to demoralise the enemy with

rapid fire at close range. In some cases, time might be taken up with manoeuvring, taking up positions and leaving them for others.

The crash of thunder of one hundred and sixty to two hundred guns stunned the ears and shook the earth, being so terrible it 'beggars description.' Amidst the fire and smoke, the dark figures of the French artillery were seen bounding about and serving their guns with frantic energy – the salute marked by 'the curling smoke rising in clouds from their brazen mouth, echoing and resounding again and again from their crested height over plain and wood and far intervening space.'

Shells rained in and at times they literally ploughed the ground and buried themselves in mud. At other times the large balls bounded along the ground, sometimes so deliberately that they could be avoided easily. A man could be knocked down by the wind of a shot, or he could be killed with the wind of the passing ball, as if he had actually been struck by it. A cannon ball makes a tremendous 'whizz,' or 'whop' as it passes you, the shell, 'tir-whit'. Two officers were both killed by the same ball which passed through both their heads, they happening to be standing a little behind one another.

Another man was killed and fell upon a shell which, exploding, drove him into the air – his knapsack, coat, shirt body and all flew in every direction. A Dublin lad looks up and exclaims with the greatest gravity: 'There's an inspection of necessaries.' There was a little spaniel running about the whole time, barking at the balls, and once smelling at a live shell, which exploded in his face without hurting him. The grape shot (actually a canister or case shot) could kill at 700 yards, taking many men and horses but still, its noise still keeps up the spirits of the soldiers.

The great black, dense body of French troops came steadily on, their columns meeting with shrapnel shells and canister shot. These burst within a hundred to a hundred and fifty yards from the head of their columns, creating chasms in their ranks, and destroying and rolling over horses and riders. Openings were drilled in their masses as if cut down with scythes, but they did not slacken their pace over the dead bodies of their comrades that lay in their way. With a cloud of Voltigeurs (light infantry) in front and on both flanks, covering their deep and dark masses, they steadily move up the incline. They were accompanied by the 'point of war', the pas de charge, beat by the French drummers advancing to the charge, and known through the British ranks as 'old trousers.' The French action:

> ...would be opened by a cloud of sharpshooters, some mounted, some on foot, who were sent forward to carry out a

general rather than a minutely-regulated mission; they proceeded to harass the enemy, escaping from his superior numbers by their mobility, from the effect of his artillery by their dispersal. Once the chink in the foe's armour had been revealed, it became the focal point for the main effort. The horse artillery would gallop up and open fire from close range with canister. Meanwhile, the attacking force would be moved up in the indicated direction, the infantry advancing in column (for it had little fire to offer), the cavalry in regiments and squadrons, ready to make its presence felt anywhere or everywhere as required. The soldiers would begin to move forward as the drums beat the charge. The sky would ring to a thousand battle-cries constantly repeated: 'En avant! En avant! Vive la République!'

British Soldiers called the French:
'Frogeaters'
'Frogs'
'Parlez Vous'
'Jack'
'Jacques'
'Beaux'
'Crapaud'
'Johnny Crappo'
'Mounseers'

French Soldiers Called the British:
'The Goddamns'
'John Bull'
Riflemen were 'Grasshoppers'

THE BRITISH SKIRMISHERS:

These were light infantry and riflemen and were deployed in pairs some 300 yards in front of the main body in the open fields. Here, all a man's wits must be about him in order to prevent the active enemy from passing his line, cutting him off and bring ruin on the army. As the French came on steadily, the riflemen fired not a shot until the enemy had turned their faces, when they served them out with a most destructive discharge and then fired away upon them. Riflemen, soon hotly engaged, loading and firing, their rifles and muskets bickering away, they were using any cover they could find, firing one moment, jumping up and running for it the next. Whenever the smoke cleared, the cannon-balls could be seen making a lane through the enemy's columns as they advanced, huzzaing and shouting like madmen. The French were now falling by fifties, but fighting and struggling hard to maintain their ground.

Our artillery mashed them up and the cavalry gave them no time to re-form. The light company, by a well directed fire, brought down some of the French officers of distinction, as they rode in front of their respective corps. There was no time to think, for all was action just at this moment; and the barrel of my piece was so hot from continual firing that I could hardly bear to touch it, and was obliged to grasp the stock beneath the iron, as I continued to blaze away.

Some light infantry were hidden below the crest of a hill, drawn back from the skyline and placed some hundreds of yards away from the edge – a tactic Wellington devised called 'Reverse Slopes.' They lay on the ground, waiting, out of sight of the enemy and secure from the artillery fire until they were wanted. With their accoutrements on, in a regular column of companies, front and rear ranks head to head and every man's firelock by his side, a formidable army can be concealed within a mile from even the sharpest of eyes.

> **Shots and shells were falling in every direction. The men were all the while lying in the ranks, and except at the very spot where a shot or shell fell, there was not the least motion – I have seen men killed in the ranks by cannon shots – those immediately round the spot would remove the mutilated corpse to the rear, they would then lie down as if nothing had occurred and remain in the ranks, steady as before.**

The riflemen retired before the enemy, moving back up the hill from boulder to boulder, slowly drawing the French columns with them up the steep sides of the hill, keeping up a constant and vicious fire, wrecking havoc on the officers and troops at the head. Reaching the top of the hill, breathless and disordered from climbing the steep and broken hillside, 'Jacques' found the riflemen gone, having doubled back behind the ridge. There was nothing to be seen but a few artillery guns and an officer, who waved his hat and bellowed, 'Charge! Huzza!' whereupon the Light Division sprang into their thin red line bristling over 2,000 bayonets. Giving a huge shout which astonished the unsuspecting French, they shot volley after volley into their compacted ranks at point blank range, while the rest of the division moved down on their right and left, pouring fire into their flanks. The British charged into the French ranks with their bayonets and the head of the French column reeled.

Other regiments extended all along the front waited in stern silence, and with unwonted patience, until the enemy come within range – a hundred yards or less.

> **I felt my mind waver; a breathless sensation came over me. The silence was appalling. I looked alongst the line. It was enough to assure me. The steady, determined scowl of my companions assured my heart and gave me determination.**

The British muskets came up and their volley roared out with a single thundering crash.

Instantly a shout, loud and protracted, rends the air, and the head of the enemy's column is annihilated by tremendous vollies. The hapless shattered mass staggers, breaks, turns, and rushed down the steep like an avalanche, while bullet, ball and shell plunge into the fugitive crowd.

We fired kneeling, to take down all the birds we could.

Fire at their legs and spoil their dancing!

Our wretched old flint firelocks would not burn powder at times until the soldier took from the pocket in his pouch a triangle screw, to knock life into his old flint, and then clear the touch-hole with a long brass picker that hung from his belt. Many a fellow was killed while performing this operation.

Firing as fast as I could, till my trigger finger was swollen as to be nearly useless. My shoulder was as black as a coal, from the recoil of my musket; for this day I had fired 107 round of ball-cartridge. In sounds of terror, the battle raged, volley following volley with deafening rapidity, while charges of cavalry and the booming of great guns swept off the warriors, on both sides brave and bold. They fell in sections, crying victory before the fight had half begun. The French masses closed on us in clouds of smoke and a stream of fire. The hill-side was soon covered with dead and dying. The battleground was shaking like an earthquake; the fire of the French sparkled along the line with terrible effect, as the many gaps in our ranks clearly showed.

The smoke, dust, and clamour, the flashing of firearms, the shouts and cries of the combatants, mixed with the thundering of the guns, was terrible.

The first thing which attracted my attention was the long melancholy whistle of the spent balls; but, as we approached

nearer the enemy, they flew past in full force, with a noise resembling the chirping of birds.

Some rockets were discharged and got amongst the Frenchmen's legs with an unheard-of-hissing, curving,

serpentining, biting, and kicking noise that they had never seen or heard before. It staggered their courage and steadiness long enough to make a rush with a cheer amongst them that they went to the right-about and fled.

The whole line of the battlefield was in a blaze – guns, mortars, cavalry, and infantry displaying double exertion and courage to win the day. The battle thickened fast, although no one could really see anything past his own brigade through the thick powder-smoke

The sun played on the arms of the enemy's battalions, as they came on, as if they had been tipped with gold. The battle soon became general; the smoke thickened around, and often I was obliged to stop firing, and dash it aside from my face, and try in vain to get a sight of what was going on, whilst groans and shouts and a noise of cannon and musketry appeared to shake the very ground. It seemed hell on earth.

The continuous cries of the wounded for water were piteous while the horses, distracted and torn with cannon-shot, were hobbling about in painful torture,

some with broken legs, and others dragging their entrails after them in mad career. One man was struck with a ball that passed through his body on the right side: you might have put a ramrod complete through the hole. He deliberately took his last shot, walked to the rear, lay down under a tree, and went to sleep in death. Asked to take a musket and join a charge on a howitzer, a drummer boy – calmly calculating the price of a drum when hundreds of balls were passing close to his body – said that were he not afraid of being obliged to pay for his drum, he too would also take a musket. Once assured it would be paid, he flung the drum away and joined the charge so as to capture the gun. A bugler whipped up an officer's pug-dog and put him in his haversack. Our feeling towards the enemy was the north side of friendly; for they had been firing upon us very sharply, greatly outnumbering our skirmishers, and appearing inclined to drive us off the face of the earth. The grenadiers were all fine-looking young men, wearing red shoulder-knots and tremendous-looking moustaches. As they came swarming upon us, they rained a perfect shower of balls, which we returned quite as sharply. Whenever one of them was knocked over, our men called out 'There goes another of Boney's Invincibles.'

The French troopers were making directly for the gap in the hedge where I was standing. I had not hitherto drawn my sword, as it was generally to be had at a moment's warning; but, from its having been exposed to the last night's rain, it had now got rusted in the scabbard and refused to come forth! I was in a precious scrape. Mounted on my strong Flanders mare, and with my good old sword in my hand, I would have braved all the chances without a moment's hesitation; but I confess that I felt considerable doubts as to the propriety of standing there to be sacrificed without the means of making a scramble for it. My mind, however, was happily relieved from such an embarrassing consideration before my decision was required; for the next moment the cuirassiers were charging, their infantry in our front giving way at the same time under our terrific shower of musketry, the flying cuirassiers tumbled in among their routed infantry, followed by, our cavalry who were cutting away in all directions. Hundreds of their infantry threw themselves down and pretended to be dead, while the cavalry galloped over them, and then got up and ran away.

The Highlanders were pitching into the French like blazes, colours flying, and their piper blowing out his national music to cheer them on. He was soon floored by a broken leg, but would not be moved, playing 'Johnny Cope' with all his might, while the blue bonnets, well supported, went into this mass with the bayonet. They stood there like a stone wall overmatched by twenty to one, until half their blue bonnets lay beside them, their dead bodies lying as a barrier to the advancing foe, the line of the killed and wounded stretched upon the heather. Their General was mortally wounded and refused to be moved from the field but had himself propped up against two knapsacks, on a point from which his dying eyes could survey the whole field, and watched the fight to the bitter end.

A cannon-ball came, and striking the right

of the company, made the arms gingle and fly in pieces like broken glass. One of the bayonets was broken off, and sent through a man's neck with as much force as though it had been done by a strong and powerful hand. I saw the man pull it out, and singular to relate, he recovered.

The red-coats were impatient and excited to be at the 'Beaux' with the bayonet. The word was delivered 'Prepare to charge.' The very hills echoed back with the mighty thundering shock of three terrifying cheers, such as is not known except amongst British troops on the battleground; drowning the clatter of musketry. All along the line it was one vast continuous uproar.

The guns were plunging shot into the French ranks until there was a flow of blood down the road. The blood was running in a stream, and the great French column continued to advance with a cloud of Voltigeurs in front and on both flanks, covering their deep and dark masses. They steadily move up the incline.

'Dead or alive, my lads, said our chief, 'we must hold our ground.' Every eye is fixed on this deadly mass, every nerve is strung. Like the gallant steed as he champs the foaming bit, ready for the charge, so was every man of ours in pain to be let loose. A howitzer, with a double charge of grape, went slap into their formost ranks; then one tremendous cheer, that only British soldiers can give with electric fire! 'Hurrah for old England!' 'Ireland for ever and the

Limerick lasses!' 'Bonnie brave Scotland, hurrah!' 'Hurrah!' from a thousand voices, as they dashed with the cold steel bayonets into the solid mass of human flesh before them. Writhing and quivering humanity lay over each other now in mortal combat, steeped in blood. The cannon-shot from each side was crushing up the living with the dead and dying. It was a horrid sight. The broken column retired, far away to the rear, while another massive column took their place and came on. The French always attacked in column.

We were like a torrent breaking bounds, following the music of the rifles. The French saw their own danger, and

fought like devils. Their first line we fairly ran over, and saw our men jumping over huge grenadiers; the second lined the side of a deep trench. A general bound was made at the chasm, and over it we went like so many beagles, snapping at them round every corner.

The men cried out (as it were with one voice) to charge. 'D—n them!' they roared, 'charge! charge!' The General desired them to stand fast, and keep their ground. 'Don't be too eager, men,' he said, as coolly as if we were on a drill-parade in Old England; 'I don't want you to advance just yet. Well done, he called out, as he galloped up and down the line; well done all. I'll not forget, if I live, to report your conduct today. They shall hear of it in England, my lads!'

A man of the 95th, at this moment rushed up to the general, and presented him with a green feather, which he had torn out of the cap of a French light-infantry soldier he had killed; 'God bless you, general!' he said; 'wear this for the sake of the 95th.' I saw the general take the feather, and stick it in his cocked hat. The next minute he gave the word to charge,

and down came the whole line, through a tremendous fire of cannon and musketry–and dreadful was the slaughter as they rushed onwards. As they came up with us, we sprang to our feet, gave one hearty cheer, and charged along with them, treading over our own dead and wounded, who lay in the front. The 50th were next us as we went, and I recollect the firmness of that regiment in the charge. They appeared like a wall of iron.

Strong posts were taken and retaken with the bayonet. It was what the Duke called 'bludgeon work.' Charge succeeded charge; each side yielded and recovered ground by turns. Regiments rushed against the crowded masses of the French, rolling them backward in disorder and throwing them down. With anything but child's play, two regiments fell upon the enemy three separate times with the bayonet, losing half their numbers. A great slaughter was going forward along the whole line of the battle. The war whoop of the charge was given and the whole mass was almost completely broken to bits. Away the parlez vous went at the double, a tempest of

lead following their heels. It was the difficulty to keep John Bull back and restrain their impatience, gamecocks as they were. Just as the French went to the right-about, a lively fellow d__d them furiously, and, all his bullets being gone, he grabbed a razor from his haversack, rammed it down, and fired it after them. The French were thrown back all along the line at the point of the bayonet, and then they were pursued and ignominiously slaughtered.

Our opponents never liked the steel, it was so indigestible, and at this part of the play the En avant (Forward) was never heard, but rather Sauve qui peut (Save yourself).

The British continued to push forward by divisions, brigades, and regiments, according to the nature of the ground and previous arrangements. Skirmishers to the front. The fusillade ran down the line like wildfire. Several points of the enemy's position were assailed at the same time, and some of their entrenchments and redoubts taken at the point of the bayonet; but these were minor works in advance, which were only taken after a sharp resistance and loss on both sides. Shells and round shot kept them uneasy on their ground, while the men were advancing in their old formidable way of renewing acquaintance with 'Johnny Crappo,' as the soldier redcoats so often called them. It was hard work charging up these sloping hills, receiving a heavy fire in the face, and losing men at every step; but if a certain number were destined to fall, the survivors only got the more excited in strength, agility, and resolution, feeling determined to win, and never looking behind. That gallant French Chef de Battalion, was leading on his men, waving them forward with his cocked hat at arm's length high in air. He rode far in front and cheered them on, while shot were rattling amongst their legs.

'Well, I'm blowed if I like to knock him over, he's so plucky.' 'Ay, Bill, but you see he must come down, for he wants to be killed.' *'Faith, and I'll make him leave that,'* says a big Irish grenadier, *'or he may be riding over us,'* when down he tumbled off his charger as dead as a stone. I was really sorry for him at the moment, but he was madly brave.

From the French perspective, the moments moved to their culmination:

When we got to about a thousand yards from the English line the men would begin to get restless and excited: they exchanged ideas with one another, their march began to be somewhat precipitate, and was already growing a little disorderly. Meanwhile the English, silent and impassive, with grounded arms, loomed like a long red wall; their aspect was imposing–it impressed novices not a little. Soon the distance began to grow shorter: cries of ' Vive l''Empereur,' 'en avant á la baionnette,' broke from our mass. Some men hoisted their shakos on their muskets, the quick-step became a run: the ranks began to be mixed up: the men's agitation became tumultuous, many soldiers began to fire as they ran. And all the while the red English line, still silent and motionless, even when we were only 300 yards away,

seemed to take no notice of the storm which was about to beat upon it.

The contrast was striking. More than one among us began to reflect that the enemy's fire, so long reserved, would be very unpleasant when it did break forth.

At this moment of painful expectation the English line would make a quarter-turn; the muskets were going up to the 'ready.' An indefinable sensation nailed to the spot many of our men, who halted and opened a wavering fire. The enemy's return, a volley of simultaneous precision and deadly effect, crashed in upon us like a thunderbolt. Decimated by it we reeled together, staggering under the blow and trying to recover our equilibrium. Then three formidable Hurrahs termined the long silence of our adversaries. With the third they were down upon us, pressing us into a disorderly retreat. But to our great surprise, they did not pursue their advantage for more than some hundred yards, and went back with calm to their former lines, to await another attack. We rarely failed to deliver it when our reinforcements came up with the same want of success and heavier losses.

The power of the bayonet consisted in its numbers as acting together as one machine in a closed compact line, an inch or two of the bayonet would generally be mortal. One regiment bayoneted eight or nine French officers and upwards of 100 men in an attack on the head of a French column coming up the road.

Once the chain was broken, nothing could stop the current of their speed. Away they fled: d___ take the hindmost; nobody wished to stop them! We had enough blood and brains on the sod for one day.

The advancing infantry now sent a shower of leaden hail into the teeth of the enemy, a cloud of dust blinded their vision accompanied by a tremendous charge of cavalry, swift and sure, sword in hand, broke in upon them in full tilt, trampled and cut them down.

The Hussars would wait for the French to charge them in their usual furious way until they were within 2 or 3 yards, perfectly steady, & then made full use of their spurs, broke them in an instant & literally cut them to pieces, for they have killed or taken prisoners nearly the whole of them – not 10 escaped. Our loss was not more than 10 killed & I suppose, as many wounded. The poor fellows are cut up in every way – some their lips off, some their noses, backs, arms, heads cut in every direction.

The enemy cavalry, twenty squadrons or so, came charging up the hill covering the road, passing and taking the British guns. The infantry, lying down behind the brow of the hill, jumped up, and came forward steadily in line. After delivering well directed fire and a shattering volley, they lowered their bayonets, and against all precedents, charged the French cavalry. Thus forcing them back down the height, recapturing the guns, and causing much confusion amongst the French troops who were trying to ascend the hill. Many red coats saw the infantry charging the French cavalry regiment.

This was the first charge of cavalry most of us had ever seen and we were all much interested in it. The French skirmishers extended against us seemed to feel the same, and by general consent both parties

suspended firing while the affair of dragoons was going on.

British infantry tended to regard their cavalry as 'more ornamental than useful' while the cavalry considered the infantry as 'extremely ungenteel.' Cavalry were not taught to charge, disperse and form while in England, where they generally never went much beyond a trot. Through long experience on outpost and piquet duty, they learned their service but in battle sometimes found it was difficult to halt their career and redeploy once in pursuit. During one charge, when the French cavalry were losing ground and also losing men, a mistaken warning sent up a cry of alarm and every man turned and made for the rear:

for a few seconds the extraordinary sight was to be seen of two forces running away from each other at the same time.

The Duke of Wellington said that he had 'never been more annoyed':

It is occasioned entirely by the trick our officers of cavalry have acquired of galloping at every thing, and their galloping back as fast as they gallop on the enemy. They never consider their situation, and never think of manoeuvering before an enemy – so little that

*one would think they cannot manoeuvre,
excepting on Wimbledon Common…*

And he added:

[These are] the best regiments in the
country, and it annoys me particularly that
this misfortune has happened to them

Cavalry was a powerful weapon in the field and
infantry in the presence of cavalry, being extremely
vulnerable, almost always retired into squares. These
were usually about 100ft on a side, formed like a
chequer board, so that the fire of one square would not
interfere with another. The first rank knelt, bracing the
butt of their muskets on the ground, the bayonets
pointing out at a 45° angle, while the second rank stood
behind them muskets to the ready, the whole offering
a bristling four sided hedgehog to the galloping
charge. Safety lay in the knowledge that horses would
not breach the unbroken thicket of bayonets if
presented by well-formed and solid infantry. The only
hope was that the men in the square would not waver,
leaving a hole, ever so small, before they fired into the
excited men and horses.

Now, my young tinkers, stand firm! While
you remain in your present position, old
Harry himself can't touch you, but if one
of you give way, he will have every
mother's son of you, as sure as you are
born!

Mind the square; you know I often told
you that if you ever had to form it from
line, in the face of an enemy, you'd be in a
damned ugly way, and have plenty of noise
about you; mind the tellings off, and don't
give the false touch to your right or left
hand man; for by God, if you are once
broken, you'll be running here and their
like a parcel of frightened pullets!

It is an awful thing for the infantry to see
a body of cavalry riding at them full gallop.

The French cuirassiers, none under six feet, mounted on
huge horses and defended by steel helmets and
breastplates, made pigeon-breasted to throw off the
balls, inspired dread, the ground shaking as their
thundering hoofs were approaching. Inside the square,
men were nearly suffocated by the smoke and smell from
burnt cartridges. It was impossible to move a yard
without treading upon a wounded comrade, or upon
the bodies of the dead; and the loud groans of the
wounded and dying were most appalling.

'Tom, Tom, here comes the calvary.'

The enemy seemed determined to force
a passage through us; and on their second
advance, they brought some artillery-
men, turned the cannon in our front upon
us, and fired into us with grape-shot,
which proved very destructive, making
complete lanes through us; and then the
horsemen came up to dash in at the
openings.

Our situation, now, was truly awful; our
men were falling by dozens every fire.
About this time, also, a large shell fell just
in front of us, and while the fuze was
burning out, we were wondering how
many of us it would destroy. When it burst,
about seventeen men were either killed or
wounded by it; the portion which came to
my share, was a piece of rough cast-iron,
about the size of a horse-bean, which took
up its lodging in my left cheek; the blood
ran copiously down inside my clothes, and
made me rather uncomfortable. Our poor
old captain was horribly frightened; and
several times came to me for a drop of
something to keep his spirits up. Towards
the close of the day, he was cut in two by a
cannon shot.

The next charge the cavalry made, they
deliberately walked their horses up to the
bayonet's point; and one of them, leaning
over his horse, made a thrust at me with his
sword. I could not avoid it, and
involuntarily closed my eyes. When I
opened them again, my enemy was lying
just in front of me, within reach, in the act
of thrusting at me. He had been wounded
by one of my rear rank men, and whether
it was the anguish of the wound, or the

chagrin of being defeated, I know not; but he endeavoured to terminate his existence with his own sword: but that being too long for his purpose, he took one of our bayonets, which was lying on the ground, and raising himself up with one hand, he placed the point of the bayonet under his cuirass, and fell on it.

The next time the cuirassiers made their appearance in our front, the Life Guards boldly rode out from our rear to meet them. It was a fair fight, and the French were fairly beaten and driven off. I noticed one of the Guards, who was attacked by two cuirassiers, at the same time; he bravely maintained the unequal conflict for a minute or two, when he disposed of one of them by a deadly thrust in the throat. His combat with the other one lasted about five minutes, when the guardsman struck his opponent a slashing back-handed stroke, and sent his helmet some distance, with the head inside it. The horse galloped away with the headless rider, sitting erect in the saddle, the blood spouting out of the arteries like so many fountains.

The French having moved to another quarter, the Duke of Wellington came riding by, asking:

'How do you get on?'
'My Lord, we are dreadfully cut up; can you not relieve us for a little while?'
'Impossible!'
'Very well, my Lord, we'll stand till the last man falls!'

In an extreme emergency with cavalry bearing down, there might not be enough time or men to form a proper square, and then the officer or NCO would shout: 'Form rallying square!' whereupon the unit would run and form a tightly-packed mass or 'Orb,' bayonet points bristling outwards.

They came with the noise of thunder. One circle wavered – some of the men abandoned their ranks – the cavalry rode through it in an instant. That in which I was stood more firm. We permitted them to approach till the breasts of the horses almost touched our bayonets, when a close and well-directed volley was poured in, and numbers fell beneath it.

With thousands of cavalry charging and surrounding infantry, retreat was especially difficult – timing the movement of the square into column, marching as far as possible bringing on the wounded while the cavalry reformed, then transforming back into square as the cavalry came galloping and screaming to attack again. The horse artillery kept up a withering fire into the charging horses. While outnumbered, the Light Infantry and Riflemen took cover and kept up a hot fire on the chaussers, the horses, the enemy gun crews, and the horse artillery. The French sustained heavy losses from the accurate fire of the riflemen, and held back, not closing with the slowly moving columns, moving in precision, with the French threatening to charge without actually executing it.

The battle lulled and the dreadful turmoil and noise subsided, and I began to look into the faces of the men close around me to see who had escaped the dangers of the hour. One feels, indeed, a sort of curiosity to know, after such a scene, who is remaining alive amongst the companions endeared by good conduct, or disliked from bad character, during the hardships of the campaign. I saw the ranks of the Riflemen looked very thin. We threw ourselves down where we were standing when the fire ceased, and down galloped the major in front, a regular good 'un – a real English soldier. The major just now disclosed what none of us, I believe, knew before, namely, that his head was bald as a coot's, and that he had covered the nakedness of his nob, up to the present time, by a flowing Caxon, which, during the heat of the action, had somehow been dislodged, and was lost; yet was the major riding hither and thither, digging the spurs into his horse's flanks. 'A guinea,' he kept crying as he rode, 'to any man who will find my wig!' The men, notwithstanding the sight of the wounded and dead around them, burst into shouts of laughter at him as he went.

Surging across a front miles wide, battles often poured around and through villages. It is always ugly, dangerous work fighting in a town; so many holes and corners, hiding-places and loop-holes, where one may be picked off by an unseen enemy. Fighting from house to house and from street to street, men were having their bones cracked, and dropping off at every corner. As the enemy retired, or were driven back, they fired the houses they left, to arrest progress, not sparing their own property. In many houses the furniture was piled up in rooms, ready for the torch. The streets were barricaded, and cannon planted at every entrance, pounding away at the first blink of any red-coat. Men dashed on through fire and smoke, and carried on the work surely and gradually – lemonade being served between the firing.

As we were forming in the gardens, a hen which seemed to have lost his way was pursued by several of the men, and ran for shelter to a thorn hedge in rear of which was a stone wall; just as two of them were making the grasp at her, a French 9 pounder interfered and carried her off a legal prize.

The fighting was deadly as the British were an obstinate foe, barricaded in houses and behind lines of stone walls. The narrow streets were encumbered with dead and wounded. The town presented a shocking sight: the Highlanders, instead of covering themselves by the walls and houses, chose to stand on the top of the former, exclaiming that they would rather, 'stand at the top of a wall, and be shot like men, than hide behind it, and be killed like dogs.' Consequently they were knocked down very rapidly, lying dead in heaps, while the other regiments, though less remarkable in dress, were scarcely so in the number of their slain.

We found by the buttons on the coats of some of the fallen foe that we had this day been opposed to the French ninety-fifth regiment (the same number as we were then) and I cut off several of them, which I preserved as trophies.

The French came leaping over a mud wall with dreadful shouts and fury. There was not a moment to hesitate, and

to it we fell pell-mell, French and British mixed together. It was a trial of strength in single combat; every man had his opponent, many had two. I got one up to the wall, on the point of my bayonet. He was unhurt. I would have spared him, but he would not spare himself. He cursed and defied me, nor ceased to attack my life, until he fell, pierced by my bayonet. His breath died away, in a curse and menace. I stood gasping for breath.

The French Grenadiers, with their immense caps and gaudy plumes, lay in piles of ten and twenty together – some dead, others wounded, with barely strength sufficient to move. Their exhausted state and the weight of their cumbrous accoutrements making it impossible for them to crawl out of the dreadful fire of grape and round shot which poured into the town. The Highlanders had been driven to the churchyard at the very top of the village, and were fighting with the French grenadiers across the graves and tombstones. The French Light Infantry had penetrated as far as the church, and were preparing to debouch upon the rear of our centre. The French gave way, yielding at every point, the British sweeping the whole village.

More than one battle was desperate – a 'close run thing' – the red coats outnumbered in men and guns.

> As we moved down in column, shot and shell flew over and through in quick succession. But we passed by a Captain who had been dreadfully lacerated by a ball, and lay directly in our path. We passed close to him, and he knew us all; and the heart-rending tone in which he called to us for water, or to kill him, could not be forgotten. All was hurry and struggle; every arm was wanted in the field. The slaughter was now, for a few minutes, dreadful; every shot told, they would make no effort. A constant feeling to the centre of the line, and the gradual diminution of our front, more truly bespoke the havock of death. We trod among the dead and dying, all reckless of them.

Standing in a blinding shower of rain and hail, gloom and blood and powder smoke – which rolled along the field and clothed the scene in partial darkness, the battle left an awful carnage on both sides. The dead lay in rows

where they had stood, the British infantry reeled and staggered and the French columns were poised to roll up the entire line – there being no reserve. The line was formed with the men approaching at quick step under a storm of shot, shell and grape, which came crashing through the ranks. Under the tremendous fire of the enemy:

> our thin line staggers, men are knocked about like skittles; but not a step backward is taken. Here our Colonel and all the field-officers of the brigade fell killed or wounded, but no confusion ensued. 'Close up;' 'Close in;' 'fire away;' 'forward.' This is done. We are close to the enemy's columns.

In vain did the hardiest French veterans break from the crowded columns and sacrifice their lives to gain time for the mass to open out on such a fair field; in vain did the mass itself bear up. Nothing could stop that astonishing red coated infantry. Their measured tread shook the ground, their dreadful volleys swept away the head of every formation, and their deafening shouts overpowered the dissonant cries that broke from all parts of the tumultuous crowd. Slowly and with a horrid

carnage the blue whole was pushed by the incessant vigour of the attack to the farthest edge of the hill and the mighty mass, breaking off like a loosened cliff, went headlong down the steep. They soon broke and rushed down the other side of the hill in the greatest mob-like confusion. Eighteen hundred unwounded men, the remnant of six thousand British soldiers, stood triumphant on the fatal hill! The dead were in heaps, one nearly three feet high, in several places whole sub-divisions or sections appeared to have been prostrated by one tremendous charge or volley. The waters of the stream so deeply tinged that it seemed actually to run blood. 1,800 of the 6,000 were still standing. The vanquished French General observed later that:

I turned their right flank, penetrated their centre;
they were completely beat and the day mine,
but yet they would not run.

After the battle, we encamped on that part of the field where the carnage had been the most dreadful, and actually piled our arms amongst the dead and dying, and collected what dead bodies were near. A kind of wall was made with them to break the wind that was very cutting, as we were very damp with sweat. The hillsides were perforated with cannon-shot, some places like a rabbit-warren, and dyed with blood. The colonel had his epaulet spoiled with a shot, and a ventilator made in his shako. The ground withersoever we went, was literally strewed with the wreck of the mighty battle. Arms of every kind, cuirasses, muskets, cannon, tumbrils, and drums, which seemed innumerable, cumbered the very face of the earth. Intermingled with these were the carcases of the slain, not lying about in groups of four or six, but wedged together, that we found it, in many instances, impossible to avoid trampling them where they lay. Those who lost accoutrements went among the dead to select such as was wanted – a belt, a bayonet, a much prized French knapsack, or a good English kit from a dead 'Johnny Newcome,' for 'Exchange is no robbery.' The wounded that could not walk were carried in blankets to the bottom of the bloody hill and laid among the wet grass, their cries and shrieks would have been dreadful if we could have heard them, but the continued discharges of the artillery, during the battle, had so affected the drums of the ears, that we could scarcely hear anything for two or three days afterwards, but the roaring of the cannon.

A Major's horse had been shot from under him and some men belonging to the Chasseurs Britannique skinned the horse, and sold the flesh at four pence halfpenny per lb. Night closed upon the saturated field of blood before we had time to light our fires and cook the wretched ration dinner. But still, with our half-gill of rum, it was an acceptable banquet. We lay down among the mire and dead men. Once I looked up out of my wet blanket, and saw a poor wounded man stark naked, crawling about I suppose for shelter. Going on rounds, I was continually stumbling over old comrades, and would then roll my head up in my cloak, and lie down amongst them for a half an hour or so, jump up and tumble over another ghost!

The day's service had been very severe, but now I took it with the coolest indifference. I felt no alarm; it was all of course. I began to think my body charmed. My mind had come to that pass; I took everything as it came without a thought. If I was at ease, with plenty, I was happy; if in the midst of the enemy's fire, or of the greatest privations, I was not concerned. I had been in so many changes of plenty and want, ease and danger, they had ceased to be anticipated either with joy or fear.

It was distressing to hear the cries and moans of the wounded and dying.

It was marvellous how quickly the dead, and often the wounded, were stripped on the battlefield by the camp-followers of the two great armies – an unhallowed trade, and there was no stopping it. I remember nearly stumbling over the bleeding body of a young French officer rolling in the dust, speechless in agony, and stark naked! The birds of prey were devouring the slain, and here I beheld a sight even more horrible – the peasantry prowling about, more ferocious than the beast and birds of prey, finishing the work of death, and carrying away whatever they thought worthy of their grasp. When light failed them, they kindled a great fire and remained about it all night, shouting like as many savages. 'My sickened fancy felt the same as if it were witnessing a feast of cannibals.

In the morning firing recommenced, and often continued until someone sent a flag of truce for leave to carry off the wounded.

In the ravine there was a small stream, at which, with the most profound harmony, and as if nothing had happened, both French and English soldiers fetched water, and, as a sign of very special mutual esteem, exchanged their forage caps. There was not the least animosity between us. One night before they attacked us, I had a long conversation with a French officer, a little brook only divided us. Both parties made a point of never firing on single officers in this way without calling to them first. The French even brought down a number of bands of music to a level piece of ground where they continued to play

As we advanced, driving them before us, a French officer, a pretty fellow, was pricking and forcing his men to stand. They heeded him not; he was very harsh. 'Down with him!' cried one near me, and down he fell, pierced by more than one ball. Our brigade-major's horse had both his fore-legs shot from under him: the poor creature began to eat grass, as if nothing was the matter with him. The Light Division came up, breaking their ranks to join us. We then mingled our shots together, and dashed forward against the foe. It was grand to see the divisions striving to out-do each other in gallantry. The enemy could not withstand the shock, but were panic-stricken, and fled in confusion: we followed them, shouting and huzzar-ing, and gave them no time to form, but drove them before us like cattle to destruction. Nothing could exceed the joy we felt, to see the enemy flying before us in dismay and confusion.

It was perfectly dark before the action finished, but, on going to take advantage of the fires which the enemy had evacuated, their soup-kettles were found in full operation, and every man's mess of biscuit lying beside them in stockings, as was the French mode of carrying them; needless to say how unceremoniously the men proceeded to do the honours of the feast.

until sunset whilst the men were dancing and diverting themselves at football.

There is never any personal animosity between soldiers opposed to each other in war. I should hate to fight out of personal malice or revenge, but have no objection to fight for 'fun and glory'

The field of battle, next morning, presented a frightful scene of carnage. It seemed as if the world had tumbled to pieces, and three-fourths of everything destroyed in the wreck. The ground running parallel to the front where we had stood was so thickly strewed with fallen men and horses, that it was difficult to step clear of their bodies, many of the former still alive, and imploring assistance, which it was not in our power to bestow.

The truce ended, sentries withdrawn, and 'and we gave our friends warning to be on their guard, and it was not long before we met again in mortal combat.'

We continued to advance, receiving a galling fire from the enemy. One of our company received a severe wound and several others fell dead at our feet. The fire coming from the enemy became dreadful, and our men fell in every direction. I really thought that, if it lasted much longer, there would not have been a man left to relate the circumstance.

The first work to be done, was to remove thousands of English and French wounded, and to bury the dead. 'Twas impossible! We had but few tools, and the ground was hard and rocky, therefore the dead were either thrown into the dry beds of winter torrents, &c., and scantily covered with earth; or, together with dead horses, gathered into heaps and burned. The smell was intolerable. As for the wounded, they perished in great numbers while lying in want of water, dressing and shelter.

I had never yet heard of a battle in which everybody was killed, but this seemed likely to be an exception, as all were going by turns. However desperate our affairs were, we had still the satisfaction of seeing that theirs were worse.

'War is a sad blunter of the feelings of men.' From a deficiency of transport, wounded soldiers were often abandoned on the field. As for the dead, there was no real grief for any one beyond a week or two – all a shadow that passed away. Their effects were sold by auction. We bought their clothes and wore them, and they were sold again perhaps in a month, being once more part of the kit of deceased officers killed in action. It was not the fashion in those days to regard the death of a poor Subaltern more than that of a cavalry charger. As to private soldiers, thousands upon thousands that joined the army from England were never heard of by their kindred or friends, dead or alive. They fought and they fell and were forgotten!

> When the prison of the soul was broken up, the poor shattered shell lay there without burial, with no kindred friend to close the late brilliant eye, or say the last leave-taking words – Requiescat in pace.

A soldier thinks of nothing that has passed by; it is only the present time that concerns him; he is a careless and thoughtless being.

Before and after a battle the two armies often marched in proximity, the French like locusts, eating up all before them.

They paid for nothing, and it was always an unlucky time for us when we got in their wake, for they cleared out the whole country as they went along, for what he can't use he will destroy from pure mischief. We followed up our friends as close as we could, sticking to them like a burr to a sheep's tail.

Their retreat resembled more that of famished wolves than men. Murder and devastation marked their way; every house was a sepulchre, a cabin of horrors! Our soldiers used to wonder why the Frenchmen were not swept by heaven from the earth, when they witnessed their cruelties. Every house contained traces of their wanton barbarity. They would regularly burn to the ground every place they pass through. In following them we find each town & village a heap of smoking ruins.

The wretched inhabitants are returning to their destroyed dwellings. The enormities committed on the property and persons of these poor people by the enemy can scarcely be recited with the expectation of gaining belief. The entire destruction of the different towns and villages they have lately passed through renders it probable that they have no intention of ever again invading the country, but the ruin and devastation they have occasioned cannot be entirely effaced in a less period than half a century.

The peasant, cleric and noble were all alike consumed and the acts committed by the French in Spain were so revolting to human nature that they could hardly be committed to paper. Their steps were traced by the conflagration of towns, villages, and quintas, and from the mountains could be seen the smoke rising from the valleys. Young women were left in their houses brutally violated; the streets were strewed with broken furniture, intermixed with the putrid carcasses of murdered peasants, mules and donkeys and every description of filth that filled the air with pestilential nausea. The few starved male inhabitants who were stalking amid the wreck of their friends and property looked like so many skeletons who had been permitted to leave their graves for the purpose of taking vengeance on their oppressors and the mangled body of every Frenchman who was to stray from his column showed how religiously they performed their mission. In one town the French burned 200 people to death in the sacristy of a chapel, some of the partially consumed bodies still kneeling or leaning against the walls; the body of a dead young child who had been strangled was in a bag, the cord still around its neck. Entering another village they found a well-dressed woman, the wife of the mayor, who had been murdered by being placed on her back in the middle of the street, with a huge piece of granite taken from the market cross, so heavy that it took seven men to remove it. The blood was running from her ears and mouth. Some cavalry found three Friars hanging to a tree by three of the branches, which had been cut and sharpened, and then the unhappy men were suspended by the insertion of the sharp points in their throats. They were daubed over with some black substance like pitch,

as if to preserve the bodies in terrorem.

Leaving a town, the French sometimes left their own dead displayed with a grotesque humour. Sometimes enclosed in large chests, placed upright in full uniform in the recesses of houses and convents, tied on the top of windmills with their arms in their hands – pointed as if levelled at those who advance, and worst of all, thrown down wells. One body, with its shako on, was found seated in the pulpit of a roofless chapel, with its musket in the position of presenting arms. Hidden away, as if a prize for the poor horses and mules, would be sacks of Indian corn filled with industriously broken glass mixed throughout – enough to have killed an ostrich. 'If the enemy could not exist in the country, they had determined that nothing should be left for others.' Wellington himself could but comment:

> *I am concerned to be obliged to add to this account, that their conduct throughout this retreat has been marked by a barbarity seldom equalled, and never surpassed.*

A French soldier rejoiced if captured by the British for they were in fear of the Spaniards. At one French hospital, the Spaniards had hacked 400 men to pieces and buried 53 alive. One French soldier who was the only survivor of some 1,200 invalids who had been butchered and mutilated, had his ears cut off and went mad as a consequence of what he had seen.

Yet, the French also returned lost children who had been sequestered in the panniers of captured donkeys, dropped off an abandoned cloak, returned wandering hounds and treated British wounded kindly, feeding them and dressing and tending wounds.

Both French and English communicated with each other by drawing caricatures of each other on the walls of deserted houses along with sarcastic remarks, and courteous retorts. A crude inscription scratched by a French prisoner in charcoal on a chapel wall, read:

> La Guerre en Espagne est la Fortune des Generaux,
> l'Ennui des Officers, and le Tombeau des Soldiats.
> (The War in Spain is a fortune for the Generals, ruin for the Officers, and the grave of the Soldiers.)

Though the combatants might only meet in full battle three or four times a year and some men nary saw a

mountainous and rocky, and thickly intersected with stone walls, and were involved in one continued hard skirmish from daylight until dark. The enemy pushed their advanced guard up close and the heavies at one point mistook some bushes for the enemy and fired at them for a half an hour. There were sharp contests for fields, villages, hills and bridges. In trying to cross a river gorged by rain, the French made many brilliant attempts although lost many.

We prided ourselves upon destroying the enemy and preserving ourselves.

While on patrol, four companies of Riflemen were posted on piquet near a most formidable pass. The French were also posted opposite. The river ran furiously in the bottom of this deep chasm over rugged rocks, causing a continued noise. At the bottom of the zig-zag pass is the bridge over the river, 100 yards long and yards wide.

The outlying piquet remained quiet. Early in the evening a tremendous firing commenced. The men were immediately ordered to fall in and move forward to the alarm post, which was on the edge of the rocky chasm. The night being dark and stormy, with rain occasionally, caused the river to make more noise in its passage over the rocky bed than usual and completely prevented the advanced sentinels hearing the approach of the enemy. Also from the obscurity of the night, it was not possible to see any object, so that the enemy passed the bridge so rapidly that only one sentinel fired before they were both knocked down. Two men were taken at

Frenchman for a year at a time, many divisions, patrols, and picquets were on everlasting skirmish, engaged every day, in petty warfare. Small groups of perhaps six troopers, to patrols of sixteen or eighteen cavalry with 150 infantry, went out to take the enemy foraging and plundering parties.

We were kept roving about the country to pot the French, kill them, and cook them in our own fashion. All was lawful in war, but they were very sharp and always slept with one eye open: we had to do the same. It was like deer-stalking at times – a glorious thing to whack in amongst a lively party with their flesh-pots on the fire of well seasoned wood, letting fly a shot into the middle of a covey who were in reality cooking their dinner. Such things happen almost every day.

There was no getting quit of these Frenchmen. They multiplied and formed new armies, always on the trot. Day by day, the French were driven from one stronghold to another, over a large track of very difficult country,

of the piquet, the French were literally scrambling up the rocky ground. They commenced firing at each other very spiritedly. Their drums beat a charge and the French attempted to dislodge the riflemen without effect. An officer who was putting on his spectacles, received a musket ball through his head and fell dead. Several were now falling and the moon shone brightly for a few minutes then disappeared and again at intervals to let us see each other. We profited by this circumstance, as their belts were white and over their greatcoats, so that where they crossed upon the breast, combined with the glare of the breastplate, gave a grand mark for our rifles. The riflemen being in dark dresses, and from their small number, were obliged to keep close together, the ground also being exceedingly rugged; all favourable circumstances. Fighting went on in this way for at least half an hour against fearful odds, when the Lieutenant Colonel brought down the three reserve companies from the village far above, who soon decided the affair. The enemy was driven in the greatest confusion back over frightful precipices, leaving two officers killed and a number of men wounded.

the bridge. However, this gave the alarm, and a small party stationed amongst the rocks kept up a fire. The sergeant being shot through the mouth and the enemy being so numerous, they could not impede their progress. In a moment, after the arrival of the main body

To provoke them further, as they were much in want of provisions most of the time, sometimes we fixed a

biscuit to the point of their bayonets and presenting it to them. At other times, individuals of the Dragoons used to engage in single combat with the horsemen of the enemy. Often whole squadrons would be brought to engage by two men beginning. There was a continued popping between the advanced posts all night.

In the day to day contests between piquets and foragers, the French at times would take off their swords and come down to say their only object was foraging. They would then complain that

> much of the way they were going on, and hoped to put an end to the business one way or another. They did not appear to think things went on well for them. They invited us to a play in Santarem they had got up, and we them to horse-races, football, and dog-hunts. The communication was put to a stop by a general order.

When advanced sentries were almost in contact, however, they would not interfere with each other. The French would copy John Bull's ways of using 'stone chatters,' instead of calling out 'All's well' by striking together twice in slow time white polished stones about two pounds weight each, repeating along the chain of sentries. The alert was three times quickly.

The Spanish guerrilla bands were forever watching the French, intercepting their convoys and detachments, and pouncing into them from the rocks and mountain passes, dealing fearful death to every victim; and this continued for six years in a charming country, amongst formerly happy, contented and amiable peasantry.

> Great ferocity existed at this time amongst the guerrilla chiefs, and indeed at all times. Mina was cruel and revengeful. The curate Merino, too, was revolting in cruelty; he took some hundred French prisoners on one occasion, and hanged fifty or sixty of them in cold blood, deliberately butchering them in order to avenge the death of three of his men, although he had no proof of their being killed at all. Then there was counter-retaliation, and so the

blood work went on continually, both parties to be condemned. Yet, make the case our own, and ask, if an enemy landed on our shores, killed, burned, and destroyed all before them, what would we do? How would we feel towards such an enemy? The poor Spaniards had very great provocation; but still no one could approve of the ferocious conduct on either side.

British Nicknames

'The' Division – The Light Division (43rd, 52nd, & 95th)
The Gentlemen's Sons – 1st Division
The Observing Division – 2nd Division
The Fighting Division – 3rd Division
The Supporting Division – 4th Division
The Enthusiastics – Also 4th Division
The Pioneers – 5th Division
The Marching Division – 6th Division
They tell us there is a 7th Division
but we have never seen it.

Other Names:

Slashers – The 28th
The Suprisers – The 2nd
The Greenjackets – The 95th
The Resurrection Men – The 3rd
The Dirty Half-hundred – The 50th
The Cumberland Gentlemen – The 34th
The Death and Glory Boys – Prussian Brunswickers

AMMUNITION

Roundshot

Roundshot, or a 'cannon ball,' was a simple iron ball that was a major projectile used by artillery in the Peninsular War against advancing columns of men as well as physical obstacles. The larger the ball, the faster and more deadly its effect could be, the 9 pounder being the primary ball used by the British. The iron balls were at times heated, producing a 'hot shot' which could set terrible fires.

Common Shell or Hollow Shot

A common shell was a hollowed iron ball which was filled with gunpowder set to explode at a specified time by an adjustable fuse, and was fired from howitzers or mortars in order to gain the necessary high-angle required. If the shell landed before the fuse had burned all of the way down, a quick man could extinguish it before it exploded.

Case Shot or Canister

Case shot was a tin canister filled with loose musket balls that ruptured as it left the muzzle of the cannon, scattering the bullets in a swath before the gun. It was limited to close range for maximum effectiveness – usually about 600 yards. Sometimes the canister was 'double shotted' with another canister or a roundshot. In land warfare, canister or case shot was often referred to as 'grape' or 'grapeshot' but authentic grapeshot was a naval shot composed of iron balls packed around a central column with a round base, all enclosed in a canvas bag, which could damage the barrels of brass cannons.

Spherical Case-shot (Shrapnel)

The practice was excellent, the shells bursting within a hundred and fifty yards from the head of their columns, creating chasms in their ranks, destroying and rolling over horses and riders, and drilling openings in their masses as if cut down with scythes.

Spherical case-shot consisted of a thin hollow round iron sphere. It was filled with 27 to 170 musket balls, depending on whether the shell was a 6 pdr or a 12 pdr, which was burst open by a small timed charge of gunpowder, set to go off above and before the advancing troops, showering them with the bullets. It could be fired from regular field artillery guns, and could be effective at 700 or even 1,500 yards. Invented by Lieutenant Henry Shrapnel of the Royal Artillery in 1784, it was first used in the Peninsula War at the battle of Rolica in 1808. It was close to a 'secret' weapon

as the French never developed or used anything like it during the war.

Congreve Rockets

The rockets went skipping about the river like mad things, and dancing quadrilles in every direction but the right one. Some of them came back to ourselves, but happily without doing any mischief. The French soldiers, at that period wholly unaccustomed to this arm, were so frightened, that they jumped overboard with all their accoutrements and were drowned.

The rockets that Sir William Congreve designed were an incendiary weapon, which consisted of a tailpiece, fuse and powder charge (packed gunpowder – potassium nitrate burning with sulphur and carbon) and a hollow warhead filled with shot or shell of varying weight. The normal shell or shot was 3 pounds, but went up to eighteen pounds. Some used case-shot holding up to 200 carbine balls sitting on bursting powder to scatter the balls. The rocket could also be used to send up a 'light-ball' that could produce a brilliant light for about ten minutes while falling back to earth on a parachute. The rocket sticks might be 15 feet long and were assembled from segments of 3 feet 6 inches (1 meter) with special tools. The rockets were usually ignited with a 'portfire' or thin iron stick about three feet long, with a pistol lock igniter on the end that was lighted by a flash of powder from a pan. This was launched from an iron-plate trough that was about a foot long, had four short legs, and weighed six pounds (the bouche á feu or 'fire mouth'). With an artillery crew and special transport carriages called 'rocket cars', carrying between 40 and 60 rockets and pulled by four horses, each car could launch two rockets in a volley from special adjustable double iron plate troughs built into the car – perhaps the first mobile rocket launchers. Mounted troopers had specially made holsters so they could carry four rockets. Targeting the rocket was done by 'eyeballing' the range from one round to the next. An experimental artillery unit called the 'Field Rocket Brigade' composed of twelve men and two *non-commissioned officers served in the Peninsula from 1808 to 1812, while a much larger group of 144 men and 105 horses was sent to Germany in 1813.*

The advantages of the rockets were that they were:

Competitive in range to field guns;
Portable;
Had no recoil;
Had impressive physical and psychological effects;

Rapid and easy operation;
Simple maintenance;
Low cost.

On the other hand, they were:

Unpredictable and erratic;
Inaccurate;
Susceptible to misfiring or exploding;
Slow, hand manufacturing process.

CAPTURING AN EAGLE

AN EXCERPT FROM 'SHARPE'S EAGLE' BY BERNARD CORNWELL

The enemy still faced away from them, still fired into the smoke, and the noise of battle became louder. At last Sharpe could hear the regular platoon volleys and knew that the second French attack had met the new British line and the dreadful monotony of the British volleys once again wrestled with the hypnotic drumming. The six-pound roundshot of the British thundered overhead and cut vicious paths in the unseen French columns, but the drumming increased, the shouts of 'Vive L'Empereur' were unabated, and suddenly they were within a hundred yards of the Eagle and Sharpe twisted the sword in his hand and hurried the pace. Surely the enemy would see them!

A drummer boy, rattling his sticks at the rear of the enemy line, turned to be sick and saw the small group coming silently through the smoke. He shouted a warning, but no-one heard; he shouted again and Sharpe saw an officer turn. There was movement in the ranks, men were swivelling to face them, but they had ramrods half down their barrels and were still loading. Sharpe raised his sword. 'On! On!'

He began to run, oblivious of everything except the Eagle and the frightened faces of the enemy who were desperately hurrying to load their muskets. Around the standard-bearer Sharpe could see Grenadiers wearing the tall bearskins, some of them armed with axes, the protectors of French honour. A musket banged and a ramrod cart-wheeled over his head; Harper was beside him, the sword bayonet in his hand, and the two men screamed their challenge as the drummer boys fled to either side and the two huge Riflemen ploughed into the centre of the enemy line. Muskets exploded with a terrible crash, Sharpe had an impression of men in green uniforms being thrown backwards, and then he could see nothing except a tall Grenadier who was lunging in short and professional jabs with a bayonet. Sharpe twisted to one side, let the blade slide past him, grabbed the muzzle of the musket with his left hand and pulled the Grenadier onto his levelled sword blade. Someone cut at him from the left, a swinging down-stroke with a clubbed musket, and he turned so that it thudded viciously into his pack to throw him forward onto the body of the Grenadier whose hands were clutching the blade embedded in his stomach. A gun deafened him, one of his own rifles, and suddenly he was clear and dragging the blade from the heavy corpse and screaming murder at the men who guarded the Eagle. Harper had cut his way, like Sharpe, through the first rank, but his sword-bayonet was too short and the Irishman was being driven back by two men with bayonets, and Sharpe crushed them to one side with his sword, slicing a vast splinter from the nearest musket, and Harper leapt into the gap, cutting left and right, as Sharpe struggled alongside.

More muskets, more screams; the white-jackets were clawing at them, surrounding them, reloading to blast the tiny band with musket fire that would crush them unmercifully. The Eagle was retreating, away from them, but there was nowhere for the standard-bearer to go except towards the musket fire of an unseen British Battalion that was somewhere in the smoke that poured from the crash of column onto line. An axeman came at Sharpe; he was a huge man, as big as Harper, and he smiled as be hefted the huge blade and then swung it powerfully down in a blow that would have severed the head of an ox. Sharpe wrenched himself out of the way, felt the wind of the blade, and saw the axe thud into the blood-wet ground. He stabbed the sword down into the man's neck, knew he had killed him, and watched as Harper plucked the axe from the earth and threw away his bayonet. The Irishman was screaming in the language of his ancestors, his wild blood surging, the axe searing in a circle so wildly that even Sharpe had to duck out of the way as Patrick Harper went on; lips wrenched back in the blackened face, his shako gone, his long hair matted with powder, the great silver blade singing in his hands and the old language carving a path through the enemy.

The standard-bearer jumped out of the ranks to carry the precious Eagle down the Battalion to safety, but there was a crack, the man fell, and Sharpe heard Hagman's customary 'got him'. Then there was a new sound, more volleys, and the Dutch Battalion shook like a wounded animal as the South Essex arrived on their flank and began to pour in their volleys. Sharpe was faced by a crazed officer who swung at him with a sword, missed, and screamed in panic as Sharpe lunged with the point. A man in white ran out of the ranks to pick up the fallen Eagle but Sharpe was through the line as well and he kicked the man in the ribs, bent, and plucked the staff from the ground. There was a formless scream from the enemy, men lunged at him with bayonets and he felt a blow on the thigh, but Harper was there with the axe and so was Denny with his ridiculously slim sword.

Denny! Sharpe pushed the boy down, swung the sword to protect him, but a bayonet was in the Ensign's chest and even as Sharpe smashed the sword down on the man's head he felt Denny shudder and collapse. Sharpe screamed, swung the gilded copper Eagle at the enemy, watched the gold scar the air and force them back, screamed again, and jumped the bodies with his bloodied sword reaching for more. The Dutchmen fell back, appalled; the Eagle was coming at them and they retreated in the face of the two huge Riflemen who snarled at them, swung at them, who bled from a dozen cuts yet still came on. They were unkillable! And now there were volleys coming from the right, from the front, and the Dutchmen, who had fought so well for their French masters, had had enough. They ran, as the other French Battalions were running, and in the smoke of the Portina valley the scratch Battalions like the 48th, and the men of the Legion and the Guards who had reformed and come forward to fight again, marched forward on ground made slippery with blood and thrust with their bayonets and forced the massive French columns backwards. The enemy went, away from the dripping steel, backwards, in a scene that was like the most lurid imaginings of hell. Sharpe had never seen so many bodies, so much blood spilt on a field; even at Assaye which he had thought unrivalled in horror there had not been this much blood.

FORMING A SQUARE

AN EXCERPT FROM 'SHARPE'S BATTLE' BY BERNARD CORNWELL

The Light Division had formed its battalions into close columns of companies. Each company formed a rectangle four ranks deep and anything from twelve to twenty files wide, then the ten companies of each battalion paraded in column so that from the sky each battalion now resembled a stack of thin red bricks.

'Form square on the front division!' the Colonel of the redcoat battalion shouted.

The Major commanding the battalion's leading division of companies called for the first brick to halt and for the second to form alongside it so that two of the bricks now made one long wall of men four ranks deep and forty men wide. 'Dress ranks!' the sergeants shouted as the men shuffled close together and looked right to make sure their rank was ruler straight. While the leading two companies straightened their ranks the Major was calling orders to the succeeding companies. 'Sections outward wheel! Rear sections close to the front!' 'The French trumpets were pealing and the earth was vibrating from the mass of hooves, but the sergeants' and officers' voices sounded coolly over the threat. 'Outward wheel! Steady now! Rear sections close to the front!' The six centre companies of the battalion now split into four sections each. Two sections swung like hinged doors to the right and two to the left, the innermost men of each section reducing their marching pace from thirty to twenty inches, while the men swinging widest lengthened their stride to thirty-three inches and so the sections pivoted outward to begin forming the twin faces of the square whose anchoring wall was the first two companies. Mounted officers hurried to get their horses inside the rapidly forming square that was, in reality, an oblong. The northward face had been made by the two leading companies, now the two longer sides were formed by the next six companies wheeling outward and closing hard up, while the last companies merely filled in the vacant fourth side. 'Halt! Right about face!' the Major in command of the rear division shouted to the last two companies.

'Prepare to receive cavalry!' the Colonel shouted dutifully, as if the sight of the massed French horse was not warning enough. The Colonel drew his sword, then swatted with his free hand at a horsefly. The colour party stood beside him, two teenage ensigns holding the precious flags that were guarded by a squad of chosen men commanded by hard-bitten sergeants armed with spontoons. 'Rear rank! Port arms!' the Major called. The innermost rank of the square would hold its fire and so act as the battalion's reserve. The cavalry was a hundred paces away and closing fast, a churning mass of excited horses, raised blades, trumpets, flags and thunder.

'Front rank, kneel!' a captain called. The front rank dropped and jammed their bayonet-tipped muskets into the earth to make a continuous hedge of steel about the formation.

'Make ready!' The two inside ranks cocked their loaded guns, and took aim. The whole manoeuvre had been done at a steady pace, without fuss, and the sudden sight of the leveled muskets and braced bayonets persuaded the leading cavalrymen to sheer away from the steady, stolid and silent square. Infantry in square were just about as safe from cavalry as if they were tucked up at home in bed, and the redcoat battalion, by forming square so quickly and quietly, had made the French charge impotent.

Men in square were safe from cavalry yet horribly vulnerable to shell and roundshot. The infantry were steady and silent, performing the intricate drill that they had practiced for hours and hours and which now was saving their lives, and doing it in the knowledge that just one mistake by a battalion commander would be fatal. If a column was just a few seconds too slow to form square then the rampaging cuirassiers would be through the gap on their heavy horses and gutting the imperfect square from the inside. A disciplined battalion would be turned in an instant into a rabble of panicking fugitives to be ridden down by dragoons or slaughtered by lancers.

The French kept searching for an opportunity. Whenever a battalion was marching in a column of companies and so looked ripe for attack a sudden surge of horses would flow across the field and the trumpets would rally yet more horse to join the thunderous charge, but then the redcoats' column would break, wheel and march into square with the same precision as if they were drilling on the parade ground of their home barracks. The troops would mark time for an instant as the square was achieved, then the outer rank would kneel, the whole formation would bristle with bayonets and the horsemen would sheer away in impotent rage. A few impetuous Frenchmen would always try to draw blood and gallop too close to the square only to be blasted from their saddles, or maybe a British galloper gun would bloody a whole troop of dragoons or cuirassiers with a blast of canister, but then the cavalry would gallop out of range and the horses would be rested while the square trudged back into column and marched stoically on. The horsemen would watch them go until another flurry of trumpets summoned the whole flux of mounted men to chase yet another opportunity far across the field and once again a battalion would contract into square and once again the horsemen would wheel away with unblooded blades.

BEFORE THE WALLS

SIEGE AND STORM

I have the honour to summons the place.
Wellington

**My Emperor gave me the town to defend,
not to surrender.**
Barrie

> Indeed, there is no duty so truly harassing to a soldier as a protracted siege, and certainly none to which he feels so marked an aversion. A general action or assault brings matters to a speedier issue, and valour and military gallantry have there a more extended field; and except a disastrous retreat, there is no situation which damps the spirit and ardour of an army so much as a tedious siege.

Napoleon's forces held a number of fortresses which controlled the vital transportation and supply routes into the interior of Spain – fortresses which had to be taken - and could only be taken by '*vive force*.' This was because Napoleon had decreed that any Governor who surrendered a fortress without it having stood at least one assault would be shot.

If the rules of siege art were strictly followed the outcome should be inevitable victory. However, the British were invariably hurried, and were ever harassed as they were lacking in almost everything – the guns, the tools, the transport, the trained sappers and miners, and the engineers capable of fulfilling the scientific

pieces. The British gradually added more modern guns supplemented with Russian naval brass guns – notwithstanding endeavours to the contrary as even Wellington could not convince the Admiral (Nelson's Captain Thomas Hardy – who served under Admiral Horatio Nelson, the hero of Trafalgar, and was with him when he died.) to give up any of the 'Great Guns' from his ships. Within this collection, the calibre varied one gun to the next, the shot being unlike and unique. Each gun had to be placed in a battery reached by a series of trenches dug gradually closer and closer to the fortress, carrying along its own allied heap of shot.

THE BATTERING TRAIN

The number of bullocks required for the draft of the whole train was 4170 pairs (8340 beasts), and over one thousand militia spent several weeks being employed merely to repair the roads so this procession could pass. It took 5 pairs of bullocks to pull one 24 Pdr gun (9 feet 6 inches long, weighing 5,544 pounds), in good weather on good roads at 1 mile per hour, and 7 to 8 pairs in wet weather over bad roads. There were 892 carts to carry the rounds; therefore making two trips. 200 carts were to move the engineer's stores, and all was to be shipped by boats where practicable, then drawn by the bullocks over land.

Battering Train in March, 1812

16 24-Pounders
20 18-Pounders (Russian)
16 5_ or 24-pound Howitzers
10 18-Pounders in Reserve

One common bullock cart could carry :

40 shot for a 24 Pdr/or
20 8 inch shells/or
21 12 10 inch do./or
10 barrels of powder/or
60 16 Pdr shot/or
1 24 Pdr Carriage/w trucks

The French left spiked and stuffed guns in their wake. So significant effort was expended unspiking this ordnance

conditions for mounting a successful siege. The men of the British army in the Peninsula considered Wellington's task in bringing a siege, as they constantly referred to it, 'Herculean.'

If an escalade of the walls using ladders was not practical, trenches had to be built, under heavy fire, to bring guns in close enough to batter down the walls creating a breach for the soldiers to climb, fighting their way into the fortress of the enemy by assault so conquering and destroying the garrison snug inside.

But, before a single shovel was ever plunged into the soil a mountain of demanding logistical work had to be accomplished to simply get the battering train into place, as ships were the 'grand magazine' - situated far from the castle. The Duke of Wellington worked out that it should take about 62 days to move the stores, 52 siege, and 40 artillery guns, powder, shells, tools, and the supporting equipment of the 'battering train.' Only once all of these necessaries and the means of their transport had been identified, examined, repaired or renovated where needed, packed, marked, recorded, and assembled.

At the start of the war, coats of arms and cyphers on the available guns in the Peninsula gave some away as being near 200 years old, and others of the more serviceable type were obsolete eighteenth century to make it fit for service, and transport it to the front. Hundreds of soldiers gathered all the spent shot they could find in ditches and around old fortifications.

During one siege, the following supplies were consumed:

2,523 90 lb barrels of powder
31,861 round shots
1,826 common and spherical 5 ½ inch shells
1,659 rounds of grape and case shot
70,000 sand-bags
1,200 gabions
700 fascines
1,570 entrenching tools

The great battering train was moved up – a laborious, slow-coach affair, the great guns moving slowly along, with only a cavalcade of bullocks and hundreds of the Spanish peasantry carrying the shot and shell. Groups of officers with unusual solemnity talked of the coming storm, when ground would be broken, who were to lead the way, what divisions to be chosen, and who would describe the fall to friends at home. No one doubted the success of the enterprise, but no one ventured to say that his life was his own after the first gun was fired. There was a terrible day approaching, but nobody was afraid, and even bets were being frequently made on the day and hour of the opening ball.

'Give me ten guineas and I will give you a guinea a day until the town falls,' or as the case might be five, six, or seven guineas.

It had been a bit more than five months from the Duke's first directive to begin work on the battering train to the first shot fired, and he was pretty close on the time it actually took to move the whole mass from sea to walls.

Trench Work

At the onset of siege operations, the French garrison did not appear to think the red coats were in earnest;

a number of their officers came out under the shelter of a stone wall, within a half musket-shot, and amused themselves in saluting and bowing to us in ridicule; but, ere the day was done, some of them had occasion to wear the laugh on the opposite side of the countenance.

Patrick's day came round as usual, and on that fighting festival-morning the band and drums enlivened all Patlanders with the national tune. The parade was magnificent and imposing. The colours of each regiment proudly, though scantily, floated in the breeze; they displayed but very little embroidery. Scarcely could the well-earned badges of the regiments be discerned yet their lacerated condition, caused by the numberless wounds that they received in battle, gave martial dignity to their appearance and animated every British breast with national pride. All the bands by one accord played the same tune, which was cheered with shouts that bore ominous. The music played was the animating national Irish air, St. Patrick's Day. The same night 1,800 men broke ground 160 yards from the outer fort, protected by a guard of 2,000. The grand battery was called to open fire on the fortress as the massy picks struck the earth, and a terrific noise followed the breaking of that ground, so that some of the Irish soldiers were not altogether disappointed in having a bit of a shindy. The trench work was as dangerous as it was arduous, and now the work of death began in reality.

One day's trench-work is as like another as the days themselves, and like nothing better than serving an apprenticeship to the double calling of grave-digger and game-keeper, for we found ample employment both for the spade and the rifle.

It was no joke travelling by daylight up to within a stone's throw of a wall, on which there is a parcel of fellows who have no other amusement but to fire at everybody they see. The Beaux fired a shell or bomb about every two minutes. The size of some of the guns and mortars used in the fortress were wide enough to admit a man's head and shoulders, so when the shot and shell fell and ex-ploded, they left holes wide enough to bury a horse.

While relieving pickets in the trenches many of our men, instead of going quietly through the trenches, or parallels, in front of the walls of the town, used to show their contempt of danger by jumping out of them and running across in the face of the enemy's fire. One day, Palmer was executing this feat with some others, when a cannon-shot fired by the French, struck the ground and hit him on the back. He fell. We thought he had been killed, but to our surprise, a moment later he jumped up unhurt. The ball had glanced off his knapsack. In commemoration of this event, he became known as the 'bomb-proof man.'

Ears and senses were astounded by the conflicting peals of the artillery and musketry, which, bursting at once on the stillness of the night, gave an appalling shock. Occasionally, the atmosphere was partially illuminated by the comet-like fusees of the bomb in their passage towards us; in a few instances they burst in the air within view, affording a momentary respite from the dread of their effects. It was possible to trace the flight of the shells through the darkness by their portentous trains, and see them bursting in the air, and shedding their 'fire-shower of ruin.'

In the meantime, gabions, (round wicker baskets filled with dirt and piled up to provide protection) continued to be brought up from the rear, and placed close to each other, six deep. Their carriage was truly a perilous service; the men were without shelter of any kind, and as they advanced with their unwieldy burthens, many were killed or wounded under the eyes of their comrades. Every minute we heard from the works going forward the cries of '*I'm wounded!*' whilst the men who still remained un-hurt, toiled on with a furious assiduity, in order to get under cover.

Siege Tools

Spunges
Ladles
Kegs of Grease
Painted Covers

Spare axle-trees
Water Buckets
Gun locks
Spare yarn and ratline
Streak nails
Spades
Felling axes
Pick axes
Bills
Sand bags
Rope
Twine for choking cartridges
Wad Hooks
Hand Spikes
Large and Small Tarpaulings
Forge Carts compleat
Spare linch pins and washers
Laboratory tents
Tool Chests
Lanthorns
Coals
Shovels
Broad axes
Hand hatchets
Hoops for powder barrels
Carpenters tools
Mallets

'Immediately a shell fell, every man threw himself flat upon the ground until it had burst.' 'Here's another brute! Look out!' Under fire from the enemy, and in the very jaws of death, many of the soldiers amused themselves by singing all manner of obscene songs; and when one of them, who was struck by a ball, and fell dead at my feet, his comrade, who was standing at his other side, looking at me, said, 'Never mind, Sir, a miss is as good as a mile.'

The shot continued to fly over with a fearful noise; and owing either to the distance they had come, different degrees of velocity, or causes unknown, they seemed to emit a variety of sounds – the soldier's music – the cannon booming forth through the calm frosty air of the night its sonorous eloquence.

They must be an unmusical pair of ears that cannot inform the wearer whither a cannon or a musket played last, but the various notes emanating from their respective mouths admit of nice distinctions. The quantity of grape and musketry aimed at our particular heads made a good concert of first and second whistles, while the more sonorous voice of the round shot, travelling to our friends on the left, acted as a thorough bass.

The elements often adopted the cause of the besieged; for scarcely had the ground been taken up when a heavy rain commenced and continued, almost without intermission, for a fortnight; in consequence thereof the pontoon-bridge connecting us with our supplies was carried away by the rapid increase of the river.

The men marched to the trenches through mud; and they worked nearly midleg deep in mud; and to make all more miserable, they had to sleep in a muddy camp.

At times, the scale of operations required every man to be actually in the trenches six hours every day, and the same length of time every night. This, with the time required to march to and from them, perhaps as much as five miles away, through fields more than ankle deep in a stiff mud, left us never more than eight hours out of the twenty-four in camp, and we never were dry the whole time.

Under cover of darkness, work parties cast up intrenchments, rose batteries, carried gabions, *fascines* (bundles of long sticks tightly tied up together), and dug with picks, spades and shovels. The enemy's light-balls were constant, aiding the musketeers planted to gall the men in the trenches, and their round shot and heavy thirteen-inch shells followed in abundance.

One day a large shell dropped into the trenches, near a Serjeant, who, to evade its effects, caught it up like a large putting-stone, and, to the terror and astonishment of many, threw it over the bastion, where it exploded without doing the smallest mischief.

A smartish frost or some snow on the ground, rendered the duties of the trenches extremely harassing. When the rain was unceasing, water accumulated in the trenches, the men being ankle-deep up to two feet of water so that

> the work of the spade was almost useless, since the liquid mud that was shovelled up ran away in streams out of the gabions into which it was cast, and refused to pile up into parapets for the trenches, spreading out instead into mere broad accumulations of slime, which gave no cover, and had no resisting power against the round shot of the garrison. The earth thus saturated with water, fell away, the works everywhere crumbled.

In a state of awful inactivity the covering patrol lay listening till near daylight; and though the firing of the artillery of the garrison continued without intermission, yet some dropped into a kind of sleep, from which many were destined never to awaken in this world.

On the noise of this explosion I started up, and the first object that met my half-opened eyes was a German soldier, whose knapsack was on fire, shouting lustily to get it off his back. It appeared that the fusee of the shell having caught his cartridge box, it blew up, setting his knapsack in a blaze, and in his terror and confusion he was unable of himself to get rid of his fiery burden.

At daybreak a large shell alighted on the brow of the hillock, and giving a few rapid rolls, burst between the legs of a sergeant, tearing off his thigh, and killing or wounding seventeen others.

Throwing up new works,

> a round shot passed pretty near my cranium, I thought I was wounded, my head ached violently. I felt the pain a long time and it was with difficulty I could perform my duty. Had I been working in a place where there was no danger I

certainly should have given up, but here I was ashamed to complain, lest any of my comrades laugh at me.

The enemy soon discovered the time fixed for reliefs, and on entering the trenches, they gave us a welcome with a pretty brisk cannonade and a fire of shells. Though we came into the trenches at *double-quick*, several were killed and wounded. When the shower of missiles was over, the men again emerged, recommencing like moles, to bury ourselves into the earth, – a curious expedient to avoid that ceremony at the hands of others.

During the day the enemy slackened their fire and as the workers were by this time nearly sheltered, little loss was for a time sustained. The chief annoyance was their shells; wherever a group sought shelter, shells were almost certain of falling immediately after; and although their near approach was announced by the smoke of their fusee, and a kind of whistling noise, men were in a state of perpetual agitation to elude them.

A shell is coming here, sir. I looked up, and beheld it approaching me like a cricket ball to be caught; it travelled so rapidly that we had only time to run a few paces, and crouch, when it entered the spot on which I had been sitting, and exploding, destroyed all our night's work.

The Portuguese knew the position of all the enemy's guns which could bear upon them, and had one man

posted to watch them, to give notice of what was coming, whether a shot or a shell, who, accordingly, kept calling out, '*bomba, balla, balla, bomba,*' and they ducked their heads until the missile past: but sometimes he would see a general discharge from all arms, when he threw himself down, screaming out '*Jesus, todos, todos!*' meaning 'everything.' In several instances the shells, after their fall, rolled about, sometimes like enormous footballs, and passing over the bodies of several who had fallen flat, exploded without doing the least injury.

An officer of ours one morning before daylight was sent opposite to one of the enemy's guns which had been doing a great deal of mischief the day before, with about thirty riflemen along with shovels to dig holes about 150 yards from the enemy's embrasures – looking like so many little graves – as near as possible to the walls, for the delectable amusement of firing at the embrasures for the remainder of the night. The enemy threw frequent fire balls among us to see where we were; but as we always lay snug until their blaze was extinguished, they were not much the wiser, except by finding, from having some one popt off from their guns every instant, that they had some neighbours whom they would have been glad to get rid of.

This officer soon had the satisfaction of knowing the effect of this practice by seeing the 'Mounseers' stopping up the embrasure with sandbags. After waiting a little he saw them beginning to remove the bags, when he made his men open upon it again, and they were instantly replaced without the guns being fired. Presently he saw the huge cocked hat of a French officer make its appearance on the rampart, near to the embrasure. Although knowing, by experience, that the head was somewhere in the neighbourhood, he watched until the flash of a musket, through the long grass, showed the position of the owner. Then calling one of his best shots, he desired him to take deliberate aim at the spot and lent his shoulder as a rest, to give it more elevation. Bang went the shot, and it was the finishing flash for the Frenchman, for they saw no more of him, although his cocked hat maintained its post until dark.

Our batteries were supplied with ammunition from the artillery park by the Portuguese militia, a string of whom used to arrive every day, reaching nearly from the one place to the other (twelve miles), each man carrying a twenty-four pound shot and cursing all the way and back again. At times there was such a shortage of ammunition that a reward was offered for every shot brought to the depot, and from this precarious source a considerable supply was obtained. The Engineers give a shilling a piece for all the large French shot that are brought and sixpence for the smaller. The men go out to look for them and stand watching the places where they hit, running the chance of being hit for the chance of getting a shilling or two.

The grand battery for the siege guns was yet uncompleted, and without cannon; the great ramparts of earth cast up preventing much injury, either by round or grape shot. Yet the situation was even more perilous and irksome than an any former occasion. By this time the besieged had arrived at such fatal precision, as to the due distance of throwing their shells, which mostly either fell on the gabions, or dropped into the trenches, rendering this place as unsafe as any other within range of their guns. In order to reconnoitre the trenches, officers had to creep on all fours to avoid the sharpshooters who were on the lookout and fired, often with great accuracy, at every head they saw.

An officer of the engineers getting on the bastion to view the enemy's fortifications, to which the guns were about to be opposed, remained standing with a spy-glass for about ten minutes. Turning round, he stooped a little, ready to jump down, when a cannon-shot carried away his head, his glass dropping from his hand as his body fell into the trenches.

We had a hard struggle for his instrument while the shot were flying over our heads: so callous had we become by custom to every sense of danger, that death had lost the greater part of his grim and grisly terrors.

The garrison fire was retaliated briskly, throwing red-hot shot against the fort - the process being very simple. An ordinary bellows will heat the furnace, from the furnace they are carried in iron crab claws and some

good wads of turn are placed between them and the powder, in less than an hour causing the buildings to be partially on fire. By taking aim at those exposed 'when loading their cannon at the embrasures this deliberate work of death was pretty successful, as was evident from the irregular discharge from those parts ex-posed to the effects of the British unceasing shot – 'our iron-tongued oratory' the most convincing.

To pass the dreary hours in the trenches, some men found amusement by putting their caps on the muzzle of their firelocks and just shewing them over the breastwork. But, sport was turned to advantage – stationing some good shots under cover, a few caps are shewn for a decoy, and some of the enemy eager to make the red coats pay for peeping would expose themselves. However, amusement could be carried too far:

> **One of our men had the misfortune to carry his death in his hands, under the mistaken shape of amusement. He thought that it was a cannon-ball, and took it for the purpose of playing at the game of nine-holes, but it happened to be a live shell. In rolling it along, it went over a bed of burning ashes, and ignited without his observing it. Just as he had got it between his legs, and was in the act of discharging it a second time, it exploded, and nearly blew him to pieces.**

Though some few of us, in the course of each night, by chance-shots, got transferred from natural to eternal sleep, after a French hit. Men were sent out to pick up dismembered limbs which had been scattered about by the shells, so as to prevent the effect it might have on the courage of the Portuguese.

SORTIES

A man working in the trenches suddenly shouted with an oath that the French were coming on, and instantly sprang out of the trench like a tiger, following his comrade, just such another fine fellow. Two or three French dragoons at that instant fired their pistols into the trenches, having approached within a few yards without being perceived. We had just entered the mouth of the parallel, and all joined in a simultaneous attack on the

enemy's infantry, without regard to trenches or anything else. The French being beaten out of the advanced lines, retired and formed line under the castle. They gained the works before our men could seize their arms. The confusion was great at the first onset. Those on guard and the working men were driven out of the trenches, and the cavalry sabred many in the depôts at the rear. The Guards immediately rallied and drove the enemy out of the works at the point of the bayonet, when many lives were lost. A part of the embankment was thrown into the trenches, and the enemy carried away almost all the entrenching tools, carrying off several shovels, etc., without asking leave. We lost one hundred and fifty men in killed and wounded during the attack.

The enemy repulsed, were next assailed in their turn. The red coats were ordered to advance, and they sprang over the rampart with alacrity. The French had by this time got under cover of their guns, which now commenced a most destructive fire; the red coats suffered severely, the grape-shot literally pouring upon them, retiring into the trenches, half-filled with the dying and the dead. Those of the French smelled strongly of brandy, of which they were reported to have had a double allowance that morning. Before the firing had entirely ceased, the light companies from the camp appeared on the road; and at the same time their commander was observed to fall from his horse, being struck on the thigh by a grape-shot.

> On returning to our former station, we had to cross the road near the bridge, where so many had fallen on our advance, on which the fort again opened its guns, but not with such destructive effect as before. Amongst the dead was recognised our fugleman, with his head and shoulder besmeared with blood and brains; and some observing that he was alive, gave him a push with their feet, on which he moved his eyes, and we hurried him into the trenches. It was soon discovered that he was not even wounded, and that the blood and brains must have been those of the person who covered him in the ranks, and whose head had been struck off by a cannon-shot, and dashed against his with a force by which he had been knocked

down and stupified. For some time he was unconscious of his situation, and at length complained greatly of his head, which we bound up, and he remained lying in the trenches till our relief arrived. He did not recover the effect of this shock for several days, though as brave a man as any in the regi-ment. On counting our files, it was found that of the eighty men who set forward to oppose the sortie made by the enemy, exactly forty were en-abled to resume their stand in the ranks.

THE STORM

We go out to look at the breach as you did the comet.

The effect of our 24-pound shot upon the wall gave notice that the breaches would soon be practicable, and, a storming party was selected for the assault on the following night.

THE FORLORN HOPE

On the eve of the storming of a fortress, when the breaches were ready, captains of companies, on private parade, would inform the men that the place was to be taken. Those men volunteering to head the stormers would step forward to the front and have their names taken down by the officer, and many of our men came forward with alacrity for this deadly service. If none offered themselves, the first men for duty were selected. The forlorn hope, designated by the French in the equally appropriate term *les enfants perdus*, or 'lost children,' always leads in the first attack. An Irishman whose only fortune was his sword volunteered to lead the forlorn hope.

An order arrived for 100 men, 2 Captains, 4 subalterns from the Division for the storming party. This is one of the highest honours the division could have received. The senior officer of each rank always has the choice. Our officers were called together & the colonel told us the business. The senior captain was not present but came up during the time of the conference. The Colonel said,

'Captain, we are to give the storming party tonight. Several captains wish to go. Will you allow it, being senior?'

He said, '*No, sir, I will go myself.*'

Two subalterns present declined. This is not esteemed a shadow of a disgrace. When an officer offers on a service of this kind it is done without any bombast; they look serious and pale. The act tells this is not from fear. The sergeants have been nearly quarrelling, saying, 'I have been on 1 & 2 (some of them 3), why may I not go on this?'

It was the rule in the services that those, both officers and men, who form the forlorn hope and the storming party, are volunteers - these being services of extreme danger - and which generally procure for the officers who survive a step of promotion. For commissions from merit in the field were like angel's visits — few and far between! Although a subaltern who led a 'forlorn hope' might reckon on death or a Company, or a Field Officer, if he survived, could reckon on a brevet-step. For all other ranks, officers, non-commissioned officers and men alike there was no prospect of advancement, for in most instances, no reward was ever given. None the less there were as many applicants for a place in the ranks of the 'forlorn hope' as if it led to the highest honours and rewards. Some of those fortunate to have survived the

forlorn hope were distinguished with a badge of laurel on the right arm, with the letters VS for 'valiant stormer' placed beneath the wreath — given by their commanding officer as a testimonial of their gallant conduct. Some received the sum of six dollars. Others received nothing.

The selection of the candidates for this service created amongst the rejected great jealousy and discontent. An offer of £20 was made and refused for an exchange, showing the value attached to this service. One bugle-major cast lots to determine who would go on this momentous errand. One of the buglers, who had been on a forlorn hope, offered the bugle-major two dollars to let him go instead. The bugle-major was reported to the adjutant for taking bribes, and he was removed from the forlorn hope.

Those who composed this forlorn hope were free from duty that day, so I went to the river and had a good bathe. I thought I would have a clean skin whether killed or wounded, for all who go on this errand expect one or the other. At 9 o'clock at night, we were paraded - it was then dark - and half a pound of bread and a gill of rum were served out to each man on parade.

A number of non-commissioned officers of the brigade met at sunset under some apple trees, for the purpose of bidding goodbye. The liquor went round in full bumpers, to the health of distant friends. With a few good songs and jokes, we parted, with hearty wishes for each other's safety.

There never was a pair of uglier men, but a brace of better soldiers never stood before the muzzle of a Frenchman's gun.

'Well,' said the Captain, 'what do you think of tonight's work?'

The Major seemed in rather low spirits. *'I don't know. Tonight, I think, will be my last.'*

'Tut, tut, man! I have the same sort of feeling, but I keep it down with a drop of this,' and he handed his calabash to the Major.

'A Lieutenant-Colonel or cold meat in a few hours.'

In the trenches in front of the city, from whence came a very smart fire of shot and shell, giving us an idea of the warm reception to be expected on our visit that night, the entire company gathered round the little party of stormers, each pressing to have a sup from his canteen. They shook hands with friendly sincerity, and speculated on who would outlive the assault.

Darkness closed over the city, and our imaginations became awake to the horrors of the coming scene. The stormers were ordered to 'fall in' and 'form,' and we moved near the walls which protected us from the enemy's shot.

'The spirit of the soldiers rose to a frightful height – there was a certain something in their bearing which told plainly that they had suffered fatigues of which they had not complained, and seen their comrades and officers slain around them without repining, but that they had smarted under the one and felt acutely for the other. They smothered both, so long as body and mind were employed, but now, before the storm, they had a momentary licence to think, and every fine feeling vanished—plunder and revenge took their place. A quiet but desperate calm replaced their usual buoyant spirits, and nothing was observable in their manner but a tiger-like expression of anxiety to seize upon their prey.'

Each arranged himself for the combat in such manner as his fancy would admit of some by lowering their cartridge-boxes, others by turning them to the front for more convenient use; others unclasped their stocks or opened their shirt collars; others oiled their bayonets. Those who had them took leave of their wives and children — an affecting sight, but not so much so as might have been expected, because the women, from long habit, were accustomed to such scenes of danger.

We felt a dead weight hanging on our minds; had we been brought hurriedly into action, it would have been quite different, but it is inconsistent with the

nature of man not to feel as I have described. The long warning, the dark and silent night, the known strength of the fortress, the imminent danger of the attack, all conspired to produce this feeling. It was not the result of want of courage, as was shown by the calm intrepidity of the advance when we came in range of the French cannon.

In proportion as the grand crisis approached, the anxiety of the soldiers increased not on account of any doubt or dread as to the result, but for fear that the place should be surrendered without standing an assault. For singular as it may appear – although there was a certainty of about one man out of every three being knocked down – there were, perhaps, not three men in the three divisions who would not rather have braved all the chances than receive it tamely from the hands of the enemy. So great was the rage for passports into eternity in our battalion on that occasion that even the officers' servants insisted on taking their places in the ranks.

Our troops were formed without knapsacks. The order of dress was trousers rolled up to the knee without socks or packs.

Pile knapsacks by companies.
Fall in and move off silently.

THE ORDER OF ATTACK:

Each Division left 1,000 men as a Reserve. The two Brigades of the Light Division were formed in 'close column of companies,' left in front. The covering-party ('firing-party') formed up in front of the Brigade. Next, four volunteers carrying ropes which they hoped to be able to pull aside the *chevaux-de-frize* of sword-blades. Then followed the 'forlorn hope.' The 'storming party' consisted of 100 men from each Regiment of the Light Division. Following close on the storming party were the rest of the Division. All was now in readiness for the signal to attack.

All 'in silent muster and with noiseless march' the soldiers moved simultaneously to the posts allotted them. Hay-bags, hatchets, and scaling-ladders were provided and distributed to each advance party according to the requirements of their respective services.

ATTACK

Soldiers! the eyes of your country are upon you. Be steady, be cool, be firm in the assault. The town must be yours this night. Once masters of the wall, let your first duty be to clear the ramparts, and in doing this keep together.

We were on the brink of being dashed into eternity, and among the men there was a solemnity and silence deeper than I ever witnessed before.

British cannon opened most musically upon the town. *Johnny* has hitherto had it all his own way in administering to the comfort of many, and most suddenly and unexpectedly sent them, I trust, to another and better world. For on this little spot all the fiercer passions of the human heart are busy in the breasts of each individual of both parties, investing and invested. Moralising will not do now; death or glory, a golden chain or a wooden leg, 'England expects every man will do his duty.' These are the only feelings that can make the

scene of death and destruction palatable to a Christian: King, Church, and Country to fight for. Every man carried his life in his hands; hope lived in the hearts of all. Many were our difficulties, and there was no suspension of the firey trial.

The night was dry and cloudy, the trenches and ramparts unusually still—lights were seen to flit here and there—while the deep voice of the sentinels proclaimed, *Sentinelles! Garde-à-vous!* – 'All's well.' The British, standing in deep columns, as eager to meet that fiery destruction as the French were to pour it down, were both alike, gigantic now in terrible strength and discipline, resolute, and determined to win or die.

ADVANCE

The expected signal, a rocket, went up from one of our batteries. The Major gave a prompt order.

> **It was no sooner said than done, and I and my front-rank men were immediately tapped on the shoulder for the ladder party, and I gave up all hope of ever returning.**

The dreadful strife now commenced. The thundering cheer of the British soldiers as they rushed forward through the outer ditch, together with the appalling roar of all arms sent forth in defiance from within, was tremendous.

With all its defects, a night attack has the advantage of concealing from the view much of danger and of difficulty that if seen might shake the nerves. But there was no time then for hesitation, no choice for the timid; the front ranks were forced onwards by the pressure from the rear, and as men fell wounded on the breach, there they found their (living) grave, being trodden into and covered by the shifting rubbish displaced by the feet of their comrades. Some few, more lucky, when wounded, rolled down the slope into the ditch, where they called in vain for that assistance which could not then be afforded them, and they added by their outcries to the wildness of the scene.

Our bugles were continually sounding the advance. The cry of 'Bravo! Bravo!' resounded through the ditches and along the foot of the breaches. The scene that ensued furnished as respectable a representation of hell itself as fire and sword and human sacrifices could make it; for in one instant every engine of destruction was in full operation.

There the balls came, as nearly as I can guess, about 20 in a minute within a yard of my head. As we were running one or two dropped on the grass every minute & were left. They now fell very fast.

Men leaped into the ditch, of whom 500 volunteers, being foremost, were dashed to pieces with shot, shell, and powder barrels. The Light Division stood for a moment in horror at the terrific sight; then, with a wild shout dashed with one accord into the fiery gulf, and, with the light of a blaze of fire-arms from above. One hundred men were drowned in the inundation (for at this time the sluices were opened, and the water let into the ditch from the river), seeking for the main breach, and got crowded and mixed together. The only light was that of the flashing guns, pouring death and destruction among them. The confusion was great, but all cheered like thunder; the French cheers also were loud and terrible. The bursting of grenades, shells, and powder-barrels, the whizzing flight of blazing splinters of barrels, the loud voices of the officers, and the heavy groans of the dying, were sufficient to create a terror in-describable.

We had about a mile to go to the place of attack, so off we went with palpitating hearts. I never feared nor saw danger till this night. As I walked at the head of the column, the thought struck me forcibly - you will be in hell before daylight! Such a feeling of horror I never experienced before. On our way to the wide ditch that surrounded the wall of the town were laid small bags, filled with grass, for each man to take up as he passed along, to throw into the ditch to jump on, that we might not hurt or break our legs, as the ditch was eight or nine feet deep. A party were in the rear with short ladders to be put into the ditch, and to be carried across for the men to ascend to the surface near the wall.

The word was now given to the ladder party to move forward. There were six of us supporting the ladder allotted to me, and I contrived to carry my grass-bag before me. We were accompanied at each side by two men with hatchets to cut down any obstacle, such as *chevaux-de-frize*, that might oppose us.

Being apprized of our intentions, the enemy threw out fireballs in every direction, and from total darkness they changed the approaches into a state light as day. By this means they were enabled to see the direction of our columns, and they opened a fire of round and grape shot which raked through them killing and wounding whole sections. We still advanced, silent as before, save for the groaning of our wounded comrades, until we reached a sort of moat about fifty feet wide formed by the inundation of the river; here we had to pass rank entire, the passage only being capable of admitting one at a time. On this place the enemy had brought their guns to bear, and they kept up such a fire of grape and musketry on it that it was a miracle that any of us escaped.

The ladders were 24 feet long. They were the common sort of ladder, such as are used by builders; and are made of *castano* (chestnut) trees in the woods nearby by the men of the Staff Corps. The whole face of the wall, being opposed by the guns of the citadel, was so swept by their discharges of round-shot, broken shells, bundles of cartridges and other missiles, and also from the top of the wall, ignited shells, &c., that it was almost impossible to twinkle an eye on any man before he was knocked down.

Just as I passed the palisade ditch there came a shot from a 24 pounder directly above this flat place and twelve men sank together with a groan that would have shook to the soul the nerves of the oldest soldier that ever carried a musket. I believe ten of them never rose again, the nearest was within a foot of me, the farthest not four yards off. It swept like a besom all within its range. The next four steps I took were over this heap.

When I got over the hill thrown up with the ditch under the wall the dead and wounded lay so thick we were continually treading upon them (I must tell the facts). The men were not so eager to go up the ladders as I expected they would be. They were as thick as possible in the ditch and, the officers desiring them to go up, I stopped about two minutes likewise. I perceived they were looking for their regiments rather than the ladders.

The storming party was soon hotly engaged. Columns moved on under a most dreadful fire of grape that mowed down our men like grass. The havoc now became more dreadful. Eight or ten officers, and men innumerable, fell to rise no more. Ladders were resting against the counterscarp from within the ditch. As fast as the men got down they rushed forward to the breaches, where a most frightful scene of carnage was going on. Fifty times they were stormed, and as often without effect, the French cannon sweeping the ditches with a most destructive fire. Lights were thrown down from the town that burnt most brilliantly, and made it easier to be shot at. This remained for a considerable time. The ditch now, to near the top of the breaches, was covered with dead and dying soldiers. If a man fell wounded, ten to one that he ever rose again, for the volleys of musketry and grape shot that were incessantly poured down made the situation too horrid for description.

We remained passively here to be slaughtered, as we could do the besieged little injury from the ditch.

The fireballs thrown into the ditches showed the advancing columns so clearly to the latent enemy that death or mortal wounds succeeded every round.

I was in a sort of frenzy stamping one of these lights out when an officer laid hold of me, saying, 'Leave it, or when the light goes out your feet will be blown to pieces, as there is a live shell connected with it.'

The storming-parties - volunteers and forlorn-hope - foremost; as they advanced they were ravaged with a tempest of grape from the ramparts, which staggered them. However, none would go back, although none could get forward, for men and officers falling fast from the withering and destructive fire choked up the passage, which every minute was raked with grape-shot, and the whizzing flight of the blazing splinters. Thus striving, and trampling alike upon the dead and wounded, these brave fellows maintained the combat. The stormers of another division, who had 300 yards of ground to clear, with extraordinary swiftness dashed along to the glacis, jumped into the ditch, eleven feet deep, and rushed on under a smashing discharge of musketry and grape, gaining the ascent; the foremost were blown to shatters, their bodies and brains plashing amongst their daring comrades behind, which only stimulated their determined exertions and doubled their strength.

Two bullets taken from the body of Private Costello, on display at the Royal Green Jackets' Museum, Hampshire.

Without a pause we dashed onwards, and precipitated ourselves into the ditch before the walls. We did not wait for the ladders for they were carried by the Portuguese, who ran away. The ladders did not make an appearance until their use had been superseded by a series of jumps made by our men into a trench 16 feet deep. When one or two ladders were procured, they were instantly placed against the scarp of the trench, and up we mounted to attack the breach. The very rungs (or steps of the ladders) were literally shot to atoms with musket balls, while underneath the dead and dying lay in heaps; some calling for a drink for God's sake. There the fire was constant and most deadly, and for some minutes, small bodies of men were swept away as they appeared. Those not knocked down were driven back by this hail of mortality to the ladders. Then ever and anon would fall upon us the body of some brave Frenchman whose zeal had led him to the edge of the wall in its defence, and had been killed by their own missiles or by the fire of our covering party.

'Let us throw down the ladders; the fellows shan't go out.' Some soldiers behind said, 'D____ your eyes, if you do we will bayonet you!'

Now the deafening shouts, crashing of broken ladders, and the shrieking of the crushed and wounded men, became loud amongst the din of war. Excited to madness, the comrades of the undaunted brave below, who swarmed again round the ladders, swiftly ran up, and were tossed over from the enemy above, who cried, 'Victory!' and 'Why don't you come in?'

So many soldiers followed on the same ladder, that it broke in two, and they all fell, many being hurt by the bayonets of their comrades round the foot of the ladder. A man's ankle was sprained, but it did not prevent his pursuing his career that night. The ladders were warm and slippery with blood and brains of soldiers dashed down from their top and lying broken in death at their foot.

> The ladder I mounted, like many others, was unfortunately too short, and I found that no exertion I could make would enable me to gain the embrasure or to descend. In this unhappy state, expecting immediate death from the hands of the ferocious-looking Frenchmen in the embrasure, I heard a voice above call out,
>
> 'Sir, is that you?'
>
> I answered 'Yes.' And the same voice cried out,
>
> 'Oh, murther! murther! what will we do to get you up at all, at all, with that scrawdeen of a ladtherr? But here goes! hould my leg, Bill;' and throwing himself flat on his face in the embrasure, he extended his brawny arm down the wall, and seizing me by the collar, with Herculean force, landed me, as he said himself, 'clever and clane,' on the ramparts. In the same manner five more were landed; and thus did this chivalrous soldier, with noble generosity, prefer saving the lives of six of his comrades at the risk of his own, one of the 'ragged rascals.'

AT THE BREACH

In the awful charnel pit we were then traversing to reach the foot of the breach. It was work of no small labour to have achieved the ascent under any circumstances, consisting as it did of a nearly perpendicular mass of loose rubbish, in which it was extremely difficult to obtain a footing.

The ramparts crowded with dark figures and glittering arms were on one side, on the other the red columns of the British, deep and broad, were coming on like streams of burning lava. It was the touch of the magician's wand, for a crash of thunder followed and with incredible violence the storming parties were dashed to pieces by the explosion of hundreds of shells and powder-barrels. Over and over, men who struggled up the steep rubble slope were met, in addition to the blast of frontal and flanking fire, by bursting shells and grenades hurled down on them besides barrels of powder and cartwheels which came bounding down among them overturning and maiming many. They tossed down lighted shells, and hand-grenades innumerable, which spun about fizzing and hissing amongst our feet. Some smashed men's heads in their descent, whilst others, exploding on the ground, tossed unlucky wretches in the air, tearing them asunder.

> The whole surface seemed to be vomiting fire and produced flashes of light alternating with momentary utter darkness.

We stood alone at the base of the breach, exposed to a tremendous fire of grape and musketry from its defences. For a minute we seemed destined to be sacrificed to some mistake as to the hour of attack – and after a moments consultation between the seniors, it was decided that it was better to die like men on the breach, than like dogs in the ditch; and instantly, with a wild hurra, all sprung upwards, absolutely eating fire.

> Major, it is as well to die in the breach as in the ditch, for *here* we cannot live.

The breaches, though large, were also very steep, and destroyed all who advanced. Thousands of live shells, hand-grenades, fireballs and every species of destructive

combustible were thrown down the breaches and over the walls into the ditches, which, lighting and exploding at the same instant, rivalled the lightning and thunder of heaven. This at intervals was succeeded by an impenetrable darkness as of the infernal regions. Gallant foes laughing at death met, fought, bled and rolled upon earth; and from the very earth destruction burst, for the exploding mines cast up friends and foes together, who in burning torture clashed and shrieked in the air. Partly burned they fell back into the inundating water, continually lighted by the incessant bursting of shells. Thus assailed by opposing elements, they made the horrid scene yet more horrid by shrieks uttered in wild despair, vainly struggling against a watery grave with limbs convulsed and quivering from the consuming fire. The roaring of cannon, the bursting of shells, the rattle of musketry, the awful explosion of mines and the flaring sickly blaze of fireballs seemed not of human invention, but rather as if all the elements of nature had greedily combined in the general havoc, and heaven, earth and hell had united for the destruction alike of the town and its furious assailants.

Now a multitude bounded up the great breach as if driven by a whirlwind, but across the top glittered a range of sword-blades, sharp-pointed, keen-edged on both sides, and firmly fixed in ponderous beams chained together and set deep in the ruins. For ten feet in front the ascent was covered with loose planks studded with sharp iron points, on which feet being set the planks moved and the unhappy soldiers falling forward on the spikes rolled down upon the ranks behind. The *chevaux-de-frize* extended the whole width of the breach, and was composed of a strong beam of wood, with sharp-pointed sword-blades fixed in every direction, they being generally about three quarters of a yard long. These were so closely set together, that it was impossible either to leap over them or penetrate between them, and the whole was so firmly fixed to the works at the top, that it could not be moved. In addition, they had fitted a number of long and thick planks, with spikes about an inch or more in length, and laid them all down the breach, but fixed at the top, so that it was impossible for any one to get up without falling on these. Every Frenchman had three or four loaded muskets at his feet, with leaden slugs over the usual bullet. Hundreds of our men had fallen, dropping at every discharge, which only maddened the living. The cheer was forever on, on, with screams of vengeance and a fury determined to win the town. The rear pushed the foremost into the sword-blades to make a bridge of their bodies rather than be frustrated in their success. Slaughter, tumult, and disorder continued. No command could be heard, just the wounded struggling to free themselves from under the bleeding bodies of their dead comrades. The enemy's guns within a few yards, at every fire opening a bloody lane amongst our people, who closed up, and, with shouts of terror as the lava burned them up, pressed on to destruction. Officers, starting forward with a heroic impulse, carried on their men to the yawning breach and glittering steel, which still continued to belch out flames of scorching death.

The fire continued in one horrible and incessant peal, as if the mouth of the infernal regions had opened to vomit forth destruction upon all around us. Even more appalling were the fearful shouts of the combatants, and cries of the wounded that mingled in the uproar.

Strange to say, I now began to feel my arms and legs were entire. At such moments, a man is not always aware of his wounds.

There was great confusion and terrible carnage under the continual fire of the French - who fought like demons. A death struggle of fiery antagonists took place at every corner, while our men most thoroughly maddened with rage and excitement, dashed at the breach with wild resolution. Here now was a crushing and most desperate struggle for the prize; the bright beams of the moon were obscured with powder-smoke. The springing of mines, powder-barrels, flashing of guns and small arms, rendered our men marks for destruction.

Small mines had been constructed all along in the ditch, which were exploded when it was filled with people, and which produced infinite mischief. On the top of the ramparts the enemy had a considerable number of shells of the largest size, ready filled and fused. When our people had filled the ditch below, these were lighted, and thrown over on their heads, each shell being capable of destroying from twelve to twenty men or more. They had beams of wood also laid on the ramparts, with old carriage-wheels, and every sort of missile imaginable, which were poured upon the unfortunate people below.

The moon rose, which cast a gloomy light round the place. Situated as I was this added fresh horrors to my view, the place was covered with dead and dying, the old black walls and breach looked terrible and seemed like an evil spirit frowning on the unfortunate victims that lay prostrate at its feet.

Around eleven o'clock, a host of Spaniards, thousands of whom, of all ages and sexes, had been collecting for some time from the neighbouring towns and villages to witness the storming and enjoy the brilliant spectacle; wherein thousands of men, women and children (including those of their own country), were to be shot, bayoneted or blown to atoms were informed the fortress had been taken.

On our right, we heard a loud cheering. This had a magical effect: regardless of the enemy's fire, and every other impediment, the men dashed in over the breach, carrying everything before them.

It was a scene sufficient to blanch the hair and to wither the heart.

At this period, also, the uproar exceeded all description; great guns roaring; musketry blazing; men shrieking from the agony of their wounds; bells ringing; and dogs barking, in such numbers, and with such fury, that it would seem that all the canine species of Estramadura were imprisoned in the fortress. Add to this, the sounding of our bugles in all directions, and the French drums beating with hurried and redoubled violence the *pas de charge*, whilst a murderous fire of shot, shell, and musketry poured on.

Supports came forward, all the officers simultaneously sprang to the front, when the Herculean

effort was renewed with a thrilling cheer, and the entrance was gained. The fighting was continued with fury in the streets, until the French were all killed, wounded, or prisoners; the town was fired in many places; many were killed in the market-place.

An Irish volunteer uttered an exclamation of surprise at the facility with which he could deprive a human being of life – his bayonet through the heart and the yell with which he gave up the ghost so terrified him that he started back, the implement of death in his hands, and apostrophising it, was heard to say: 'Holy Moses! How easy you went into him!' As the first taste of blood rouses the latent fierceness of the tiger's whelp, so this event seemed to have altered his nature.

The town was virtually ours. A voice was heard to shout above the uproar, 'They run, they run!' The enemy's resistance slackened, and they suddenly fled from before us, escaping right and left by boards laid across cuts, through the terre-pleine, by which the breach was isolated: the boards they left behind in their panic.

When the first fire ball was thrown it was about half past 9 o'clock, a quarter to 10 when we got over the bridge, quarter past 10 when the grape shot came, half past 10 when we got into the citadel, and near 12 before all was silent.

We have indeed done the Beaux.

IN THE CITADEL

I found myself standing amongst several French soldiers, who crowded round the gun in the embrasure. One of them still held the match lighted in his hand, the blue flame of which gave the bronzed and sullen countenances of these warriors an expression not easily forgotten. A grenadier leaned on the gun, and bled profusely from the head; another, who had fallen on his knees when wounded, remained fixed in astonishment and terror. Others, whose muskets lay scattered on the ground, folded their arms in deep despair; and the appearance of the whole group, with their huge bushy moustaches, and mouths blackened with biting the cartridges, presented to the eye of a young soldier at least an appearance sufficiently formidable.

> Don't mind them fellows, Sir, they were all settled jist afore you came up; and, by my soul, good boys they war for a start, and fought like raal divils, so they did, till Mr. S. and the grenadiers came powdering down on them with the war-whoop. Och, my darlint, they were made smiddreens of in a crack, barring that great big fellow you see there, with the great black whiskers, bleeding in the side, and resting his head on the gun-carriage. He was the bouldest of' them all, and made bloody battle; but 'tis short he stud afore Jim. He gave him a raal Waterford pucks that tumbled him like a nine-pin in a minute; and, by my own sow!, a puck of the butt-end of Jim's piece is no joke, I tell you, for he tried it on more heads nor one.

The Lieutenant was without a cap, his sword scabbard was gone, and the laps of his frock coat were perforated with balls. Indeed everyone who returned bore evident marks where they had been. Their caps, belts, firelocks, etc., were more or less damaged. I had three shots pass through my cap, one of which carried away the rosehead and tuft, my firelock was damaged near the lock, and a ball had passed through the butt. I had been some seconds at the *revêtement* (wall) of the bastion near the breach, and my red-coat pockets were literally filled with chips of stones splintered by musket-balls.

THE BUTCHER'S BILL

The sun rose in majesty and splendour, as usual in the blooming month of April, which in that climate is as our May. The country around was clothed in luxuriant verdure, refreshed by recent dew, which still clinging to each green leaf and blade in diamond drops reflected the verdant hue of the foliage upon which it hung till diamonds seemed emeralds. A thousand nameless flowers, displaying as many lovely colours, were on all the earth.

The great breach was fairly stained with gore, which through the vivid reflection of the brilliant sun, whose glowing heat already drew the watery vapours from its surface, gave it the appearance of a fiery lake of smoking blood. 'There lay a frightful heap of fourteen or 1,500 British soldiers, many dead but still warm, mixed with the desperately wounded, to whom no assistance could he given. There lay the burned and blackened corpses of those that had perished by the explosions, mixed with those that were torn to pieces by round shot or grape, and killed by musketry. Stiffening in their gore, body piled upon body, they involved and intermixed into one hideous and enormous mass of carnage; whilst the morning sunbeams, falling on this awful pile, seemed to my imagination pale and lugubrious as during an eclipse. There stood still the terrific beam across the top, armed with its sharp and bristling sword blades, which no human dexterity or strength could pass without impalement. The smell of burned flesh was yet shockingly strong and disgusting.

Elsewhere, the dead lay in heaps, numbers of them stripped, with every variety of expression in their countenance, from calm placidity to the greatest agony. They displayed the most ghastly wounds. Here and there, half-buried under the blackened fragments of the wall, or reeking on the surface of the run, lay those who had been blown up in the explosions, their remains dreadfully mangled and discoloured. Strewed about were dissevered arms and legs. In one spot lay nine officers. A colonel came and he looked very dull. 'Do you not know that my brother was killed last night?' In a flood of tears he pointed to a body. 'There he lies.' He had a pair of scissors with him. 'Go and cut off a lock of his hair for my mother. I came for the purpose, but I am not equal to doing it.'

I retraced my steps of the night before. I passed many wounded, indeed there were some in every place. I saw 8 or 10 shot through the face, their heads one mass of clotted blood, many with limbs shattered, some shot in the body & groaning most piteously and, oh shame to the British soldiers, the fatigued officers could not get the men moved all day from their plunder &

intoxication! I went two or three times to the town, the last time the smell was horrible. You were continually treading upon feet or heads.

> Let any man picture to himself this frightful scene of carnage taking place in a space of less than a hundred square yards. Let him consider that the slain died not all suddenly, nor by one manner of death; that some perished by steel, some by shot, some by water, that some were crushed and mangled by heavy weights, some trampled upon, some dashed to atoms by the fiery explosions; that for hours this destruction was endured without shrinking, and that the town was won at last.

When the extent of the night's havoc was made known to Lord Wellington, the firmness of his nature gave way for a moment, and the pride of conquest yielded to a burst of grief for the loss of his gallant soldiers, he commented that

'Our loss has been very great. The truth is, that equipped as we are, the British army are not capable of carrying on a regular siege.'

In one siege and storm he had lost over 4,000 killed and wounded out of some 17,100 men – about 24%.

THE SACK

> *Sweet is*
> *Pillage to soldiers, prize-money to seamen.*
> *Lord Byron*

Soon after daylight, the bugle sounded for two hours plunder.

By the laws of war we are allowed to kill all found in a town that stands a storm.

> *I believe it has always been understood that the*
> *defenders of a fortress stormed*
> *have no claim to quarter.*
> *The Duke of Wellington*

A storm seemed to be a signal from hell for the perpetration of villainy which would have ashamed the most ferocious barbarians of antiquity. The surviving soldier, after storming a town, considers it as his

165

indisputable property, and thinks himself at liberty to commit any enormity by way of indemnifying himself for the risking of his life. The bloody strife has made him insensible to every better feeling; his lips are parched by the extraordinary exertions that he has made, and from necessity, as well as inclination, his first search is for liquor. This once obtained, every trace of human nature vanishes, and no brutal outrage can be named which he does not commit.

Confusion and uproar prevailed in the town. The scenes were of a most deplorable and terrific nature: murders, robberies, and every species of debauchery and obscenity were seen, notwithstanding the exertions of the officers to prevent them. The howling of dogs, the crowing of cocks, the penetrating cackle of thousands of geese, the mournful bleating of sheep, the furious bellowing of wounded oxen maddened by being continually goaded and shot at and ferociously charging through the streets, were mixed with accompaniments loudly trumpeted forth by mules and donkeys and always by the deep and hollow baying of the large Spanish half-wolves, half-bloodhounds which guarded

the whole. Add to this the shouts and oaths of drunken soldiers in quest of liquor, the reports of fire-arms, the crashing in of doors, and the appalling shrieks of hapless frantic women, the shrill screaming of affrighted children, the piercing shrieks and groans of the wounded, the savage and discordant yells. An uproar such as could issue only from the regions of Pluto that made you think you were in the regions of the damned.

The infuriated soldiery resembled rather a pack of hell-hounds vomited up from the infernal regions for the extirpation of mankind. Lust and rapine were perpetrating every crime and at the moment trampling upon every principle sacred and civil, moral and religious; at that very instant were the demons of rage ruining everything good and virtuous, destroying the properties and violating the rights of every family and of every habitation.

No house, church, or convent, was held sacred by the infuriated and now ungovernable soldiery, but that priests or nuns, and common people, all shared alike, and that any who showed the least resistance were instantly sacrificed to their fury. They had a method of firing through the lock of any door that happened to be shut against them, which almost invariably had the effect of forcing it open; and such scenes were witnessed in the streets as baffle description.

For two days the town was in possession of the victorious. A siege is always terrible, but the sacking of a town is an abomination. Here the inhabitants suffer the terrible vengeance of all the ferocity of the human species. An English army is perhaps, generally speaking, under stricter discipline than any other in the world; but in proportion as they are held tight while they are in hand, if circumstances occur to give them liberty, I know of no army more difficult to restrain when once broke loose. The moment that is the most dangerous to the honour and the safety of a British army is that in which they have won the place they have assaulted. While outside the walls, and linked together by the magic hand of discipline, they are heroes – flushed by victory; hurried on by the desire for liquor, and eventually maddened by drink, they will stop at nothing. They are literally mad, hardly conscious of what they are doing in such a state of excitement, and once they have forced themselves inside they become demons or lunatics – for it is difficult to determine which spirit predominates.

I was hoarse in endeavouring to restore order – my voice no longer audible.

There was no safety anywhere. The wine-shops were all in demand. If the men were not all drunk there were none of them quite sober, but very able to go on with the plunder. One fellow might be seen with a bag of dollars; another cove would take him into a wine-house, make him stupidly drunk, and carry off the douros; one or two more working in concert would knock this chap down, and rob him of his treasure. They brought all sorts of things into the camp, until the tents were supplied with furniture such as was never seen in a camp before. One fellow with a tattered red coat, grasping his firelock, was groaning under an old-fashioned eight-day clock; while another had a broad looking-glass on his back; chairs and tables, priests' vestments, ladies' dresses, beds, blankets, and cooking-pots, with sausages, and pig-skins of wine.

'Stop, Jack, and give us a dhrink ov that wine', some fellow would say (dressed in his half-bloody uniform, and on his head the sombrero of an old priest).

'Devil a drop, now; it's going to the camp.'

'Faith an' I'll tapt it for my-self, then', and slap goes his bayonet into the skin and out flows the wine. Then there is a wrangle, then they are friends, and both get jolly drunk and lie there helpless long enough. There were watches amongst them, gold and silver, some valuable ornaments, doubloons, and dollars. They were fond of parading their treasure, and more fond of drinking to excess; consequently these articles changed hands frequently as they got drunk, and the sober ones saved them the trouble of looking after their stolen goods.

The Duke rode into the town with his staff, on the evening of the second day, and was immediately recognised. A dozen or so of half drunken fellows collected to salute him, firing a volley of ball cartridge over his head, with a cheer, saying, 'There goes the owl chap that can leather the French!' and then they all cut away and hid themselves out of his sight.

But still the truth must be told: the besieging army were promised the sacking of the town when taken, and, notwithstanding all the devotion and bravery of the British soldier, this promise of pillage adds to his courage and determination. Therefore it became their reward, and as all the Spaniards in the city had timely notice of the siege, and were offered a free and safe escort away to any place of safety, those who chose to remain stayed at a fearful risk.

A PERSONAL REFLECTION

I shall now give you my feelings upon the affair & I doubt not that I shall have your sympathy. I marched into the town in good spirits. When the balls began to whiz I expected every one would strike me. As they increased I minded them less. I viewed calmly the town & to the whizzing of the balls soon became accustomed. When upon the bridge I was thinking where I should be struck. At the bottom of the hill I was accustomed to danger & would have marched up to a cannons mouth. When the grape shot came I felt much more for those that fell than I did for myself. When I trod upon the heap it was horrible. In the next 20 or 30 steps I trod

upon many dead that was not half so bad. I assure you my reflections were very serious ones and at the moment when I expected instantly to be summoned before the Judge that knows every thought as well as deed. These reflections threw shells into my soul that were more formidable than all the balls that were fired from the French batteries that night. I have the greatest reason for gratitude that at least I was not groaning with a shattered limb but, thank God, not a hair of my head was hurt and I caught no cold. I was never in better health in my life. I have walked through the hospitals, I have seen limbs amputated on the field, the dead lying in heaps like rats after a hunt, some thrown into a ditch. I have seen them afterwards putrid. This horrible scene I have contemplated over & over again.

OFFICER'S REFLECTIONS

Among the officers and staff, however, there was much bitterness about what were felt to be unnecessary losses sustained in the Peninsular sieges. They believed that the wondrous power of discipline could bind the whole together as with a band of iron, and in the pride of army none doubted their might to bear down every obstacle that man could oppose to their fury. However the losses attendant on the advance of a siege were blamed on the useless and most disgraceful tools furnished by the Storekeeper General's office in England, and a dearth of skills and trained men.

The considered opinion was that no army was ever so ill provided with the means of prosecuting such an enterprise. The ablest officers trembled when reflecting how utterly destitute they were of all that belonged to real service. Without sappers and miners they were compelled to attack fortresses defended by the most warlike, practised, and scientific troops of the age. The commonest materials, and the means necessary for their art, were denied the engineers, of which the army was deficient in any case, there not being more than thirty engineering officers in the whole Peninsula and almost no rank and file to serve under them for most of the War.

Wellington wrote back to England that the capture of this fortress:

affords as strong an instance of the gallantry of our troops as has ever been displayed. But I anxiously hope that I shall never again be the instrument of putting them to such a test as that to which they were put last night. I assure your lordship that it is quite impossible to carry fortified places by '*vive force*' without incurring great loss, and being exposed to the chance of failure, unless the army should be provided with a sufficient trained corps of sappers and miners. The consequence of being so unprovided with the people necessary to approach a regularly fortified place are, first, that our engineers – though well-educated and brave, have never turned their minds to the mode of conducting a regular siege, as it is useless to think of that which it is impossible, in our service, to perform. They think they have done their duty when they have constructed a battery with a secure communication to it, which can breach the place. Secondly, these breaches have to be carried by *vive force*, at an infinite sacrifice of officers and soldiers. These great losses could be avoided, and, in my opinion, time gained in every siege, if we had properly trained people to carry it on. I declare that I have never seen breaches more practicable in themselves, and the fortress must have surrendered with these breaches open, if I had been able to 'approach' the place. But when I had made the third breach on the evening of the 6th, I could do no more. I was then obliged either to storm or to give the business up, and when I ordered the assault, I was certain that I should lose our best officers and men. It is a cruel situation for any person to be placed in, and I earnestly recommend to your lordship to have a corps of sappers and miners formed without loss of time.

THE BATTLE GAINED

Next to the battle lost, the greatest misery is
a battle gained.
The Duke of Wellington

WOUNDED –
HORS DE COMBAT:

There was scarcely a man who had not
been wounded –
the prison of many a soul was broken up.

The roar of the battle is hushed; the hurry of action is over; let us walk over the corse-encumbered field. Look around, - behold thousands of slain, thousands of wounded, writhing with anguish, and groaning with agony and despair. Not long ago, the trampling of horses, the shout, the cry, the prayer, the death-stroke, all mingled their wild sounds on this spot; it is now, but for a few fitful and stifled groans, as silent as the grave. What is this? A battered trumpet; the breath which filled, this morning, its haughty tone, has fled, perhaps, forever. And here again, a broken lance. Is this the muscular arm that

wielded it? 'Twas vigorous, and slew, perhaps, a victim on this field; it is now unnerved by death. Who are these that catch every moment at our coats, and cling to our feet, in such a humble attitude?

We came to an open space where a number our badly wounded were lying wrapped in their blankets. They heard the rustle of our feet.

Where are you going?
We are retreating.
Will you leave us here?

We stole away, and left them to the mercy of the enemy and the mountain wolves, not being able to take them off. We tore ourselves away, and hurried to get out of sight. We could not bear it.

When a man is wounded, the corps he belongs to is generally in action and cannot spare from the ranks the necessary assistance, so that he is obliged to be left to the tender mercies of those who follow after. They generally pay him the attention due to a mad dog, by giving him as wide a berth as they possibly can – so that he often lies for days in the field without assistance of any kind. Those who have never witnessed such scenes will be loth to believe that men's hearts can get so steeled; but so it is – the same chance befals the officer as the soldier. Although the fate of those around might have been ours the next instant, our common weal, our honour, and our country's, alike demanded that every thing should be sacrificed to secure the prize which was now within our grasp; and our onward movement was therefore continued with measured tread and stern silence, leaving the unfortunate sufferers to doubt whether the stone walls around had not been their only listeners.

WOUNDS

Shots are very strange things. They fly fast and those struck by a ball do not always feel it at the time — a Sergeant of the Rifles received a ball in the head:

> **Am I dead? Am I dead?**

Poor fellow. He was mortally wounded, and it was with difficulty that I extricated myself from his deadly grasp.

> *You are wounded, Sir.*
> **God bless me! So I am.**

CLOSE CALLS:

Some fellows were always being hit, while others - a few others - went through all the war without a scrape, and it was not unusual for some men to receive two or three wounds each. Even the Duke of Wellington was hit more than once by a spent shot. Once it hit him in the leg, but he pushed on early next day after his friends, when there was another row and some slaughter, the common reaction. He probably did not even "return" the incident as a wound. Though all of these close calls were regaled around camp fires many times over in jokes and awe.

Every now and then some poor fellow was hit and tumbled over, the case resulting in no more than many a one carrying weight over the course, i.e. a bullet or two in the back of his knapsack. The ledden ball did have its way of bringing discomfort as well as salvation as it did for the Lieutenant who had his horn full of brandy slung on his back going into action, and was about to rejoice over it, but alas, the bottle was empty. A musket-ball played one of those practical tricks one hears of after a big fight. One passed through the horn during the row, and let off the brandy without any notice. He knew that he had been slightly wounded in the side, little knowing it was a cow's horn saved him!

A sergeant-major found his arm very stiff about the crook, as he said; no blood, nor mark of a shot-hole. He pulled off his jacket and found a ball lodged in his elbow-joint, which had run up his sleeve in this playful way. A young officer was shot through the nose, which, as he jocosely said, made him sneeze a bit!

Some men were generally in great luck, having their legs and arms broken by musket-shot, and none of them killed outright except Tim Casey, and he was only kilt. But he made a most horrible whilalaloo about it, crying out,

'Oh, murdher, I'm kilt entirely. I'll never see home — I'm ript up!' holding his bloody hand to his stomach.

'Let me see where you're kilt, Casey. There is no murdher here, everybody kills everybody—that's the order.' A ball struck one of his buttons, turned off, and ripped open the surface of his bread-basket from right to left without in the least spoiling his appetite.

Another bullet proved to be no more than a button off the front row of my jacket, which were very large! The ball had struck against my breast, and driven the button off into my left arm, leaving the shank on the jacket.

In the line of a narrow escape, a ball aimed to go right through one man's head, was turned by the scale of brass on his cap, opened a furrow across his forehead, baring the bone and passing away on the other side.

It was wonderful the multitude of extraordinary wounds that men received. Wounds in the feet and in the groin were the most painful and dangerous. A Lieutenant had both his eyes shot out. Another Lieutenant narrowly escaped the same dreadful calamity; the ball passed close under the eyes, breaking the bridge of his nose, and spoiling his beauty. I have seen men wounded in every part of the human frame — some wounds most extraordinary and severe — and yet the men recovered.

When wounds were abundant it was not considered a disadvantage to be low and lean in flesh, for the poorer the subject the better the patient! A smooth ball or a well polished sword will slip through one of your transparent gentlemen so gently that he scarcely feels it, and the holes close again of their own accord. But see the smash it makes in one of your turtle or turkey fed ones! The hospital is ruined in finding materials to reduce his inflammations, and it is ten to one if ever he comes to the scratch again.

During a brisk action, as I was in the act of pulling my trigger I received a wound in both legs, the ball glanced or scraped the skin just above the outside ancle of the left foot and passed through the gristle behind the ancle of the right just missing the bone, down I fell. I endeavoured to rise but found I could not stand and that my shoe was full of blood.

'The Devil's luck to ye' said Ned Eagan, 'For a fool, now can't ye be easey and lay quiet for a minute or so til we give them another charge, and send them in double quick over the hill.'

At this moment Hooker came to me and said, 'I hope Bill you are not much hurt, take some of this rum.'

'Arrah Tom' says Eagan 'now you would be the best fellow alive and so you would if you would just be after letting me wet my trottle with a drop of the crature.'

Hooker gave him his canteen saying 'you are welcome Ned.'

Ned wetted his 'trottle,' gave Tom the canteen shouting to the Frogs:

'Och my jewels, then bad luck to me if one of ye don't get this ledden pill through ye, then you may say that old Eagan's son is the biggest liar in all Ireland.' So saying he put in the cartridge. Hooker was employed in empting some of the rum into my canteen, and Eagan was busy in sending down the charge, when down he came on top of us. They did not give him time to fulfill his promise, he was shot through the body and in a moment was a corpse. I felt stunned, and, in a few moments, became faint, and dizzy, and fell. The first sensation which I was conscious of after my fall, was that of a burning thirst, universally felt after gunshot wounds.

The wounded were groaning on the heather all night,

and not a drop of water within reach. They always suffer extremely from thirst, and their cry is, "Water for God's sake!" I remember drinking more water on an occasion of this kind than I had done for a month previous.

FIELD HOSPITALS:

Directly after a battle, some of the wounded would have been carried off the field into a churchyard or such. Two long tables had been procured from some houses near, and were placed end to end amongst the graves, and upon them were laid the men whose limbs it was found necessary to amputate. Both French and English were constantly lifted on and off these tables. As soon as the operation was performed upon one lot, they were carried off, and those in waiting hoisted up: the surgeons with their sleeves turned up, and their hands and arms covered with blood, looking like butchers in the shambles. I saw as I passed at least twenty legs lying on the ground, many of them being clothed in the long black gaiters then worn by the infantry of the line. The surgeons had plenty of work on hand that day, and not having time to take off the clothes of the wounded, they merely ripped the seams and turned the cloth back, proceeding with the operation as fast as they could.

Many of the wounded came straggling into this churchyard in search of assistance, by themselves. I saw one man, faint with loss of blood, staggering along, and turned to assist him. He was severely wounded in the head, his face being completely incrusted with the blood which had flowed during the night, and had now dried. One eyeball was knocked out of the socket, and hung down upon his cheek.

A cavalry officer came up, perfectly sensible and had walked about half a mile. He asked the surgeon if he should make up his mind [that he was dying]. The surgeon told him he must not let his spirits droop. A cannon ball had taken his right breast off & his arm was smashed to a mummy close to the shoulder. He died 3 hours after. 5 minutes after a private of dragoons was brought in a blanket with his leg shot completely off at the knee, & the leg & foot lying by his side.

Owing to the Army having advanced and the few means of transport, many of the wounded suffered horribly. For three days after the battle, a great many were stilly lying, who had received no assistance nor were likely to till the next day, and had lain scorching in the sun without a drop of water or the least shade. On the ground were several patrols of Prussians shooting their own and the French wounded soldiers, who were beyond recovery. Although it seemed a piece of barbarity at the time, I am sure it was a great act of charity, as their sufferings must have been truly awful, with the heat and lack of anything to quench their thirst for three days under scorching sun. Many begged us to put them out of their misery.

The wounded, among whom there was a multitude of hurts (as the doctors called them), great and small, from the amputation of limbs to the scalping of heads were moved to the rear, some crawling off as well as they could, some making crutches of the barrels of the firelocks and their shoes – as the bullock drivers often ran away with their beasts and left the poor wretches. It is curious to observe that, in the rear of an army in battle, confusion and uproar generally exists while all in front is order and regularity; being thus a generally a queer place – the day is won and lost there a dozen times, unknown to the actual combatants. Fellows who have never seen an enemy in the field, are there to be seen flourishing their drawn swords, and "cutting such fantastic tricks before high heaven, to make angels weep," while others are flying as if pursued by legions of demons.

When possible, men tried to find shelter in nearby peasant homes, though this was hard won for the accessible was often horridly overcrowded once attained.

Lucky enough to get an old man to take me on his back, he carried me into his house, and placed me by a good fire. The first thing I did was to write with chalk on the door in large letters:

Provost Martial

This was the complete tallisman, the house was spelbound against Marauders.

The only conveyance for these poor cripples, with broken legs and arms and shattered shells, were some mules sent up by the Commissary. Two men were placed on each mule, with their broken limbs bandaged up in a way and dangling down. No help for it; the poor fellows were groaning with their sufferings all the way.

The bullock car was a mixed blessing. The men suffering the most severe torture from the jolting motion sustained at almost every movement, though a better answer than the English spring waggon.

> The springs of this machine were very strong, and the rough ground we passed over made them dance up and down in an awful manner. Bad as the movement of the bullock car was, this was ten times worse, if possible.

When night came on the assistant-surgeon got the wounded dismounted as quietly as was possible, and laid some upon dry ferns. We had nothing to eat or drink and not a spoonful of water for the dying men. I could not sleep for their moaning and groaning all night. I could not see them nor help them in the dark. When the morning was welcomed in, I found that many had passed away to the promised land; the mortal part was left where the spirit took its leave. We had no means here to bury the dead.

Those who had performed a long journey, through a barren country, and under a broiling sun – and their wounds remaining unattended and undressed all this while, were often in such a state as to defy description, soldiers on the march to the front doing what was possible within their means.

> There was no lack of willingness on our parts to assist them. We cleaned out the best houses in the place; spread straw, and, where we could find it, linen, for them on the floors, and gave ourselves up to the business of cleansing their hurts, the smell proceeding from which was fearful. Over and over again we were forced to quit the miserable patients in a hurry, and run out into the open air, in order to save ourselves from fainting; while they, poor fellows, reproached us, with a degree of bitterness which none of us cared, even in thought, to resent for a moment. We did our duty faithfully by our mutilated countrymen; so faithfully, indeed, that weeks passed away

ere I was able entirely to overcome the effect which the distressing occupation had produced upon me. I could neither eat nor sleep, for every thing seemed to be tainted with effluvia from those cankered wounds, and my dreams were all such as to make sleep a burden. Fortunately for us, however, we were not long condemned to the torture; for war must be fed for ever with new victims, and we turned our backs upon those already smitten, on the morning after we had met them.

Wounds festered from ignorance and neglect, and several of the poor soldiers died upon the road.

> Soldiers in general are like children, and must be directed as such; although they were frequently told if they exposed their wounds, the flies would deposit their eggs upon them, still they took no notice, and there was no officer present to enforce this command, so their wounds became completely alive with myriads of large maggots, the sight of which made me really shudder again. Oil was found the best thing to take them away, as when applied it killed them, obstructing their breathing. We had no means of keeping off the swarms of insects, and the slow pace that the bullocks went, made you feel the

vertical rays of the sun with redoubled force. We had some salt meat as rations, which, in the feverish state of our existence, we turned from with disgust; we very seldom got bread, generally biscuit, and that full of worms or mouldy.

Once arrived, the wounded came under the hand of the doctors. In this army there were men in charge of sick now who till they came never prescribed in their lives, and there are others who have had no practice beyond answering a prescription in an apothecary shop in England. Such are the men entrusted with the lives of soldiers, but it must always be the case in a great degree while the pay remains so small as to induce those only to enter the service who would starve at home. A surgeon was heard to say that he had no doubt that two-thirds of the deaths in this army were due to the inattention and ignorance of the medical officers.

'Oh, doctor dear!' he said, 'it's murdering me you are! Blood an''ounds! I shall die! — I shall die! For the love of the Lord don't cut me all to pieces!'

French and English soldiers were laid up together in the hospitals. In a long, broad room with a table down the centre were lying some twenty or thirty poor fellows, under the operation of the doctor's knives.

I must confess that I did not bear the amputation of my arm as well as I ought to have done, for I made noise enough when the knife cut through my skin and flesh. It is no joke I assure you, but still it was a shame to say a word, as it is of no use. For want of light, and from the number of amputations he had already performed, and other circumstances, his instruments were blunted, so it was a long time before the thing was finished, at least twenty minutes, and the pain was great. I then thanked him for his kindness, having sworn at him like a trooper while he was at it, to his great amusement.

An English soldier belonging to the 1st Royal Dragoons, evidently an old weather-beaten warfarer, while undergoing the amputation of an arm below the elbow, held the injured limb with his other hand, without betraying the slightest emotion; near to him was a Frenchman bellowing most lustily while a surgeon was probing for a ball near his shoulder. When the Englishman's arm was amputated, he struck the bawling Frenchman a smart blow across his cheek with the bloody part of the lost limb, holding it at the handwrist, then said, "Take it, and make soup with it, and stop your damned bellowing."

While lying in hospital — at all times a wretched place, from the groans of the numerous sufferers — I was placed under the immediate attendance of Sergeant Michael Connelly who, having recovered sufficiently from a slight wound, had been appointed sergeant to the hospital, and was in charge of our ward. He was one of the most singular characters I ever met with. If an awkward person and uncouth face had gained him the preferment, then his match could not be found anywhere.

Mike was exceedingly attentive to the sick, and particularly anxious that the dying British soldier should hold out a pattern of firmness to the Frenchmen, who lay intermixed with us.

'Hold your tongue, ye blathering devil,' he would say, in a low tone. 'Don't be after disgracing your country in the teeth of these 'ere furriners by dying hard. You are not at Elvas to be thrown into a hole like dog. You'll be buried in a shroud and coffin; you'll have the company at your burial, won't you? You'll have the drums beating and the guns firing over you, won't you? Marciful God! what more do you want? For God's sake, die like a man before these 'ere Frenchers.'

Mike, however, had a great failing - he drank like a whale, and as he did not scruple to adopt as gifts or legacies, the wine rations of the dying and the dead, he drank himself out of the world. As his patients remarked, he died like a beast.

The news of Mike's death spread like wildfire, and all his old friends, and the convalescents, crowded around to do honour to his remains. The coffin carrying the deceased sergeant, borne by four bearers, and with the usual complement of soldiers with the arms reversed, slowly wound its way through the city. Cavalier and foot soldier, drum boy and trumpeter, and all the women, children and camp followers in the locality, flocked to follow his remains. They reached the burial-ground, near the French battery, which had been taken by us some time previously. The bearers were about to enter the gateway, when they were suddenly aroused by a slight cry. It came from within the coffin, and was accompanied by a kind of scraping noise. They halted, paused, and listened. Surely it was Mike scraping! On they moved again doubtfully, but for a second time they heard the voice.

'Whist!' ejaculated the bearers, their caps moving almost off their heads.

'Oh blood and ouns!' said the voice. 'Where am I? Oh, bad luck to yer souls! Let me out, won't you? Oh, merciful Jasus, I'm smothered.'

The bearers bolted out from under the coffin, and in an instant a dozen bayonets were sunk under the lid to lift it. The crowd crushed forward to take a look. There lay Sergeant Michael Connelly, as stiff as a fugleman, but somewhat colder. One of the bearers was that blackguard, the cockney ventriloquist, and he joined in the astonishment as 'innocent' as you please! He winked at me, and I winked back.

'Ned,' he said, 'I'm blessed if I think he's dead. Why don't some of them there chaps go for a doctor?'

'To be sure,' cried the crowd, 'send for the doctor.'

Meanwhile a regular rush was made to press Mike to swallow some of his favourite liquor, but his teeth so obstinately opposed the draught, that when the doctor arrived, they pronounced that poor Mike was 'not himself'.

For some, wounds were but a pause in a war to which they returned to fight again — for others, it was war's end.

I was carried out of Spain, borne in a blanket, broken in body and depressed in mind, with all my brilliant prospects like myself fallen to the ground. Such is glorious war.

You grow familiar on service with death and sorrow; you do not weep –
but if he have an eye to observe, and a heart to feel,
few men see or suffer more than a soldier.

THE CRUCIBLE OF WAR

War, with all its terrible accompaniments, is a fearful sounding thing - a drama that has many subordinate plots - yet it is, nevertheless, a complicated and delicate web, the meshes of which require to be as delicately handled as if they were composed of the finest materials. The least false touch may destroy all its arrangement; and that which cost so much time and labour to render perfect, may be undone by falling into hands unable to appreciate its texture. If any one part give way, the whole machinery become unhinged — broken up; and the repairing of it oftentimes costs more than the original outlay, and the end sought for is lost!

Those unaccustomed to warfare, are apt to imagine that a field of battle is a scene of confusion worse confounded, but that is a mistake, for, except on particular occasions, there is in general no noise or confusion any thing like what takes place on ordinary field days in England. In soldiering, as in every thing else, except Billingsgate and ballad singing, the cleverest things are done quietly, and that seat of cleverness, that soul of armies, the mind of a great commander was all on the British side, in Wellington's knowledge-box! And nothing retarded his progress.

His plan was always to run no risks that were not absolutely necessary and to harass the enemy by placing him in situations where he must unavoidably suffer by privation and fatigue. This he did with "that Article," the British soldier, who, when let loose in the field with all his steam up, the difficulty was to keep him in check, to stop his onward rapidity. When he sees the enemy in his front, he fights for his Queen, fights for Old England, fights for victory, and always wins. The British soldier is a queer sort of biped, fierce in battle, full of a child's simplicity and kindness when over. He will tear the shirt off his back to bind up the bleeding wounds of his fallen foe, carry him away on his back to some quiet spot for medical care, lay him gently down, and divide with him the contents of his flask.

They say Wellington committed faults—what were they? England had no army until he made one. He landed in Portugal with 9,000 men, and beat back the armies of France to their own firesides. He had rare qualities as a commander. He overthrew the great conqueror Napoleon, the swell and dash of a mighty wave, before whom kingdoms fell. If you fight for England you should always win, and what English General was ever so victorious as Wellington?

After conquest one begins to count the cost. War is a great evil, and a very expensive trade. In this one England expended more than a hundred millions sterling money on her own operations, besides an immense expenditure on Spain and Portugal. Her land forces fought and won eighteen pitched battles, besides affaires and combats without number, took four great fortresses by siege, and sustained ten others. Two hundred thousand of the enemy were killed, wounded, and prisoners.

FIRST VICTORY

The whole French army had taken to their heels. As they passed on they broke down the bridges to impede our line of march. But we never came up with them again, nor smelt the perfume of tobacco and onions which tainted the air behind them. We halted, and there we heard by an express from Paris that Napoleon the Grand had abdicated, and that the Allies were in the capital of la belle France, and all the rest of it. This was all very serene, and I believe joyful news to most of us, for in reality we had enough fighting and marching and starving for a long time to come.

The general and universal feeling was that, for the present, we had had enough of campaigning, and that a little rest and time to refit would be desirable. The feeling of no war, no picquets, no alerts, no apprehension of being turned out, was so novel after six years' perpetual and vigilant war, it is impossible to describe the sensation. It was so novel that at first it was positively painful.

The news of the peace at this period certainly sounded strange in our ears, for it was a change that we never had contemplated. We had been born in war, reared in war, and war was our trade; and what soldiers had to do in peace was a problem yet to be solved among us.

There is nothing in this life half so enviable as the feelings of a soldier after a victory. Previous to a battle, there is a certain sort of something that pervades the mind which is not easily defined. It is neither akin to joy or fear, and probably anxiety may be nearer to it than any other word in the dictionary; but when the battle is over and crowned with victory the soldier finds himself elevated for a while into the regions of absolute bliss!

I do think that after all was over that I strutted about as important a personage, in my own opinion as ever trod the face of the earth; and had the ghost of the renowned jack-the-giant-killer itself passed that way at the time I'll venture to say that I would have given it a kick in the breech without the smallest ceremony.

There was no end to gaiety. There were balls, concerts, and evening parties, and entrée into all the theatres to any part of the house for a franc. The people seemed happy and rejoiced over the new order of things. The town had not suffered in the least during the killing and slaying outside. The Duke did not suffer a shot or shell to be thrown into the city when held by the vanquished troops, and of course gained the respect and esteem of the citizens for his consideration and humanity.

We would have remained willingly for weeks if we could. The situation was so charming, so peaceful. No parades nor drills, nor a chance of one's bones being broken with shot or shell. How wonderful was the feeling of quiet; no trampling of horses, nor clashing of arms, nor tir-whit of a shell, or the whop of a cannon-ball, splashing the mud in one's face, or perhaps the brains of your camarado. The first stage, homeward bound—it all appeared as a holy dream.

After six weeks of refreshing jollification, we got the route for Bordeaux. I sold my three horses to raise the wind and pay my debts.

In some districts, the men were on excellent terms with the French quartered in the neighbourhood. There were several little balls and hops; and here, for the first time, several young men began to dance quadrilles; in short, there was no want of amusement among this gay and lively people. To while away the time there were constant matches in running, jumping, and gymnastic exercises - dinners and feasts, the French bands playing "Patrick's Day" - former enemies singing and enjoying themselves in the French quarters until three in the morning.

Yet in other places there was much unpleasant work and bad feeling between French and English officers. Some were so habituated to fighting it seemed quite out of their power to give it up – like two game-cocks who meet on the same path, they must have a kick at each other! There was a feeling of deep jealousy amongst the French against the British as the ladies favoured the British officers with smiles, which made things worse. There were many quarrels, and the Duello came into practice. The French ladies not appearing to countenance any but those big Irishmen, sharp words were spoken against all red-coats, a great many frowns.

177

Swords were half unsheathed and dashed back into the metal scabbard with a sort of clang of defiance—the blood of St. Patrick was roused. Those gentle creatures, whose trade was killing and slaying, did not require much fuel to get up their steam. One, a battering-ram of himself, drew his stick half-way up through his left hand, and sent it down again with a bang on the floor, looking pistols and daggers. There were some sarcastic words, then a shove and a scuffle, which soon increased to something like an Irish row at Donnybrook Fair, when the Frenchmen were banged out wholesale. As the last of the blue-coats went rolling down the stairs, some one cried out, 'Exeunt omnes!' and all was quiet. Next morning was fixed for the Duello, the general finale of such sports. Blood was spilt on both sides very freely, and one or two gentlemen were qualified for a wake. Preparations were being made for a great fighting field-day on the following morning, but the whole of the campaign being reported to the Commander-in-Chief, hostilities were suspended by a general order. The French officers were ordered by their chiefs to retire to

their own quarters. An issue of six months' back pay in gold now opened the eyes, and the mouths, and the hands, and the hearts of the whole army, and the matter became how to spend it. Soldiers like sailors win their money like horses, and spend it like asses.

Soon there was to be another parting scene exhibited. The Portuguese were ordered to leave, and proceed towards their own country. The Spanish and Portuguese women who had followed the men were either to be sent home from hence, or their protectors were to consent to marry them. Some adopted the latter alternative, having had children by them, and some others who had not, and the remainder, of course, were compelled to separate.

There was much weeping and wailing on the part of the señoras. Many men, bound by the charms of the señoritas who had followed their fortunes through the war, took this opportunity to desert their country's cause, to take up that of their Dulcineas. Not content with the 'arms' offered by these 'invincibles', they took rifles and all with them, and we never saw or heard of them after.

The divisions drew up in the morning they marched, and honoured the brave Portuguese (for indeed, they had always behaved well in the field) with three cheers, as they turned their faces towards Portugal. Many were the heavy hearts in both armies on this occasion; for it is not easy to conceive how the circumstance of passing through scenes of hardship, trial, and danger together, endeared the soldiers of the two armies to each other. It was perhaps never before felt so fully how much each was attached to the other; but the departure of the poor women caused many heavy hearts, both among themselves, poor creatures, who had a long and dreary journey before them, and among those with whom they had lived, and who had shared in all their good and bad fortune. Among these, several on both sides were not oppressed with too fine feelings. The women marched down to Spain and Portugal forming a column of 800 or 900 strong. They were regularly told off into companies; and the commanding-officer, a major, and all the captains, were married men, who had their families with them - all excellent arrangements; but they were the

most unmanageable set of animals that ever marched across a country. The officers had to draw rations for them all the way; but many of them left the column and went wherever they pleased. Few reached Portugal in the order in which they started.

Finally, the anchor was weighed, and we left Spain, the country in which we had endured so much and so long, and as if we had not fighting enough, certain regiments were selected to embark for America, to begin a new war with people who could speak English.

I had marched through Portugal, all over Spain, and well into France. I had been in thirteen engagements with the next best troops in the world, and escaped for three years out of the hands of the Philistines without any broken bones, a providential and rare occurrence in those days, when one considers the rough usages of war, and that we left in Spain and France the bones of nearly 100,000 men; most of them bleaching in the sun, after being picked bare by the vulture and the wolf.

On leaving, there were no tears shed, unless they were tears of joy. For my own part, I was filled with gratitude, that Divine Providence had so far acceded to my wishes, and had thus preserved me from death in its most terrific forms. I could not help rejoicing that I was once more on my way to the best of nations. When I thought of landing in England, my heart fluttered with a sort of joy, which cannot be described. With what great pleasure did I walk the decks of the vessel, my mind being occupied with the thoughts of home, and all its delights.

Safely returned to England, and quartered in Dover barracks, our men soon forgot the fatigues of the Peninsula campaigns. Being joined by a batch of recruits, and supplied with new clothing, the old soldiers once more panted for fresh exploits; peace became irksome to them. Their souls were strong for war, and they were not long disappointed. At the end of April, we received orders to embark at Dover for Ostend — and Waterloo, and Paris.

FINAL VICTORY AND HOME

The final bloody and decisive battle at Waterloo over, victory was declared again. The Prussian bands played, among other tunes, "The Downfall of Paris" and the British "God save the King" as the great armies marched into that City under its gates and through its streets, spilling into interminable encampments and bivouacs which overspread them. The countless rows of huts which everywhere crowded upon the eye; the unceasing noise of drums, trumpets, clarions, and other musical instruments; the hubbub of voices which assailed you, as men of all nations conversed or sported together: these things together with the passing and repassing of thousands of men and women, as if some huge ant-hill had been disturbed. Although instead of ants, human beings came fourth from its recesses and created such a scene as cannot be conceived. These included grand military reviews, and here all the great ones of the earth assembled to witness this imposing spectacle; exhibited, no doubt, as much as anything, for

the purpose of showing the French the power of those who now held them in subjection.

Some officers were billeted in the city, but the infantry were kept in bivouac in the Bois de Boulogne and the Champs Elysées, no private soldier being allowed to enter the City without a pass signed by his Commanding Officer. But it didn't matter, as

> **certainly, the sights we witnessed this far-famed capital amply repaid us for our trip to France. Suffice it to say, that in Paris, with plenty of money, and with an inclination to enter into all the gaieties of the place, no city on earth, I believe, is so fruitful of the means of pleasure and dissipation.**

During the winter many of the troops were sent to the northeastern frontier or to adjacent villages — nothing very material happening.

> **The French people were greatly attached to the British and I assure you I never spent so pleasant a time during my soldiering, many of the men, being discharged, went back and got married.**

In July of 1815, Napoleon, vanquished, had given himself up to a British man-of-war, Bellerphon, and sailed for England; hence St. Helena's — his life's end.

The beginning of the winter of 1818 witnessed the evacuation of France by British troops, which were immediately afterwards scattered all over the world like dust before the wind.

The meanest soldier, fired by glory's rage,
Believes his name enroll'd in history's page;
O ! dear deceit — the statesman's finest friend,
By which the rabble crowd promote their end.

Sound, sound the clarion! fill the fife,
To all the sensual world proclaim —
One crowded hour of glorious life
Is worth an age without a name!

So now the business of the field is o'er,
The trumpets sleep, and cannons cease to roar,
When every dismal echo is decay'd,
And all the thunder of the battle laid.

Thomas Mordaunt (1730-1809)

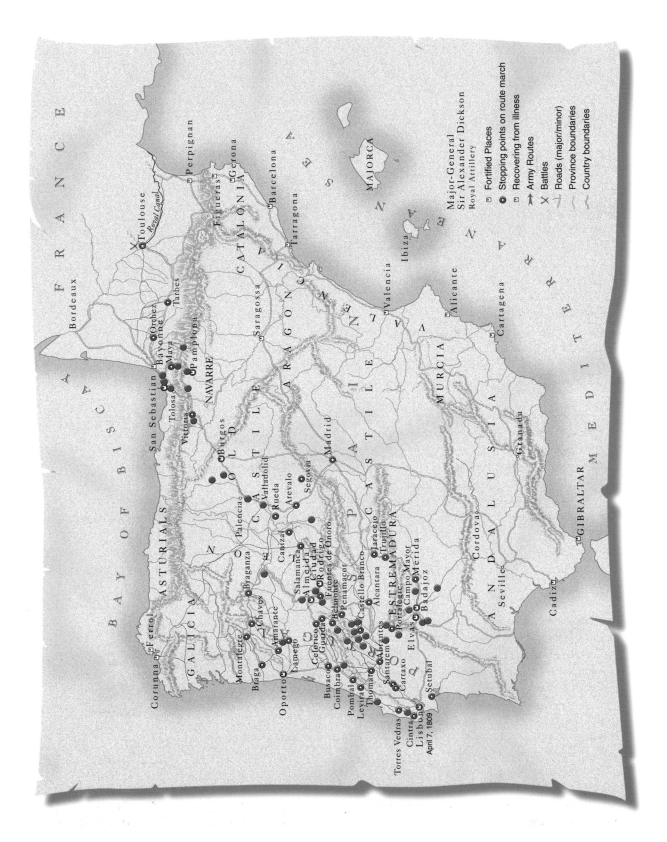

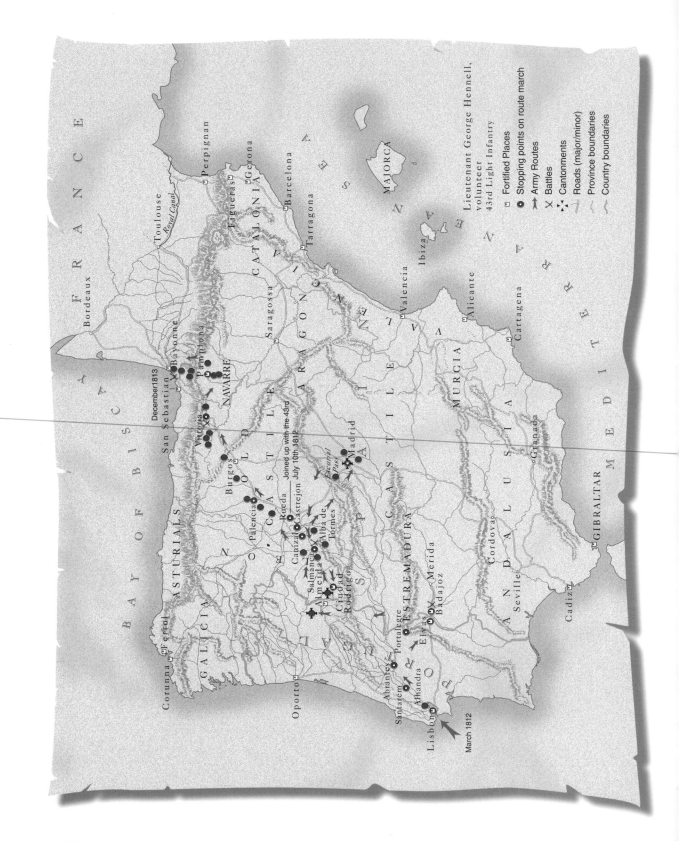

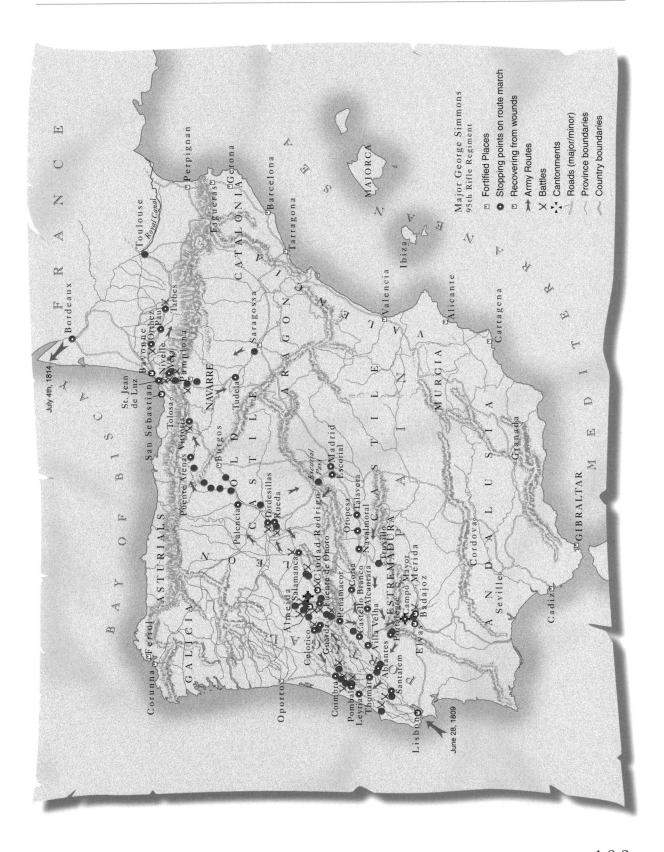

Major George Simmons
95th Rifle Regiment

□ Fortified Places
● Stopping points on route march
□ Recovering from wounds
→ Army Routes
✕ Battles
✳ Cantonments
╱ Roads (major/minor)
〈 Province boundaries
〈 Country boundaries

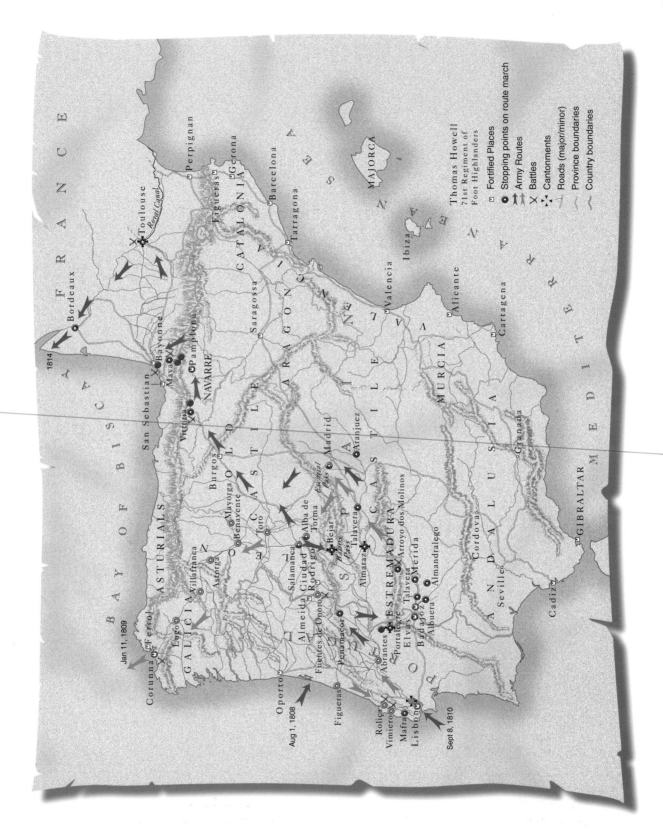

APPENDICES

CHRONOLOGY

1775 American Revolution

1783 Great Britain Recognizes Independence of the United States

1789 French Revolution

1793 France declares war on England

1795 Napoleon appointed Commander in Chief, Italy

1797 Napoleon directed to invade England

1798 Nelson defeats the French fleet in Aboukir Bay

1800 Formation of the Experimental Rifle Corps
Napoleon declares himself First Consul

1801 Act of Union between Britain and Ireland

1802 Peace of Amiens between England and France

1803 England declares war on France

1804 Napoleon proclaimed Emperor of the French
Spain declares war on England

1805 Nelson defeats the French/Spanish fleet at Trafalgar; Nelson killed.

1806 Napoleon declares blockade of Britain in Berlin Decrees
England blockades French ports

1807 France invades Portugal; English remove royal family to Brazil

1808 British arrive in Portugal
Battle of Rolica
Battle of Vimeiro

Convention of Cintra
Revolt in Spain
Napoleon enters Madrid

1809 Battle of Corunna; British troops evacuate
Sir John Moore killed
Arthur Wellesley in command of British troops
Battle of Oporto
Battle of Talavera
Napoleon divorces Josephine
Construction of the Lines of Torres Vedres

1810 Battle of Busaco
French held by Lines of Torres Vedres

1811 Battle of Barrosa
French leave Portugal
Battle of Fuentes de Onoro
Battle of Albuera

1812 Storm of Ciudad Rodrigo
Storm of Badajoz
War of 1812 with America
Battle of Salamanca
British enter Madrid
Siege of Burgos
Napoleon defeated in Russia

1813 Battle of Vittoria
Battle of the Pyrenees
Storm of San Sebastian

	Battle of Bidassoa		End of war between Britain and America
	Wellington enters France	1815	Napoleon returns to France
	Battle of Nivelle		Battle of Quatre Bras
	Battle of Nive		Battle of Waterloo
1814	Battle of Orthez		Napoleon abdicates and is exiled to St. Helena
	Wellington enters Bordeaux		Allied forces enter Paris
	Battle of Toulouse	1818	Allied forces leave France
	Napoleon abdicates and is sent to Elba		

SELECTED ITEMS OF EXPENDITURE FROM DICKSON'S PETTY CASH BOOK, 1809-11

June, 1809

June		Dollars	Vintems
13	Tea, sugar, and butter	1	35
	3 knives and forks		36
	3 table and 3 tea spoons		20
	cups and saucers, plates and a mug		29
	3 tumblers		10
	Portuguese cockade		3½
15	Cheese and bread for march		24
	Sausages, &c		2
16	Cherries at St Domingos		3
19	Calico for shirts	5	9
20	Paid Taylor for repairing my coat		25
	Washing		9
23	A Boliero [driver] going to examine road to Villa de Rey		8
24	A Portuguese Artilleryman going to Abrantes		
	with a letter from me to May		24
	Gave two English soldiers in distress at Villa de Rey		24
26	Fowls, &c	1	32
	A pair of gloves	1	
29	Lost at cards Captain Mor's at Thomar		
30	Red cloth for cuffs and collar of coat		2

July 1809.

July		Dollars	Vintems
5	Cloth and leather for a pair of overhauls	8	
	Cutting hair		24
8	Fish hooks, &c		5
9	Share of expense with Arentschild of party we gave to family of Custodio Jacomo in garden...	6	
11	Amount of Joseph's [Joseph was Dickson's servant. Ed.] expenditure for house account rom 27 June to this date per memorandum	22	21
12	Gave Driver Dickenson left in hospital at Thomar	5	
	Justina [Dickson's land-lady. Ed.] at Cacharias	1	
14	Poor man at Memoria		3
20	Breakfast at Ponte de Murcella		19
	Old man at Galizes		5
21	Guides going from Pinhancos to Mangoalde...		24

August, 1809.

August		Dollars	Vintems
1	10 dozen anchovies	2	
6	Gave a French prisoner	1	
14	Fishing in Ocreza	1	
16	Breakfast at Villa Velha		30
17	Man that found my spur		24
	A pen knife and pocket clasp ditto	1	20
25	Fishing in Ocreza		24
	2 clasp knives	1	
29	3 bottles Gin	3	24
31	Lost cards	1	15

September, 1809

September		Dollars	Vintems
2	Housemaid at Billet Castello Brando	1	
8	Bought at Sobreira Formosa fair 11¾ Covadas of brown suragoca at 32 vintems per cova	9	16
12	Supper at Certaa two fowls	1	29
14	Paid Mr. Rozierres for two lbs. tea purchased at Thomar	4	0
17	Settled Joseph's account from 20 July to this date	50	0
28	Guide to Figueiro dos Vinhos		2
	Ferry man at Barca de Boncar		5

OCTOBER 1809.

October		Dollars	Ventims
2	A ham	1	27½
4	½ hundred quills		20
6	A Bottle ink		26
8	Old woman		6
1	A large ham 17lb at 9 vintems	3	34
	Gave a poor soldier of Lusitanian Legion		24
14	Making my Portuguese uniform	3	30
13	Gave man at Pereira for explaining country		12
15.	Two turkeys		12
16	Bought fish caught in river		6
31	Gave house-keeper of my billet at Certaa	4	0
	Servant girl do. (ditto)		8

NOVEMBER 1809.

November		Dollars	Vintems
5	Lost cards		24
7	Hair cutting		12
10	6 *covas* of linen for shirts	5	0
13	Medicine	1	34
14	A silver purse bought at fair	4	20
15	Making two shirts	1	8
	Cambric for frills for 6 shirts	1	20
	Ribbon for a cockade		11
	Two pairs concave spectacles	1	0
	A compass with dial	1	30
	A pair Gallowses [braces.]	1	
20	8 dozen small round buttons	2	16
21	Cocked hat	13	
	An Epaulette	12	

DECEMBER 1809.

December		Dollars	Vintems
10	Gave man that remained to take charge of sick at Certaa	2	16
	Four fowls	2	
17	Paid taylor for making jacket	2	16
18	Paid Captain Kelly for ham bought at Abrantes, deducting his share of Mess	2	16
23	Wine		24

JANUARY 1809.

January		Dollars	Vintems
1	To Joseph and the Drummers on Christmas Day	1	33½
2	Soap and combs		15
4	Boatman crossing to Chamusca		10
15	A sash purchased for me by Arentschild	9	
	A pair of grey pantaloons	2	20
23	A Waiter at Santarem		23
24	Putting shoe on mule at Castanheira		3
28	Opera at San Carlos	1	20
30	Paid Taylor for new great coat	17	3

FEBRUARY 1810.

February		Dollars	Vintems
7	Hair cutting		12
	Paid for a lb. of tea purchased at Thomar	3	
9	Taylor for making pantaloons	2	4
12	Gave sick woman in hospital		12
13	Toys for Rozierres children	1	
24	Old coin at Meidobriga		6

MARCH 1810.

March		Dollars	Vintems
1	Pastry, day German Artillery dined with me,	1	
12	Oranges, etc		5
15	Guide going to Valencia de Alcantara		
20	Two bottles rum	1	24
22	Present of rum for Mr Arriaga	8	
	Joseph either willfully or by neglect has omitted entering in his accounts money received from me	3	6

APRIL 1810.

April		Dollars	Vintems
1	Gave painter that gave information about painting knapsacks		12
2	6 bottles gin	7	4
	Two tongues	2	16
	A salmon	1	
14	Oldman		2

		Dollars	Vintems
16	Bought a knife		24
18	Child at Herdade de Mosqueiros		2
23	Taylor on account of making new coat and put ting new lining to old one	3	
25	Two coins at Meidobriga, one of Constantine, the other of Maximian		12

MAY 1810

May		Dollars	Vintems
2	Fowl		24
7	Paid Rettberg for a quarter veal	1	
8	Little girl		5
12	Share of expences on trip to Alburqucrque and Campo Major with Hartmann	3	
17	Servant at billet at Elvas	1	
18	Dinner at Villa Viçoza	1	
19	Breakfast at do	1	12
22	Manoel at Sou.zel	1	
25	Paid Major Hartmann for 16 bottles of brandy Brown brought me from Lisbon	6	
30	Paid Costa for tea-pot, coffee-pot, arid 6 cups	2	13

JUNE, 1810

June		Dollars	Vintems
12	Paid Mr Manoel Souza for a pair of epaulettes he brought me from Lisbon	15	
21	Two pound tea	4	30
23	Joseph has expended on house account since the 18 December 1809	139	11
	Paid wages on discharging him, from 16 March 1809, to 16 June 1810, at 10 shillings per month per account	33	27
27	Cutting hair, etc		15
28	Stuff for a pair of pantaloons sent me from Lisbon by José Pedro	8	
	A pair of boots do	7	
	8 bottles Hollands sent by Cunha which José Pedro paid for	8	
9	Taylor for making pantaloons	2	

191

July, 1810

July		Dollars	Vintems
9	12 coloured crayon pencils	2	
11	A riding whip	2	
	A cag of brandy	8	
	A ring as present to Donna Maria at my billet at Portalegre	5	
17	Gave old arrieiro (Port. Muleteer) who had been wounded	1	
	Wine at Alpalhao	8	

Receipts			
3	The boots I received from Lisbon not fitting		
	Captain Rozierres took them	7	
22	Gratification for April (gratuity)	4	20
	Received to purchase an additional horse, by		
	Virtue of an order from the Regency	50	

August 1810

August		Dollars	Vintems
1	10 dozen anchovies purchased at Tinalhas	2	
6	Gave a French prisoner	1	
14	Millar fishing in Ocreza	1	
17	Man that found my spur		24
20	Three bottles of gin	3	24
31	Bread, butter, etc., bought at Sobreira	2	
	Lost at cards	1	15

September 1810

September		Dollars	Vintems
1	Paid for guides when I went to Villa Veiha	1	24
	Two pound best tea for Squire	2	
18	An *almude* [Portuguese wine measure.] of wine		
	Senhor Liogo brought me from Coimbra	6	
25	Bullock driver that dislocated his arm	2	

October 1810.

October		Dollars	Vintems
10	Stuff for a pair of pantaloons blue net	8	
	Gave Manoel Henriques for executing my commissions		
	at Lisbon	5	
11	Three ducks	1	5

20	Gave Gunner who had his arm cut		
26	My subscription for the ransom of captives at Algiers	25	
29	A pair boots	10	

NOVEMBER, 1810

November		*Dollars*	*Vintems*
12	4 bottles gin	3	10
	Two lb. refined salt		15
	¼lb. pepper		10
	Purchased by Lieut. Theodoro in Lisbon.		
	A cheese	4	13
	A large bass basket	3	
	A fine table cloth	3	
	8 *canadas* (Portuguese wine measure. Ed.) brandy	8	
	A hat cover	1	5
	Two cockades		35
	Blue cloth to make saddle cloth	6	35
	A pair silver spurs	6	35
	Purchased at Lisbon by Antonio Henriques.		
	dozen knives and forks	1	32
	Butter, sugar, potatoes, &c	3	
	A ham	2	32
	A tureen		
	Wax candles	1	12
20	Gave dragoon at Vallada for finding my horse	1	

FEBRUARY, 1811

February		*Dollars*	*Vintems*
6	Hat ornaments	2	20
	Lace for do	1	25
	Ribbon for cockades		22
	Opera with Fisher	2	
12	A pair of boots	6	
15	Gunner who brushed my clothes for 2 days	1	
	Poor woman		8
23	2 lb. raisins ; 1 lb. figs; 1 lb. almonds	1	21

MARCH, 1811

March		*Dollars*	*Vintems*
6	2 bottles brandy; 2 do. gin	4	
8	Small barrel biscuit	1	20
14	Oranges		10
20	Cakes at the nunnery		15

JULY, 1811.

July		Dollars	Vintems
4	Bought a grey horse	72	
12	Two turkeys	3	20
	Four chickens	1	8
	3 dozen eggs	1	5
23	Bread and milk at Villa Veiha		6
24	Fowl at Lardosa	1	20
30	Dinner at Trancoso	2	
31	Dinner at Moimenta	1	20

AUGUST, 1811.

August		Dollars	Vintems
3	Gave boatmen on reaching Oporto	2	0
10	6 shirts and two pair pantaloons	47	0
	Horse medicine	2	0
12	Pair gloves	12	20
18	Pair trousers		
28	Expenses during my illness that I have no account of	40	30
29	Paid Dr Ogilvie the physician who attended me	50	0
30	Paid nurse for 15 days	15	0

SEPTEMBER, 1811

September		Dollars	Vintems
2	3 tongues	1	20
	3 quire paper	2	20
	Two sticks sealing wax		10
3	One dozen *Porto* [port wine.]	3	24
	Paid Diogo for 3 dozen Porlo he procured me	12	5
4	Artillery driver who assisted in my stable	2	
9	Gave boy that accompanied Mr Boyes's mules	1	24
18	Sowing silk		30
21	Paulo bought at Lamego		
	5 lb. marmalade		35
	Pears and lemons		24
	Ribbon		
24	Mrs Holder for cooking dinner	1	
27	Sent Mr Boyes price of litter that came from		
	Larnego 3 days at 4000 per diem	26	0

October 1811

October		Dollars	Vintems
1	Walnuts		10
3	A teakettle	1	
6	Two ducks	1	20
5	A turkey and bringing from Penedono	2	24
13	Lost at cards	1	8
22	Poor family	2	
24	Poor women		27
28	Bought Lindseys gun	26	

BIBLIOGRAPHY

Anonymous. Journal of a Regimental Officer during the Recent Campaign in Portugal and Spain under Lord Viscount Wellington, with a correct Plan of the Battle of Talavera. 1810.
    Memoirs of a Sergeant late in the Forty-Third light Infantry Regiment, previously to and during the Peninsular War; including an Account of his Conversion from Popery to the Protestant Religion. John Mason. London. 1835. Facsimile of 1835 edition published by Ken Trotman, Cambridge, 1998.

Anton, James, Late Quartermaster-Sergeant, Forty-Second or Royal Highlanders. Retrospect of A Military Life During The Most Eventful Periods of the Last War. Facsimile of the 1841 edition published by Ken Trotman, Cambridge, 1991.

Aitchison, John. An Ensign in the Peninsular War. The Letters of John Aitchison. Edited by W.F.K. Thompson. Michael Joseph Ltd. London. 1981.

Bell, Major-General Sir George. Soldier's Glory being 'Rough Notes of an Old Soldier.' Edited and arranged by his kinsman, Brian Stuart. G. Bell and Sons, Ltd. London. 1956.

Baker, Ezekiel. Remarks on Rifle Guns. 2nd Ed. London. 1804.

Barber, Captain T.H. , British Army. Instructions for Sharpshooters.

Barrett, C.R.B. History of the XIII Hussars. 2 Vols. Blackwood. Edinburgh and London. 1911.

Beaufroy, Captain Henry (A Corporal of Riflemen). Scloppetaria. London, 1808.

Barrès, J.-B., Memoirs of a Napoleonic Officer, ed. M. Barrès. Trans. B. Miall. London. 1925.

Blackmore, Howard. L. British Military Firearms. 1650-1850. New York. Arco Publishing Company, Inc. 1961.

Blakiston, Major J. Twelve Years' Military Adventure in Three quarters of the Globe: or, Memoirs of an Officer who served in the Armies of his majesty and of the East India Company, between the years 1802 and 1814 in which are contained the campaigns of the Duke of Wellington in India, and his last in Spain and the South of France. 2 Vols. 1829.

Blakeney, Robert. A Boy in the Peninsular War. Edited by Julian Sturgis. John Murray. 1899. Facsimile of the 1899 edition by Greenhill Books, Lionel Leventhal Limited, London. 1989.

Boutflower, Charles. The Journal of an Army Surgeon During The Peninsular War. UK. 1912. Facsimile of the 1912 edition by Spellmount Ltd. Staplehurst. 1997.

Brett-James, Anthony. Life in Wellington's Army. Tom Donovan Publishing Ltd. London. 1994.

Brotherton, Gen. Sir Thomas. A Hawk at War. The Peninsular Reminiscences of General Sir Thomas Brotherton CB. Edited by Bryan Perrett. Chippenham, Picton. 1986.

Bryant, Arthur. C.H. Jackets of Green: A Study of the History, Philosophy, and Character of the Rifle Brigade. Collins. London. 1972.

Buckham, P.W. Personal Narrative of Adventures in the peninsula during the War in 1812-1813. 1827.

Bunbury, Lieut.-General Sir Henry, K.C.B. Narratives of Some Passages in the Great War with France from 1799-1810. Peter Davies. London. 1927.

Call, Captain George Issac. Diary of Captain George Issac Call, 27th (later 24th) Light Dragoons, from September 1811 to

February 1812. National Army Museum 6807/150.

Campbell, Brevet-Major, 23rd Regiment, Late D.A.Q.M.G. to the Light Division, and Captain Shaw, 43rd Regiment, Late A-D-C. to General Crauford (sic), publishers. *Standing Orders as Given Out and Enforced by the late major-General Robert Crauford, for the use of the Light Division, During the years 1809, 1810, and 1811, then serving under his command in the Army of the Duke of Wellington*. 1831.

Churchill, Winston S. *A History of the English-Speaking Peoples; The Age of Revolution*. Dodd, Mead & Company. New York. 1957.

Cooke, John. *Memoirs of the Late War: Comprising the Personal Narrative of Captain Cooke of the 43rd Regiment of Light Infantry. 2 Vols*. 1831.

Cooper, John Spencer. *Rough Notes of Seven Campaigns in Portugal, Spain, France and America During the Years 1809-1815*. UK. 1869. Facsimile of 1869 edition published by Spellmount Ltd. Staplehurst. 1996.

Cooper, Leonard. *The Age of Wellington. The Life and Times of the Duke of Wellington 1769-1852*. New York. Dodd, Mead & Co. 1963.

Cooper, Capt. T.H., *A Practical Guide For The Light Infantry Officer*. T. Egerton at the Military library, near Whitehall. 1806. Facsimile edition published by Frederick Muller, Ltd., Fleet Street, London., 1970.

Cope, Sir William H., Bart. Late lieutenant Rifle Brigade. *The History of the Rifle Brigade (The Prince Consort's Own) Formerly the 95th*. Chatto & Windus, Piccadilly. London. 1877

Costello, Edward. *The Adventures of a Soldier, or Memoirs of Edward Costello of the Rifle Brigade, comprising narratives of Wellington's Campaigns in the Peninsula, etc*. Colbourn & Co. London. 1841

Daniel, J. *Journal of An Officer in the Commissariat Department of the Army: comprising a Narrative of the Campaigns Under His Grace The Duke of Wellington, in Portugal, Spain, France, and the Netherlands, in the years 1811, 1812, 1813, 1814, & 1815; and a short account of the Army of Occupation in France, During the Years 1816, 1817, & 1818*. Porter and King. Walbrook. 1820. Facsimile of 1820 edition published by Ken Trotman, Cambridge, 1997.

Darling, Anthony D. *Red Coat and Brown Bess*. Museum Restoration Service. Alexandria Bay, N.Y. 1971.

Dawson, Lionel. "Hunting in the Peninsular." *The Age of Napoleon*. Vol. 20. Pp. 34-37. n.d.

Dickson, Major-General Sir Alexander. Royal Artillery. *The Dickson Manuscripts. Being Diaries, Letters, Maps, Account Books, with various other papers. Series "C" – From 1809-1818*. Edited by Major John H. Leslie. Royal Artillery Institution Printing House. Woolwich. 1905. Facsimile of 1905 edition published in 5 Vols. by Ken Trotman, Cambridge, 1987.

Donaldson, Joseph. *Recollections of the Eventful Life of a Soldier. (A Sergeant in the 94th Scots Brigade.)* Edinburgh. 1845.

Douglas, John. *Douglas's Tale of the Peninsula and Waterloo. (former Sergeant, 1st Royal Scots)*. Edited by Stanley Monick. Leo Cooper. Pen & Sword Books Ltd. Barnsley. 1997.

Dundas, Col. David. *Principles of Military Movements, Chiefly Applied to Infantry*. 1788.

Farmer, George. *The Light Dragoon*. Edited by George C. Gleig. Henry Colburn, Publisher. London. 1844. 2 Vols. Facsimile of 1844 edition published by Ken Trotman, Cambridge, 1999.

Fletcher, Ian. *Craufurd's Light Division*. Spellmount. Ltd. Tunbridge Wells, England. 1991.
  In Hell Before Daylight. The Siege and Storming of the Fortress of Badajoz, 16 March to 6 April 1812. Spellmount. Staplehurst. 1994.

Foy, General M. S. *Histoire de la Guerre de la Péninsule sous Napoleon*. 4 Vols. Paris. 1827.

Frazer, Augustus. *Letters of Colonel Augustus Frazer, K.C.B., commanding the Royal Horse Artillery in the Army under the Duke of Wellington, written during the Peninsular and Waterloo campaign*. Edited by major-General Edward Sabine. Longman. London. 1859.

Fuller, Colonel J. F. C. *British Light Infantry in the Eighteenth Century (An Introduction to "Sir John Moore's System of Training")*. Hutchinson & Co. London. 1925. Facsimile of 1925 edition published by Terence Wise, Doncaster, 1991.

Gardyne, Lieut.-Colonel C. Greenhill. *The Life of a Regiment. The History of the Gordon highlanders from its Formation in 1794 to 1816*. Douglas. Edinburgh. 1901.

Gates, David. *The British light infantry Arm c. 1790-1815 its creation, training and operational role*. B.T. Batsford Ltd. London. 1987.

Glieg, G. R. *The Subaltern*. Edinburg. 1872.

Glover, Richard. *Peninsular Preparation The Reform of the British Army 1795-1809*. Cambridge University Press. Cambridge. 1970.

Gordon. Alexander A. *A Cavalry Officer in the Corunna Campaign 1808-09. The Journal of Captain Gordon of the 15th Hussars*. Felling. Worley. 1913. 1990 ed.

Graham of Fintry. *Supplementary Report on the manuscripts of Robert Graham, Esq., of Fintry*. Edited by C. T. Atkinson. Historical Manuscripts Commission. Series 81. London. 1940.

Grattan, William. *Adventures in the Connaught Rangers*. Edited by Charles Oman. Edward Arnold. London. 1902.

Gronow, Capt., *The Reminiscences and Recollections of Captain Gronow*. Frome. Surtees Society. 1984.
  United Service Journal. 1831. II. P. 181

Green, John. *The Vicissitudes of a Soldier's Life, or a series of Occurrences from 1806 to 1815; together with an introductory and a concluding chapter; the whole containing, with some other matters, a Concise Account of the War in the Peninsula, from its commencement to its final close.* J. and J. Jackson and Simpkin and Marshall. London. 1827. Facsimile of 1827 edition published by Ken Trotman, Cambridge, 1996.

Guedalla, Philip. *Wellington*. Harper & Brothers Publishers. New York and London. 1931.

Greener, William. *The Science of Gunnery, as applied to the Use and Construction of Fire Arms*. Longman and Co., London. 1841.

Gurwood, John. *The General Orders of Field Marshall the Duke of Wellington in Portugal, Spain and France, from 1809 to 1814; in the Low Countries and France, in 1815; and in France, Army of Occupation, from 1816 to 1818.* 1837.

Hall, Basil. "When I Beheld These Men Spring from the Ground. 1809." Dean King, with John B. Hattendorf, Editors. *Every Man Will Do His Duty. An Anthology of Firsthand Accounts from the Age of Nelson.* Henry Holt and Company. New York. 1997. (Pp. 234-254).

Hall, John A. *A History of the Peninsular War. Volume VIII. The Biographical Dictionary of British Officers Killed and Wounded, 1808-1814.* Greenhill Books. London. 1998.

Hanger, Col. George. *To All Sportsmen and Particularly to Farmers and Gamekeepers*. London.

Harris, Benjamin. *Recollections of Rifleman Harris*. Edited by Henry Curling. Robert M. McBride & Co. New York. 1929.

Hart, Liddell. *The Ghost of Napoleon*. Yale University Press. New Haven. n.d.

Hathaway, Eileen. *Costello. The True Story of a Peninsular War Rifleman*. Shinglepicker Publications. Swanage. 1997.

Hay, Captain William, C.B. *Reminiscences 1808-1815 Under Wellington*. Edited by His Daughter, Mrs. S.C.I. Wood. Facsimile of the 1901 edition published by Ken Trotman Ltd., Cambridge. 1992.

Haythornthwaite, Philip J. *The Armies of Wellington*. Brockhampton Press. London. 1996.

"That Unlucky war : Some aspects of the French experience in the Peninsula." In Ian Fletcher, editor. *The Peninsular War. Aspects of the Struggle for the Iberian Peninsula.* Spellmount. Staplehurst. 1998.

Weapons & Equipment of the Napoleonic Wars. Arms & Armour Press. London. 1979, 1996.

Wellington's Military Machine. Spellmount Limited. Staplehurst. 1989.

Henry, Walter. *Surgeon Henry's Trifles; Events of a Military Life.* Edited by Pat Hayward. Chatto & Windus. 1843. 1970ed.

Howell, Thomas. *A Soldier of the Seventy-first. The Journal of a Soldier in the Peninsular War.* Edited by Christopher Hibbert. Leo Cooper. 1975. Reprinted by The Windrush Press. Moreton-in-Marsh. 1997.

Hennel, George. *A Gentleman Volunteer. The Letters of George Hennell From the Peninsular War 1812-1813.* Edited by Michael Glover. William Heinemann Ltd. London. 1979.

Jackson, Inspector-general Robert, *British Army Hospitals. A Systematic View of the Formation, Discipline, and Economy of Armies.* London. 1804.

Jones, Lt-Col. H. 'Narrative of Seven Weeks' Captivity in St. Sebastian' in *United service Journal*, 1841, I.

Keep, William Thornton. *In the Service of the King. The Letters of William Thornton Keep, at Home, Walcheren, and in the Peninsula, 1808-1814.* Edited by Ian Fletcher. Spellmount. Staplehurst. 1997.

Kincaid, Captain J. *Adventures in the Rifle Brigade, in the Peninsula, France, and the Netherlands, from 1809 to 1815.* First Published in 1830. Republished by Leo Cooper, London. 1997.

Kincaid, J. *Random Shots From a Rifleman*. T. and W. Boone, 29, New Bond-Street. London. 1835

Larpent, F. Seymour. *The Private Journal of F. Seymour Larpent, Judge-Advocate General, attached to the Head-Quarters of Lord Wellington during the Peninsular War, from 1812 to its close.* Edited by Sir George Larpent. 2nd ed. 2 Vols. Richard Bentley. London. 1853.

Lawrence, William. *Autobiography of Sergeant William Lawrence.* Edited by George Nugent Bankes. 1886. Reprinted as *A Dorset Soldier. The Autobiography of Sergeant William Lawrence 1790-1869.* Edited by Eileen Hathaway. Spellmount Limited. Staplehurst. 1993.

Leach, Captain Jonathan. *Rough Sketches of the Life of an Old Soldier during a Service in the West Indies, at the Siege of Copenhagen in 1807, in the Peninsular and the South of France in Campaigns from 1808 to 1814, with the light Division; in the Netherlands in 1815; including the Battles of Quatre Bras and Waterloo, &c.* Longman, Rees, Orme, Brown, and Green, Paternoster Row. London. 1831. Facsimile of 1831 edition published by Ken Trotman, Cambridge, 1986.

Leetham, Lieutenant-Colonel Sir Arthur, 'Old Recruiting Posters' in *JSAHR*, I (1922) p. 120.

Longford, Elizabeth. *Wellington: The Years of the Sword.* Weidenfeld and Nicholson. London. 1969.

Mackinnon, late Major-Gen. Henry. *A Journal of the Campaign in Portugal and Spain, Containing Remarks on the Inhabitants, Customs, Trade, and Cultivation, of those Countries, From the Year 1809 to 1812.* Charles Duffield, Bookseller. Bath. ND. Facsimile edition published as *Two Peninsular War Journals* by Ken Trotman, Cambridge, 1999.

Malcolm, John. Late of the 42nd. Regt. "Reminiscences of the Campaign in the Pyrenees and South of France, in 1814" in *Memorials of the Late War.* 2 Vols. Constable & Co. 1831. Facsimile edition published as *Two Peninsular War Journals* by Ken Trotman, Cambridge, 1999.

Manningham, Colonel. *Regulations for The Rifle Corps formed at*

Blatchington Barracks under the command of Colonel Manningham. August 25th, 1800. Printed for T. Egerton, at the Military Library, Near Whitehall by C. Roworth, Hudson's Court, Strand. 1801. Facsimile of 1801 version reprinted around 1890 by Willoughby Verner.

Maxwell, W.H. Esq. Ed. *Peninsular Sketches; by Actors on the Scene.* Henry Colburn, Publisher. London. 1844. 2 Vols. Facsimile of 1844 edition published by Ken Trotman, Cambridge, 1998.

Mills, John. *For King and Country. The Letters and Diaries of John Mills, Coldstream Guards, 1811-1814.* Edited by Ian Fletcher. Spellmount Ltd. Staplehurst. 1995.

Moore, Lieut.-General Sir John. *A Narrative of the Campaign of the British Army in Spain, Commanded by His Excellency Lieut. -General Sir John Moore, K.B. Authenticated by Official Papers and Original Letters.* Edited by james Moore. Joseph Johnson. London. 1809.

Moore Smith, G.C. *The Life of John Colborne, Field-Marshal Lord Seaton.* Dutton. New York. 1903.

Morris, Thomas. *The Recollections of Sergeant Morris.* Edited by John Selby. 1967. Reprinted by The Windrush Press. Moreton-in-Marsh. 1998.

Myatt, Frederick. *British Sieges of the Peninsular War.* Spellmount. Staplehurst. 1987.

Napier, G.T. *Passages in the Early Military Life of General Sir George T. Napier.* Edited by W.C.E. Napier. John Murray. London. 1884

Napier, Major-General Sir W.F.P. *History of the War in the Peninsula and in the South of France from the year 1807 to the year 1814.* 6 Vols. Frederick Warne and Co. London. 1828-1840.

Nosworthy, Brent. *With Musket, Cannon and Sword. Battle Tactics of napoleon and His Enemies.* Sarpedon. New York. 1996.

Oman, Carola. *Britain Against Napoleon.* Faber and Faber Limited. London. 1942.

Oman, Sir Charles. *A History of the Peninsular War. Vols. I-VII.* Oxford. 1901-1930. Facsimile of the 1902-1930 editions by Greenhill Books, Lionel Leventhal Limited, London. 1995-1997.

Wellington's Army, 1809-1814. Edward Arnold, London. 1913. Facsimile of the 1913 edition by Greenhill Books, Lionel Leventhal Limited, London. 1986.

Page, Julia V. *Intelligence Officer In the Peninsula. Letters and Diaries of Major the Hon Edward Charles Cocks. 1787-1812.* Spellmount Ltd. Turnbridge Wells. 1986.

Parkinson, Roger. *The Peninsular War.* Book Club Associates. London. 1973.

Reynolds, Captain "The Fortification of England's South Coast: The Martello Towers." Public Record Office., WO/30/62

Rous, John. *A Guards Officer in the Peninsula. The Peninsula War letters of John Rous, Coldstream Guards, 1812-1814.* Edited by Ian Fletcher. Spellmount Ltd. Turnbridge Wells. 1992.

Schaumann, August Ludolf Friedrich. *On the Road With Wellington. The Diary of a War Commissary.* Edited and translated from the German by Anthony M. Ludovici. William Heinemann Ltd., London. 1924. Facsimile of the 1924 edition by Greenhill Books, Lionel Leventhal Limited, London. 1999.

Sherer, Col. Joseph Moyle. *Recollections of the Peninsula.* Longman, Hurst, Rees, Orme, Brown, and Green. London. 2nd. Ed. 1824.

Simmons, Major George. *A British Rifle Man. Journals and Correspondence during the Peninsular War and the Campaign of Wellington.* Edited by Lieut.-Colonel Willoughby Verner. A&C Black. London. 1899. Facsimile of the 1899 edition by Greenhill Books, Lionel Leventhal Limited, London. 1986.

Smirke, Robert. *Review of a Battalion of Infantry, Including the Eighteen Manoeuvres, Illustrated by a Series of Engraved Diagrams: to Which are Added the Words of Command with an Accurate Description of Each Manoeuvre.* London. 2nd Ed. 1803.

Smith, Sir Harry. *The Autobiography of Sir Harry Smith 1787-1819.* Ed. G. C. Moore Smith. London. 1910. Facsimile of the 1910 edition by Constable and Company Limited. London. 1999.

Smyth, Lieut. B. *History of the 20th Regiment 1688-1888.* 1889.

Stepney, John Cowell. *Leaves From the Diary of An Officer of the Guards.* Chapman and Hall. London. 1854. Facsimile of 1854 edition published by Ken Trotman, Cambridge, 1994.

Stewart, William. *Outlines of a Plan for the General Reform of the British Land Forces.* 1806.

Surtees, William. *Twenty-Five Years in the Rifle Brigade.* Blackwood, Edinburgh, and T. Cadell. London. 1833. Facsimile of the 1833 edition by Greenhill Books, Lionel Leventhal Limited, London. 1996.

Tomkinson, Lieut.-Col. *The Diary of A Cavalry Officer in the Peninsular War and Waterloo Campaign 1809-1815.* Edited by his Son James Tomkinson. Frederick Muller Ltd. London. 1894. 2nd Edition, 1971.

Thoumine, R. H. *Scientific Soldier. A Life of General Le Marchant 1766-1812.* Oxford University Press. London. 1968.

Verner, Colonel Willougby. *History & Campaigns of the Rifle Brigade. Part I – 1800 –1809; Part II – 1809 –1813.* John Bale, Sons & Danielsson. London. 1919. Facsimile of the 1919 edition by Buckland and Brown, Old Bond Street. London. 1995.

Ward, Mrs. (Tidy). *United Service Journal. 1840. II.*

Warre, Lieut.-Gen Sir William. *Letters From The Peninsula 1808-1812.* First edited by his nephew The Rev. Edmond